Fodor's In

YELLOWSTONE & GRAND TETON NATIONAL PARKS

1st Edition

Where to Stay and Eat
for All Budgets

Must-See Sights
and Local Secrets

Ratings You Can Trust

Fodor's Travel Publications New York, Toronto, London, Sydney, Auckland
www.fodors.com

FODOR'S IN FOCUS YELLOWSTONE & GRAND TETON NATIONAL PARKS

Series Editor: Douglas Stallings

Editor: Douglas Stallings

Editorial Production: Astrid deRidder

Editorial Contributors: Gil Brady, Steve Pastorino

Maps & Illustrations: Rebecca Baer, Bob Blake and William Wu, *map editors*

Design: Fabrizio LaRocca, *creative director*; Guido Caroti, *art director*; Ann McBride, *designer*; Melanie Marin, *senior picture editor*

Photography:

Cover Photo (big horn sheep, Yellowstone National Park): Gavriel Jecan/ Danita Delimont

Production/Manufacturing: Matthew Struble

COPYRIGHT

1st Edition

ISBN 978-1-4000-0746-2

ISSN 1941-0271

SPECIAL SALES

This book is available for special discounts for bulk purchases for sales promotions or premiums. Special editions, including personalized covers, excerpts of existing books, and corporate imprints, can be created in large quantities for special needs. For more information, write to Special Markets/Premium Sales, 1745 Broadway, MD 6-2, New York, New York, NY 10019, or e-mail specialmarkets@randomhouse.com.

AN IMPORTANT TIP & AN INVITATION

Although all prices, opening times, and other details in this book are based on information supplied to us at press time, changes occur all the time in the travel world, and Fodor's cannot accept responsibility for facts that become outdated or for inadvertent errors or omissions. **So always confirm information when it matters,** especially if you're making a detour to visit a specific place. Your experiences—positive and negative—matter to us. If we have missed or misstated something, **please write to us.** We follow up on all suggestions. Contact the In Focus Yellowstone & Grand Teton editor at editors@fodors.com or c/o Fodor's at 1745 Broadway, New York, NY 10019.

PRINTED IN THE UNITED STATES OF AMERICA

10 9 8 7 6 5 4 3 2

Be a Fodor's Correspondent

Your opinion matters. It matters to us. It matters to your fellow Fodor's travelers, too. And we'd like to hear it. In fact, we *need* to hear it. When you share your experiences and opinions, you become an active member of the Fodor's community. Here's how you can help improve Fodor's for all of us.

Tell us when we're right. We rely on local writers to give you an insider's perspective. But our writers and staff editors also depend on you. Your positive feedback is a vote to renew our recommendations for the next edition.

Tell us when we're wrong. We update most of our guides every year. But things change. If any of our descriptions are inaccurate or inadequate, we'll incorporate your changes in the next edition and will correct factual errors at fodors. com *immediately*.

Tell us what to include. You probably have had fantastic travel experiences that aren't yet in Fodor's. Why not share them with a community of like-minded travelers? Share your discoveries and experiences with everyone directly at fodors.com. Your input may lead us to add a new listing or a higher recommendation.

Give us your opinion instantly at our feedback center at www.fodors.com/feedback. You may also e-mail editors@ fodors.com with the subject line "Yellowstone & Grand Teton Editor." Or send your nominations, comments, and complaints by mail to Yellowstone & Grand Teton Editor, Fodor's, 1745 Broadway, New York, NY 10019.

Happy Traveling!

Tim Jarrell, Publisher

CONTENTS

ABOUT THIS BOOK

Our Ratings

We wouldn't recommend a place that wasn't worth your time, but sometimes a place is so experiential that superlatives don't do it justice: you just have to be there to know. These sights, properties, and experiences get our highest rating, **Fodor's Choice**, indicated by orange stars throughout this book. Black stars highlight sights and properties we deem **Highly Recommended**, places that our writers, editors, and readers praise again and again.

Credit Cards

Want to pay with plastic? **AE, D, DC, MC, V** after restaurant and hotel listings indicate whether American Express, Discover, Diners Club, MasterCard, and Visa are accepted.

Restaurants

Unless we state otherwise, restaurants are open for lunch and dinner daily. We mention dress only when there's a specific requirement and reservations only when they're essential or not accepted—it's always best to book ahead.

Hotels

Unless we tell you otherwise, you can assume that the hotels have private bath, phone, TV, and air-conditioning. We always list facilities but not whether you'll be charged an extra fee to use them, so when pricing accommodations, find out what's included.

Many Listings

★	Fodor's Choice
★	Highly recommended
⊠	Physical address
⊹	Directions
⌂	Mailing address
☎	Telephone
🖷	Fax
⊕	On the Web
✍	E-mail
🎟	Admission fee
☉	Open/closed times
Ⓜ	Metro stations
⊟	Credit cards

Hotels & Restaurants

🏨	Hotel
🛏	Number of rooms
⚴	Facilities
⊠	Meal plans
✕	Restaurant
⚶	Reservations
⊻	Smoking
🍸	BYOB
✕🏨	Hotel with restaurant that warrants a visit

Outdoors

⚷	Golf
⛺	Camping

Other

☺	Family-friendly
⇨	See also
⊠	Branch address
☞	Take note

WHEN TO GO

Hotels in both parks book up early, especially in July and August. It would not be imprudent to make reservations at least one year in advance if you want to stay in either park at one of the top properties. Even in winter it's important to make reservations because of limited accessibility—and winter is the height of the ski season in the Jackson area. Even then, cancellations are common, so if you plan a last-minute trip don't despair on being able to find a good place to stay inside the park. Just be persistent.

If you don't mind capricious weather, spring and fall are opportune seasons to visit either Yellowstone or Grand Teton—prices drop and crowds thin out tremendously. Spring's pleasures are somewhat limited, since snow usually blocks the high country well into June. But spring is a good time for fishing, rafting on rivers swollen with snowmelt, birding, and wildlife viewing. In fall, aspens splash the mountainsides with gold, and wildlife comes down to lower elevations. The fish are spawning, and the angling is excellent.

Climate

Summers in this part of the country begin in late June or early July. Days are warm, with highs often in the 80s F, and nighttime temperatures fall to the 40s and 50s. Afternoon thunderstorms are common over the higher peaks. Fall begins in September, often with a week of unsettled weather around mid-month, followed by four to six gorgeous weeks of Indian summer—frosty nights and warm days. Winter creeps in during November, and heavy snows close many park roads by early December. Winter tapers off in March, though snow often lingers into early June and into July on mountain passes.

Forecasts National Weather Service (⊕www.wrh.noaa.gov). **Weather Channel** (⊕www.weather. com).

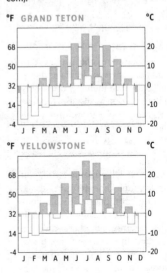

Welcome to Yellowstone & Grand Teton National Parks

WORD OF MOUTH

"There are just too many great experiences in Yellowstone, but last summer we got to the Old Faithful area just as a pending thunderstorm turned the skies a very dark gray and old faithful started going off. That dark gray sky made for such a beautiful background."
—utahtea 6/2007

LIKE FAMILY HOLIDAY TRADITIONS or the magnificent oral history of Native Americans, trips to Yellowstone and Grand Teton national parks are a rich part of the American dream. Yellowstone and Grand Teton are remote places, as inaccessible as any place in the lower 48 states. Still, for more than 130 years, we have been drawn to the incomparable combination of natural beauty, rugged wilderness, majestic peaks, abundant wildlife, and geothermal activity.

We are drawn to Old Faithful as an enduring American icon, just as we are drawn to the Grand Canyon or Mount Rushmore. We are drawn to the bears and roadside feedings that still linger in our nostalgia for the 1950s and '60s, even though those feedings are strongly discouraged now. We are drawn to the region's lakes, rivers, towering mountains, and backcountry. We are drawn by the hulking, peaceful bison, so uniquely patriotic they should be painted red, white, and blue.

America's first national park is as popular as ever—with an average of 3,000,000 visitors per year in the past decade. In many ways, it's the same park your parents and their parents visited. The park's signature icons, Old Faithful and the Grand Canyon of the Yellowstone, haven't changed perceptibly in the last century.

Grand Teton National Park is much younger than Yellowstone. Parts of the current national park were set aside in 1929 and 1942, but the park as a whole celebrated its 50th anniversary in 2000, and it's no less spectacular than its sister park to the north. The Teton Range has no foothills; instead, they rise directly up from the Jackson Hole valley floor, allowing a close-up, unimpeded view of the magnificent, jagged, snowcapped peaks. The massif is long on natural beauty. Before your eyes, mountain glaciers creep imperceptibly down 12,605-foot Mt. Moran. Large and small lakes gleam along the range's base. As in Yellowstone, many of the West's iconic animals (elk, bears, bald eagles) call this park home.

What has changed the most in both parks in the past 50 years are landmark wildlife management programs. The National Park Service has drastically altered habits and numbers of bears, bison, wolves, and elk in a largely successful effort to restore one of the world's largest remaining intact ecosystems. In fact, with the reintroduction of wolves in 1995, Yellowstone reigns as the only ecosystem in the nation essentially intact to its pre-settler days of the 18th century.

If you're looking for novelty in the parks, go see the gleaming Yellowstone Canyon Village Visitor Center, ride restored "Old Yellow Buses" reintroduced in 2007, or learn about the submarine navigating Yellowstone Lake's bottom in search of geothermal and volcanic discoveries. In Grand Teton, you can see the re-created Menor's Ferry, so you can once again experience how it provided transportation across the Snake River before there were even bridges.

Otherwise, the world's greatest concentration of geysers and hot springs still beckon at Old Faithful and a dozen other basins. You can still hike to Artist Point and view Lower Falls from the same vantage point used by Thomas Moran in the 19th century. The terraced formations of Mammoth Hot Springs are unlike anything you'll see anywhere else in America. In Grand Teton, you can hike or simply take a float trip on the Snake River, or paddle a canoe or motorboat onto Jackson or Jenny lake. If you seek active leisure, fishing, hiking, camping and winter sports are just a few reasons why America's "backyard" is also one of its foremost playgrounds as well.

Plan your time well—the only disappointment in Yellowstone and Grand Teton is when you have to depart.

HISTORY OF THE PARKS

YELLOWSTONE: AMERICA'S FIRST NATIONAL PARK

Yellowstone was established in 1872 as America's first national park. It's popularly believed that early-19th-century French trappers called the region Yellowstone when they heard a Sioux description of the yellow rock varieties in the deep canyon along the Yellowstone River. Only one small Shoshone band, the Sheepeaters, lived on the land now occupied by the park, but for thousands of years the Blackfeet, Crow, Bannock, Flathead, Nez Perce, and Northern Shoshone traversed the park and knew about the area's plentiful wildlife.

Mountain man John Colter became the first white American to explore Yellowstone, in 1807–08. His descriptions of geysers and boiling rivers prompted some mapmakers to dub the uncharted region Colter's Hell. Reports coming out of the region in the 1820s through the 1860s eventually prompted exploration by the federal government and designation of the area as America's first national park. Dispatches from three prominent expeditions between 1869 and 1871 thrust Yellowstone into America's consciousness. These expeditions were largely funded by railroads looking to build demand for their new service to the region from both coasts. Ulysses S. Grant signed the bill declaring Yellowstone a national park in 1872. The official approval process and designation had taken only two years. In the early days, the U.S. Army administered national parks such as Yellowstone; the creation of the National Park Service in 1916 began the modern era of conservation and preservation.

Yellowstone's history is preserved in the park, particularly at Norris's Museum of the National Park Ranger and in the displays and archives at the Albright Visitor Center in Mammoth and Canyon Visitor Center.

GRAND TETON: BORN FROM CONTROVERSY

Proposals to expand the boundaries of Yellowstone National Park begin in the late 19th century but went nowhere. When the National Park Service was established in 1916, one of the earliest proposals from the first director, Stephen Mather, was to add parts of the Tetons and Snake River, as well as Jackson Lake, to Yellowstone. However, some ranchers and Jackson Hole businessmen opposed this move, and the original bill died in Congress in 1919. Soon, however, it became clear that only some kind of national park designation would save the pristine area from overdevelopment and commercialization, and many of these very people joined the effort to have Grand Teton protected, though most still opposed the national park designation.

Parts of the Teton range were designated a national park in 1929, but efforts continued to purchase private land around Jackson Hole to extend the park's boundaries further south. John D. Rockefeller, Jr. purchased much of this land and, after a protracted political stalemate, donated it to become Jackson Hole National Monument in 1943, after 20-some years of turmoil. The two parks were merged and enlarged only in 1950, when it became clear to the local business people in Jackson Hole that the best future development of the region lay in tourism rather than mining or ranching.

Three Expeditions

Accounts delivered by three bands of 19th-century explorers brought validity to decades-old reports of "wild, hellish lands" from tall-tale-telling trapper Jim Bridger and John Colter, who explored Yellowstone after leaving the Lewis & Clark Expedition. The following three expeditions explored, recorded, and mapped the park, and you'll see their legacy everywhere in Yellowstone: **COOK–FOLSOM–PETERSON (1869).** Setting off from Bozeman the three mine workers named Charles W. Cook, David E. Folsom, and William Peterson followed the Yellowstone River to Tower Fall, the Grand Canyon of the Yellowstone, Mud Volcano, and Yellowstone Lake. They followed the lake to West Thumb, then to Shoshone Lake, and then to the Firehole River.

WASHBURN (1870). Surveyor-General Henry Washburn and businessman Nathaniel P. Langford retraced much of the 1869 expedition but also followed Yellowstone Lake's eastern and southern shores. They explored the Lower, Midway, and Upper geyser basins—naming Old Faithful in the process. Truman Everts, a member of the expedition, was separated from the party and lost for 37 days; when found, Everts was ungrateful and refused to pay the reward offered by his family for rescuing him. Washburn died shortly after the expedition.

HAYDEN (1871). Ferdinand V. Hayden, head of the U.S. Geological and Geographical Survey of the Territories, led an expedition in 1871. His survey brought back scientific corroboration of earlier accounts, but it was the visual proof from William Henry Jackson's photographs—and paintings by Henry W. Elliot and Thomas Moran, two artists who also accompanied the expedition—that cemented Yellowstone's place in the American public's mind.

GEOLOGY OF THE PARKS

Cataclysmic volcanoes erupted in the Yellowstone area 2 million years ago, 1.3 million years ago, and again 600,000 years ago, helping to create the steaming, vaporous landscape of today. The heat from the magma (molten rock) under the Yellowstone Caldera continues to fuel the park's bubbling mud pots, hissing steam vents and famous geyser basins. West Thumb, Upper, Lower, Midway, and Norris geyser basins contain most of Yellowstone's active geysers.

Other traces of the geological past include the basaltic columns near Tower and the steam that hisses from Roaring Mountain. The molten lava beneath the Yellowstone Caldera, one of the world's most active volcanoes, has created two resurgent domes: Sour Creek, forming the eastern edge of Hayden Valley, and Mallard Lake, which overlooks Old Faithful from the Upper Geyser Basin, at Observation Point. In Firehole Canyon, the Firehole River runs between two lava flows; at West Thumb, a minor eruption created the Lake Yellowstone bay lined with hydrothermal features; in the park's forests, volcanic soils nurture lodgepole pine.

In Grand Teton National Park, the Snake River valley is known as Jackson Hole. Looming over the valley are the massive peaks of the Teton Range, which began their ascent between 2 and 13 million years ago. Some glaciers still remain in the higher elevations. Wetlands are abundant in the flat regions of the valley, and glacial lakes stand at the feet of the mountains.

FLORA & FAUNA

Eighty percent of Yellowstone is forest, and the great majority of it is lodgepole pine. Miles and miles of the "telephone pole" pines burned in the massive 1988 fire, but its heat also creates the ideal condition for its serotinous cones to release their seeds. Note the contrast between 20-year-old and 100-year-old lodgepole pines throughout the park. Whitebark pine is found above 7,000 feet, where its purple-brown cones produce important nutrients for bears and squirrels. Look for wildflowers in open meadows or sagebrush steppes, including glacier lilies in the spring and goldenrod in the fall.

Grand Teton's short growing season and arid climate create a complex ecosystem and hardy plant species. The dominant elements are big sagebrush—which gives a gray-green cast to the valley—lodgepole pine trees, quaking aspen, and ground-covering wildflowers such as bluish-purple alpine forget-me-nots. Yellowstone and Grand Teton are home to 61 species of mammals including bears, wolves, wolverines, moose, elk, bison, bighorn sheep, otter, bats and many rodents. Moose, beaver, pronghorn antelope, and bison are prevalent in Grand Teton; on almost any trip to Grand Teton you will see bison, antelope, and moose. Bears, mountain lions, and wolves are less com-

Park Passes

An annual pass, available for $50, gives unlimited access to both Yellowstone and Grand Teton national parks for 12 months from the purchase date. However, your best bet is the America the Beautiful–National Parks and Recreational Lands Pass (☎888/275–8747, Ext. 1; ⊕ store.usgs.gov/pass), available for $80, which gives unlimited access to all federal recreation areas and national parks for 12 months from pur-chase date. The America the Beautiful Senior Pass has the same benefits for U.S. citizens age 62 or older for the cost of $10. As of January 2007, The America the Beautiful–National Parks and Recreational Lands Pass replaces all previous National Parks passes, including the Golden Eagle Passport, Golden Eagle Hologram, Golden Access Passport, and Golden Age Passport.

mon in Grand Teton than they are in Yellowstone. Rangers in both parks offer one-page guides to help identify species. The best chances of sighting the large "trophy" mammals in Yellowstone are in Lamar Valley and Hayden Valley. In Grand Teton, the best place to see elk in the summer is on Teton Park Road. Oxbow Bend and Willow Flats are good places to look for moose and beaver. Jackson Hole Highway and Antelope Flats Road are good routes for spotting bison and antelope. Bird watchers can study bald eagles, ospreys and a dozen other raptors, as well as more than 300 species recorded in the parks.

FLORA

Engelmann spruce (*Picea englemannii*) and *Subalpine fir* (*abies lasiocarpa*). Yellowstone's Absaroka Range does not have the volcanic, silica-rich soil (prominent in the Yellowstone caldera) where hardy lodgepole pines thrive. In the non-rhyolitic soil of the Absarokas, the Englemann spruce and subalpine fir thrive and can soar to 100 feet in height. You will also see Engelmann spruce in the canyons between Teton peaks, while Subalpine firs are more common in the higher elevations of the Teton range.

Evert's, or Elk, Thistle (*Cirsium scariosum,* in the aster family). This spiny plant is nicknamed for Truman Everts, who allegedly survived on eating it when lost for a month during the 1870 Washburn Expedition. According to the U.S.

Forest Service, it grows up to 4 feet in height in open meadows up to 8,000 feet.

Lodgepole Pine (*Pinus contorta*). The signature tree of Yellowstone National Park, the lodgepole is also the most common tree in Grand Teton. New- and old-growth lodgepoles occupy about 80% of the land in Yellowstone, and they grow on the lower slopes of the Tetons. These straight trees crave sunlight, so lower branches wither and fall off in dense forest, leaving long straight trunks that are perfect for lodges and teepees. Lodgepoles have serotinous cones, which means their seeds are released only when subject to great stresses such as fire. When 36% of the park burned in the 1988 fires, many of the scorched trees were lodgepoles. However, the blackened trees released millions of seeds that effectively reseeded the park much more quickly than many doomsayers had predicted.

Quaking Aspen (*Populus tremuloides*). Look for smooth-bark quaking aspen on level, moist ground as well as on dry slopes. The bark of these trees is smooth, and they get their name from the leaves, which seem to quiver in a light breeze. **Ross's Bentgrass** (*Agrostis rossiae*). Yellowstone is the only place on the planet where the inquisitive botanist might find Ross's bentgrass. You'll only find it on thermal ground along the Firehole River and near Shoshone Lake—in patches where the ground temperature is close to 100 degrees. The grass may bloom as early as January, with full bloom occurring in late May and early June.

Sagebrush-Steppe. Like much of Wyoming, Montana, Utah, Idaho, and Nevada, the high plateaus of Yellowstone and Jackson Hole feature **sagebrush** (*Artemisia tridentate*) and wild grasses such as **Idaho fescue** (*Festuca idahoensis*). Yellowstone's many enduring images of buffalo roaming Hayden Valley showcase the subtle beauty of these plains.

Thermophiles. Yellowstone's hydrothermal features create some of the most extreme habitats for life on the planet. Millions of microbes, in the form of bacteria, viruses, and algae thrive in microclimates with a wide range of acidity, heat, and surface temperatures.

Whitebark Pine (*Pinus albicaulis*). Appropriately named for their chalk-colored, spongy bark, these pines flourish above 7,000 feet. Hike to the summit of Yellowstone's Mt. Washburn to see broad stands of whitebark pines; they can also be seen through the higher elevations of Grand Tetons.

Their cones provide important food for squirrels, bears, and Clark's nutcrackers.

FAUNA

BIRDS

Bald Eagle (*Haliaeetus leucocephalus*). Yellowstone and Grand Teton are two of the few places in the lower 48 states where sightings of the majestic bald eagle are fairly common. Look for them high in trees above Lake Yellowstone and along several rivers, including the Madison at the west entrance, as they prey on fish and waterfowl. In Grand Teton, they will be found most often near one of the many lakes, or along the Snake River near Menor's Ferry. More common golden eagles are often found chasing rodents in park meadows and open spaces.

Great Blue Heron (*Ardea herodias*). These large wading birds are the largest of the herons in North America. The birds are blue-gray in color, with black feathers underneath; the head is almost white, but there are two black streaks running back from the eyes. They nest near Oxbow Bend.

Great Gray Owl (*Strix nebulosa*). The gray owl hunts at dusk and can startle campers as it emerges with a "whoosh" from a tree in pursuit of a mole, hare, or weasel. Wingspans can reach nearly 5 feet on both males and females.

Osprey (*Pandion haliaeetus*). Often spotted in the Grand Canyon of the Yellowstone during the summer, the black-and-white osprey nests in the adjacent canyon and descends to the river for its diet of fish. They also nest at Oxbow Bend in Grand Teton and can be seen hunting fish in the Snake River near Menor's Ferry. According to Yellowstone biologists, once it catches a fish, it arranges the prey "head-first" to make it less wind resistant as it carries the prey back to its nest.

Pelicans (*Pelecanus erythrorhynchos*). The broad-winged white birds spend the summer fishing at the Yellowstone Lake and Yellowstone River. They're easy to spot with their massive wingspan and black-tipped wings. They can also be spotted at Oxbow Bend and Grand View Point in Grand Teton.

Trumpeter Swan (*Cygnus Buccinator*). "Snow" white with black webbed feet and bill, trumpeter swans are a visual treat for visitors in winter, when hundreds of swans descend on the park. During the rest of the year, the several dozen swans that inhabit the park are much harder to spot. They sometimes nest on Christian Pond in Grand Teton.

FISH

Arctic Grayling (*Thymallus arcticus montanus*). Another of the native fish to the Greater Yellowstone Ecosystem, this rare and protected species is found in several lakes including Grebe Lake in Yellowstone.

Cutthroat trout (*Oncorhynchus clarki*). The world's largest native concentration of cutthroat trout is found in Lake Yellowstone and the Yellowstone River; you'll also find the Snake River cutthroat trout (the only species native to Grand Teton) there. A dream catch for fishermen—as well as bears and eagles—they're off-limits to humans in Yellowstone, especially in sensitive spawning areas such as the LeHardy Rapids near the mouth of the Yellowstone River. But you can fish for cutthroat and other nonnative species in the Snake River with a Wyoming fishing license. Identify cutthroats by red or orange markings under their mouth and black spots towards the tail of their golden bodies.

Lake Trout (*Salvelinus namaycush*). This nonnative fish was first caught in Yellowstone Lake in 1994 and is considered one of the greatest threats to the Yellowstone ecosystem in recorded history. Much larger than cutthroats, lake trout devour dozens of other fish (including cutthroats) annually. Unlike cutthroats, they reside deep in the lake and do not spawn in shallow rivers, depriving natural predators such as grizzly bears, eagles, and otters of a significant portion of their diet. Any angler who catches a lake trout must kill it. Lake trout can also be found in Grand Teton's lakes.

Mountain Whitefish (*Prospium williamsoni*). This slender silver fish lives in Yellowstone's and Grand Teton's rivers and streams. It requires deep pools with clear and clean water. Unlike trout, it spawns in the fall.

Suckers (Longnose, Mountain, and Utah). Three species of this bottom-dwelling fish inhabit the park. The mountain suckers are found in cold, fast, rocky streams. The longnose sucker ranges from Yellowstone Lake to rivers that drain in and out of the lake. Utah suckers are found in the Snake River drainage in the southern half of the park and in Grand Teton.

Bringing Your Pet

CLOSE UP

1

Most national parks are not particularly pet-friendly. In Yellowstone, pets are allowed in private vehicles and your campsite, but not on park trails. Park historian Lee Whittlesley tells a particularly gruesome story about a pet dog and its owner who perished in Fountain Paint Pots when the overeager canine leaped out of a vehicle and into scalding water. Think twice before bringing your pet to the park.

Pets are similarly restricted in Grand Teton. The National Park Service suggests that an appropriate rule of thumb is that pets can go anywhere cars can go (i.e., not on trails, not inside visitor centers, etc.) as long as they are kept on a leash. Although Grand Teton doesn't have the thermal hazards of Yellowstone, animals can be drawn to pets and their noises, so it's important that they be kept safe and secure. Owners are required to pick up and dispose of all pet feces.

There are several private kennels in Jackson, Wyoming, where you can board your pet while you explore Grand Teton and Yellowstone national parks.

MAMMALS

Bighorn Sheep (*Ovis canadensis*). Look for the rams (male) and ewes along side the cliffs and mountain slopes of Gardner Canyon, Yellowstone Canyon, and Mt. Washburn in Yellowstone; they are uncommon in Grand Teton but may be seen along the higher slopes. Look and listen for their dramatic mating "rut" in late fall and early winter, when 300-pound males may challenge one another in loud, jarring, head-banging collisions.

Bison (*Bison bison*). It's hard to believe that the thousands of bison that symbolize Yellowstone were on the verge of extinction less than 100 years ago. The bison have rebounded from less than two dozen to approximately 3,600 since the early 20th century. North America's largest mammals can exceed 2,000 pounds yet can run 30 miles per hour. They roam the park's valleys throughout the summer, and congregate near geothermal areas for warmth in the winter. They can be seen in the grassy meadows along the Snake River in Grand Teton. Be careful—human-bison encounters cause more injuries in the park each year than human-bear encounters.

Black Bear (*Ursus americanus*). Once near extinction, more than 500 black bears now roam Yellowstone's forests and meadows, and they can be found in Grand Teton as well. These omnivores may forage for berries, grass, and nuts or patiently fish for trout. Elk calves are vulnerable to these quick hunters—and they may fight wolves for their kill as well.

Coyote (*Canis latrans*). Smaller, but otherwise similar in shape and coloring to gray wolves, the coyotes are the species that has most suffered from the wolf restoration in Yellowstone. Their numbers are estimated to be down 30% to 50% since the return of the wolves beginning in 1995; they still roam Grand Teton, where wolves are still rare. The coyotes have few other predators and roam the park in packs of six to eight animals. Coyotes prey upon rodents, birds, elk calves, and carrion. Look for them in park grasslands and meadows.

Elk (*Cervus elaphus*). More than 10,000 elk call Greater Yellowstone home in the summer. The majority migrates to the northern meadows (Lamar Valley and Gardiner Valley), south to Jackson Hole or out of the park in the winter. The annual elk rut galvanizes visitors to Mammoth Hot Springs in the fall, where dozens of elk may congregate on the sweet, manicured lawns of Ft. Yellowstone and the surrounding buildings. In the summer, elk are common in Grand Teton, especially near Timbered Island. Elk bugling can be heard throughout the park, especially during the rut.

Gray Wolf (*Canis lupus*). Their reintroduction in the 1990s has been well documented in books such as *Decade of the Wolf*. The wolves were hunted to extinction in the early 20th century, contributing to the Greater Yellowstone Ecosystem's imbalance. In 1995 and 1996, 31 wolves were relocated to Yellowstone from Canada. The wolves flourished and now number nearly 150 inside the park boundary and nearly 400 in the ecosystem, which includes Grand Teton. The mysterious, graceful wolves travel in packs that average 11 members. Ninety percent of their diet is elk.

Grizzly Bear (*Ursus arctos horribilis*). One of the most feared American predators, grizzlies are less common than black bears in Yellowstone and Grand Teton but more popular among photographers and visitors. Male grizzlies can weigh 300 to 700 pounds, while black bears top out at about 350 pounds. They are voracious eaters with rodents, insects, roots, berries, elk calves, and carrion among their favorites.

Moose (*Alces alces shirasi*). Long-legged herbivores, this largest member of the deer family depends on old-growth fir forests for winter foliage—and thus suffered greatly due to the deforestation caused by the 1988 fires. Moose now number less than 500 in Yellowstone but are still found in Grand Teton in about the same numbers they always have been (look for them in Willow Flats and Oxbow Bend). They are usually found adjacent to either park's many creeks and rivers.

Yellow-bellied Marmot (*Marmota flaviventris*). The marmot is one of Yellowstone and Grand Teton's largest rodents. It inhabits rocky areas from valleys to high-altitude valleys feeding on grasses, seeds, and insects. Look for its reddish-brown body, yellow underbelly, and prominent tail during its short season above ground—the marmot may hibernate for as much as eight months.

Pronghorn Antelope (*Antilocapra americanus*). With a sprint that appears almost effortless as it bounds across meadows of the northern section of Yellowstone and the sagebrush flats of Grand Teton (look for them near Timbered Island), the pronghorns are a beautiful sight to behold. The herd within the park has fallen drastically in recent years to less than 300 animals, which has park officials concerned.

IF YOU LIKE

HIKING

There are more than 1,000 miles of trails and 300 backcountry campsites. Take a hike to find secluded fishing spots, enjoy hidden waterfalls, view animals in their natural state, or for the finest peak-top views of the park. Trailheads are located on each of the park's entrance roads, plus all along the Grand Loop Road. For an incredible wilderness experience, contact the backcountry office prior to your arrival to plan a journey suiting your abilities and desires.

CAMPING

Twelve campgrounds in Yellowstone and five in Grand Teton give you the unparalleled experience of waking up to the chatter of birds and crisp, clean cool air (another, Flagg Ranch, is in the John D. Rockefeller Memorial Parkway, near both Grand Teton and Yellowstone). Larger

CLOSE UP

Tips for RVers

Fishing Bridge RV Park is the only full-service RV park inside Yellowstone's boundaries. It offers utility hook-ups, pull-through sites, and dumps. Fishing Bridge sites do not have picnic tables or fire rings, so plan to be self-sufficient for meal preparation and dining. Also, only hard-sided campers are allowed at Fishing Bridge due to the high level of bear activity in the area. All other campgrounds in Yellowstone welcome RVs, but check the park's Web site or call ahead regarding site availability, sizes, and services.

In Grand Teton's boundaries, only Colter Bay RV Park is a full-service campground for RVs, with full hook-ups, showers, and a dump station.

There is even a self-service laundry nearby. Flagg Ranch Campground on the John D. Rockefeller Memorial Parkway between Grand Teton and Yellowstone also has RV sites with full hook-ups, as well as fire rings and picnic tables. Many of the campgrounds in Grand Teton can accommodate self-contained RVs, but Jenny Lake Campground does not permit RVs at all.

In Yellowstone and Grand Teton (or really any national park), it's important to do your homework and make reservations for hook-up sites whenever possible. These are usually in high demand and short supply during the busy summer season.

campgrounds operated by Xanterra in Yellowstone and by Grand Teton Lodge Company in Grand Teton can be reserved in advance and have amenities like showers, laundry, ice, and evening campfire ranger programs. Smaller campgrounds operated by the National Park Service offer a quieter, more peaceful experience—but lack any amenities other than bathrooms, bear-proof food storage boxes, picnic tables, fire rings, and potable water.

ARCHITECTURE

Robert Reamer designed and built Old Faithful Inn in 1903–04 ushering in a century of landscape-inspired natural buildings dubbed "Parkitecture." The Inn is a gem, as are Lake Yellowstone Hotel, Lake Yellowstone Lodge, several ranger stations and even some 100-year-old stores. The remnants of Mormon homesteaders in Grand Teton can still be seen in the cabins the barns and ranch building they left behind (and also at the re-created Menor's Ferry).

OUTDOOR EXERCISE

Summer is short, but millions make their way here to hike, fish, bike, ride horses, or canoe. The snows fall as early as September, and the park closes for six weeks in November and early December to prepare for the winter. Snowmobiles, snowshoers, and cross-country skiers descend on Yellowstone during Christmas week, using Old Faithful Snow Lodge and Mammoth Springs Hotel as bases for adventures until the park closes again from early March to early May. Although the Jackson area is a major winter ski destination, most of Teton Park Road closes from late October through early May, but Highways 89/191 and 26/287 are plowed and usually remain open. Snowmobiles are allowed on the Continental Divide Snowmobile Trail and on Grassy Lake Road (as well as on Jenny Lake, but only for ice-fishing).

GAZING AT SCENERY

The late Paco Young's painting over the Old Faithful Inn dining room fireplace captures the essence of the park with bison grazing in the foreground of America's most famous geyser. Bison, elk, or deer might similarly visit your campsite, your Lake Yellowstone Lodge sunrise view or your creekside walk. If you drive along the Snake River in Grand Teton, you'll see abundant wildlife. There is no better landscape in America for natural beauty and abundant wildlife.

FAMILY FUN

National parks are great family destinations, and Yellowstone and Grand Teton are no exceptions. Before you even arrive at the park, kids can explore the park's Web site as "virtual rangers." Once you arrive at the park, Junior Ranger newspapers offer creative and fun ways for kids to enjoy the park—from wildlife-watching to meeting and learning from park rangers.

IN YELLOWSTONE

Yellowstone has countless ways to enjoy the park with your family. Elementary-age children can enjoy short hikes like Trout Lake or Storm Point, while active teenagers will enjoy dozens of longer hikes. Although the water can be freezing, there are many beaches on the shores of Yellowstone Lake and Lewis Lake, including several picnic areas.

Each of Yellowstone's visitor centers demonstrates a different aspect of the park, with the all-new Canyon Visitor's Center featuring exhibits on volcanic activity, geology, Native American history, and wildlife. Finally, many tour operators, including Xanterra (the park's official concessionaire) offer family-based trips via horseback, historic yellow buses, or on foot. "Yellowstone for Families" is an award-winning summer camp offered by the park's educational arm, the Yellowstone Association Institute.

IN GRAND TETON

Families going to Grand Teton will enjoy float trips down the Snake River aboard big rubber rafts, though these are not suitable for very young children. Horses can be rented for a couple of hours, or you can take guided tours at either Colter Bay or Jackson Lake. Nearby guest ranches offer more intensive horse opportunities. Rides on old-fashioned stagecoaches are available in Town Square in nearby Jackson. During the winter, you can see thousands of elk while riding a horse-drawn sleigh through the National Elk Refuge, south of Grand Teton; during the summer, the elk can be seen along many of the park roads.

Exploring Yellowstone National Park

WORD OF MOUTH

"I was blown away by Yellowstone . . . it was so much more than I expected it to be: elk harassing tourists at the Mammoth area, a griz[zly bear] on a bison carcass. The whole trip was magic. But if I had to pick one moment, it would be our sighting a grizzly on the shore of Lake Yellowstone. Lucky I had the camera handy (like I wouldn't). You are in for the treat of a lifetime!"

—peterboy 6/2007

By Steve
Pastorino

YELLOWSTONE'S GRANDEUR can be seen the moment you enter the park through any of its five entrances. Lamar Valley and Madison Valley are wildlife-rich refuges alongside the Northeast and West entrance roads, respectively. Roosevelt Arch and the ornate thermal terraces of Mammoth Hot Springs greet visitors from the north. Lewis Lake and Yellowstone Lake beckon in the south. The Absaroka Mountains and Sylvan Pass capture the immediate attention of visitors from the east.

Then you hit the Grand Loop Road—a figure-eight park "highway" with eight developed areas—for the rest of the park's highlights. The most famous of the developed areas is Old Faithful Village, on the park's west side; it has the widest variety of lodging, dining, and visitor services. To the north, Madison and Norris areas have active geyser basins, ranger stations, and campgrounds. Mammoth Hot Springs is the northernmost village and the only one accessible year-round by car. Continuing clockwise, Tower–Roosevelt offers limited services but serves as the gateway to the bison habitat of Lamar Valley. Canyon Village is centrally located in the park, has all essential visitor services, and is adjacent to one of America's most scenic canyons. Fishing Bridge, Lake Village, and Bridge Bay Marina are the three developed areas on Yellowstone Lake's northern shore. Finally, Grant Village is the only community in the southern half of the park and a popular stopping point for visitors from Grand Teton National Park. Each of the developed areas has a Visitor Center and/or ranger station, and this is always a good first stop in your park travels. You'll find gas stations, hotels, restaurants, and stores in the more developed areas.

Before you begin your visit, assess your desires and endurance. If your time is limited, don't try to cover the whole park. Instead, read through this book and pick an area to concentrate on, such as the Old Faithful in the west or Grand Canyon of the Yellowstone in the east; or plan to drive either the lower or upper part of the Grand Loop. Make plans to get out of your car and take advantage of many short hikes, roadside picnic areas, self-guided trails, and beautifully designed buildings. Make time for listening, too, for an elk bugling, a nuthatch clamoring, or silence; these are rare aural pleasures in contemporary America and are every bit as worthwhile as the eye-popping scenery.

As you explore the park, keep this thought in mind: Yellowstone is not an amusement park. It is a wild place. The altitude and changing weather can be as lethal as the animals. Respect the wildlife—they may seem docile or tame, but every year careless visitors are injured or killed when they venture too close. Particularly dangerous are female animals with their young; bison in particular can turn and charge in an instant. (Watch the bison tails: when they are standing up or crooked like a question mark, the bison is agitated.)

PARK INFORMATION. The park newspaper, *Discover Yellowstone*, is a valuable resource with details about lodging, camping, visitor centers, ranger-led programs, and current road conditions, amenities, and regulations. Read it! The official **Yellowstone National Park** (☎ 307/344–7381 ⊕ www.nps.gov/yell) Web site is somewhat cumbersome but is a great starting point for trip-planning, and you can download a "Yellowstone Trip Planner" in PDF form, and there are maps of all the major developed areas. You can also call the park's visitor information line for the very latest information at any time.

MADISON & NORRIS AREAS

Madison is 14 mi (23 km) east of Yellowstone's West Entrance; Norris is 14 mi (23 km) northeast of Madison.

The West Entrance Road follows the Madison River as it winds below Mt. Haynes and National Park Mountain to the south, and Mt. Jackson and Purple Mountain to the north. The grassy valley in Madison Canyon is one of the prime spots in the park for seeing elk, deer, and bison.

The Madison Ranger Station, a National Historic Landmark, is a worthwhile stop. The Hayden Expedition of 1871 stopped in a field just west of where the ranger station now stands. According to the historical marker, the group pondered the (priceless!) economic value of the land before agreeing altruistically that the entire area be put aside as a park for the nation's enjoyment. Contemporary historians now consider this to be park legend, but it is indisputable that less than two years later, President Ulysses S. Grant signed the law declaring Yellowstone the nation's first national park.

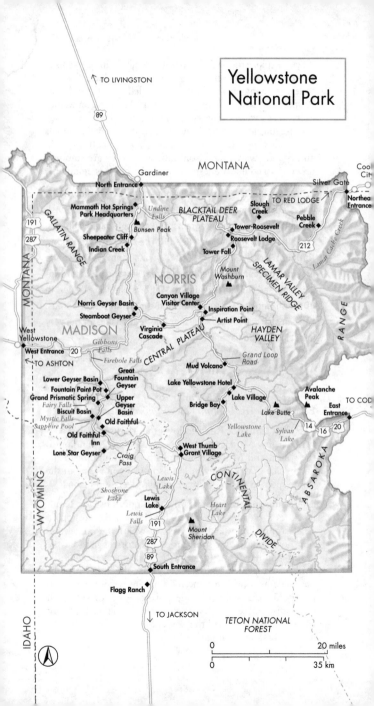

Yellowstone National Park

TO LIVINGSTON

89

MONTANA

Coo Cit

Gardiner

North Entrance

Silver Gate

Northea Entrance

TO RED LODGE

191

287

GALLATIN RANGE

MONTANA

Mammoth Hot Springs
Park Headquarters

Undine Falls

BLACKTAIL DEER PLATEAU

Slough Creek

Pebble Creek

Sheepeater Cliff

Bunsen Peak

Tower-Roosevelt

212

Indian Creek

Roosevelt Lodge

Lamar Cache Creek

Tower Fall

LAMAR VALLEY

SPECIMEN RIDGE

NORRIS

Mount Washburn

RANGE

Canyon Village
Visitor Center

Norris Geyser Basin

Steamboat Geyser

Inspiration Point

West Yellowstone

MADISON

Virginia Cascade

Artist Point

HAYDEN VALLEY

West Entrance

20

Gibbous Falls

CENTRAL PLATEAU

Grand Loop Road

TO ASHTON

Firehole Falls

Mud Volcano

Great Fountain Geyser

Lake Yellowstone Hotel

Lower Geyser Basin

Fountain Paint Pot

Grand Prismatic Spring

Upper Geyser Basin

Bridge Bay

Lake Village

Avalanche Peak

East Entrance

TO COD

Fairy Falls

Biscuit Basin

Mystic Falls

Sapphire Pool

Old Faithful

Lake Butte

14

16

20

Old Faithful Inn

Yellowstone Lake

Sylvan Lake

Lone Star Geyser

Craig Pass

West Thumb

Grant Village

WYOMING

CONTINENTAL

ABSAROKA RANGE

Lewis Lake

Shoshone Lake

Heart Lake

Lewis Lake

Lewis Falls

191

287

89

Mount Sheridan

DIVIDE

South Entrance

Flagg Ranch

IDAHO

TO JACKSON

TETON NATIONAL FOREST

0   20 miles

0   35 km

YELLOWSTONE TOP 5

Geysers and Other Hot Spots: With more than 10,000 thermal features powered by a massive volcanic "hot spot," Yellowstone is in perpetual upheaval. Old Faithful Geyser is the most famous, but don't miss fascinating steam vents, bubbling mud pots, and crystal clear hot springs.

Fishing: Anglers love Yellowstone's 2,000 mi of streams and countless lakes, home to several types of trout, grayling, and mountain whitefish.

American History: When President Ulysses S. Grant declared Yellowstone the world's first national park, he launched the conservation ethos that persists a century later. Historical highlights include the Museum of the National Park Ranger, a collection of Thomas Moran's work at the Albright Visitor Center, and historical markers where the Nez Perce Indians crossed through the park.

Hiking: By foot, snowshoe or ski, you can easily escape the crowds on more than 1,000 mi of trails. Venture to peaks, lakes, geysers, and meadows—each alive with the largest concentration of mammals in the continental United States.

Yellowstone in Winter: Yellowstone can be a truly amazing place during the winter months, and navigating the park by snowmobile or snow coach allows you to see all park attractions like Old Faithful, Mammoth Hot Springs, and the Firehole River.

There are several excellent hikes in this area. On the entrance road from West Yellowstone, Harlequin Lake (0.5 mi each way) is a short hike suitable for walkers of all ages. The Purple Mountain Trail (7 mi round-trip) offers excellent vistas of the park's western mountains and valleys. The Gneiss Creek Trail (12.5 mi one-way) cuts through more than 12 mi of the Madison River Valley and nearby meadows; the hike ends at U.S. 191, and most people arrange to be picked up there rather than doing the round-trip.

The Norris Area, at the western junction of the Upper and Lower Grand Loop roads, is an excellent example of terrain, hiking, and camping opportunities that would be cherished in their own right if found in any other place in America. Yet here in Yellowstone, the Norris region is often bypassed in favor of Mammoth Hot Springs area to the north, and the Old Faithful complex to the south. If

GREAT ITINERARIES

YELLOWSTONE IN ONE DAY

Don't fret what you'll miss in one day in Yellowstone. Rather, enjoy its bounty for as much time as you can. **Old Faithful** is one of the most iconic destinations in America, so don't miss it. Plan on at least two hours for Old Faithful. Eruptions are approximately 90 minutes apart, so spend the time between exploring the surrounding geyser basin and Old Faithful Inn.

You'll have plenty of time to explore the Madison River and look for elk, bison, osprey, and eagles at numerous turnouts. Use the **Madison Ranger Station** (skipping Old Faithful's crowds) for orientation, seasonal tips, maps, and books. Enjoy **Firehole Canyon Drive** off the Grand Loop Road. Cross the Continental Divide between Old Faithful and **West Thumb,** where you can see an active geyser basin that extends into Yellowstone Lake. Choose one short hike and enjoy the wilderness.

From the north, spend an hour getting oriented while exploring in and around the **Albright Visitor Center** and **Fort Yellowstone** in Mammoth Hot Springs. Take another hour to explore the complex geothermal features at **Upper Terraces** and **Lower Terraces** before starting the 75-minute drive to Old Faithful. Break it up with stops at **Obsidian Mountain, Roaring Mountain, Norris Geyser Basin** and/or **Firehole Canyon Drive.** And make time for a short hike.

If you enter from the east, enjoy stops at **Lake Butte, Fishing Bridge,** and the wildlife-rich **Hayden Valley** as you cross the park to Old Faithful. At **Canyon Village,** enjoy lunch and a hike along one of the rims of the **Grand Canyon of the Yellowstone.** Do ask a ranger how to make the most of your experience. If you hike any trail in the park for a couple miles, you will increase your chances of seeing wildlife exponentially. (In the north, try Beaver Ponds or Hellroaring Creek. In the south and west, try Riddle Lake, DeLacy Creek, Lone Star Geyser, or Mystic Falls.) If you MUST see wolves or bears, call ahead and find out when/if rangers or volunteers might be stationed at roadside turnouts in Hayden or Lamar valleys, which have spotting scopes. If you love the water, the one-hour **Lake Queen Scenic Cruise** from **Bridge Bay** is enjoyable and informative. Don't forget to make dinner reservations.

GREAT ITINERARIES

YELLOWSTONE IN THREE DAYS

Explore Yellowstone for three days, and you'll be enthralled—and your appetite whetted for a return visit. Where you enter and exit the park will determine the order of this itinerary, but follow it one way or another to cut down your driving.

Mammoth Hot Springs, with its geothermal terraces is definitely worth two hours of your time. If wildlife watching is a priority, continue on to the **Lamar Valley,** near Tower-Roosevelt. Look for park rangers or wolf-watching volunteers with their spotting scopes on turnouts between Tower Junction and **Pebble Creek.** Bring your binoculars and/or telephoto lenses for the long view, then hike a few miles of the **Slough Creek Trail** to see what you can find up close. Head south for a quick view of **Tower Falls** (on your way to the even more dramatic Upper and Lower Falls in the Grand Canyon of the Yellowstone). Be sure to explore the comprehensive visitor center at **Canyon Village;** check out the many nearby trails and services. Don't neglect the **Hayden River Valley** and the **Mud Volcano** area.

Spend a second day along the **Yellowstone River** and **Yellowstone Lake.** During Spring, watch the trout leaping upriver as they spawn between **LeHardys Rapids** and historic **Fishing Bridge** (don't miss then "then and now" pictures of the bridge). **Lake Yellowstone Hotel** is an option for lunch, or you can grab something fast and look for eagles as you wait to board the Lake Queen scenic cruise at **Bridge Bay Marina.** Gull Point Road, **West Thumb Geyser Basin,** and the Continental Divide are interesting stops on your way to the Old Faithful.

On day three, watch an eruption of **Old Faithful Geyser** at dawn or after dark to avoid the theme-park feel of thousands of fellow spectators. Hike or bike to **Lone Star Geyser** to see a reliable geyser in a pleasant forest above burbling **Kepler Cascades.** Xanterra's Firehole Basin Adventure, a three-hour ride on a historic Old Yellow Bus, is a relaxing way to experience many of the geyser basins on the park's west side. If you'd prefer to do things on your own, explore the **Upper Geyser Basin** near Old Faithful, **Grand Prismatic Spring** at **Midway Geyser Basin,** and **Norris Geyser Basin** for a rich variety. Picnic at **Madison Ranger Station, Nez Perce Picnic Area** or along Firehole Canyon Drive for a complete day.

2

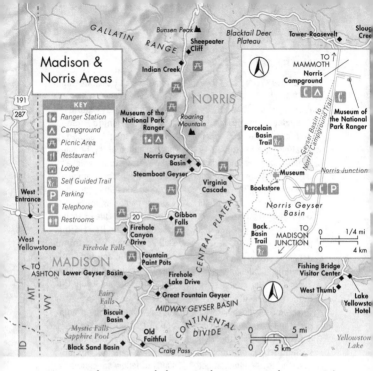

you have a couple hours and want to see the most active geyser basin in the park, Norris is a delight.

Norris Geyser basin is divided in two parts: Back Basin and Porcelain Basin. Make time for at least one. The underground plumbing is constantly changing here, with ground temperatures occasionally heating to 200°F, and the activity of its thermal features always evolving. Consult with rangers at the Norris Geyser Basin Museum (it's really more of an information kiosk than a museum) for geyser eruption predictions, as well as any closed areas.

One of the prime fishing spots in the nation, the Madison River, is formed by the joining of the Gibbon and Firehole rivers. Fly fishermen will find healthy stocks of brown and rainbow trout and mountain whitefish. The park policy allows for catch-and-release fishing only.

VISITOR CENTERS

Madison Information Center. In this National Historic Landmark, the ranger shares the space with a Yellowstone Association bookstore, which features high-quality books, guides, music, and learning aids. You may find spotting scopes set up for wildlife viewing out the rear window; if this is the case, look for eagles, swans, bison, elk, and more. Rangers will answer questions about the park, provide basic hiking information and maps, and issue permits for backcountry camping and fishing. Picnic tables, toilets, and an amphitheater for summer-evening ranger programs are shared with the nearby Madison campground. Regrettably, there is no coffee available here. ⊠*Grand Loop Rd. at West Entrance Rd., Madison* ☎*307/344–2821* ☉*June– Sept., daily 9–5.*

LANDMARK RANGER STATIONS. Built in the 1920s, the Madison, Norris, and Fishing Bridge ranger stations were the nation's first "trailside" interpretive museums. The low-slung timber and rock buildings ushered in a new way for the public to enjoy America's natural resources. Prior to their construction, natural science education was limited to museums and academic settings.

SCENIC DRIVES

You might find gorgeous lookouts, geothermal activity, and wildlife around any bend in Yellowstone, but the west entrance offers an exceptional variety of all three. The park's pulse beats in its thriving rivers—and the Madison, Gibbon, and Firehole rivers converge near Madison Junction to give visitors three picturesque driving options.

Grand Loop Road from Madison to Norris. Traveling from West to East, you'll climb slowly as you straddle Yellowstone Caldera, the 30 x 45 mi (48 x 72 km) crater formed by a volcanic eruption 640,000 years ago. Pull over to see the Gibbon River as it tumbles into the caldera at 84-foot **Gibbon Falls.** You'll also pass several roadside geothermal features (stop at Monument Geyser and Artists Paintpots) before you arrive at Norris Geyser Basin. ⊠*Drive begins at Madison campground, 14 mi east of West Entrance on Grand Loop Rd.*

West Entrance Road. One of the park's four grand drives through wildlife-filled valleys, this road follows the Madison River for 14 mi (23 km). From late summer through winter, you'll see bison and elk. Look up, too! Eagles, osprey, and even trumpeter swans may be seen here. **CAUTION At sunset, the drive west can be blinding.** ⊠*Drive begins at the West Entrance, West Yellowstone, MT.*

Firehole Canyon Drive. Pick up this one-way, 2-mi (3-km) detour off Grand Loop Road just south of Madison Junction. The narrow asphalt road twists through a deep canyon and passes the 40-foot Firehole Falls. In the summer, look for a sign marking a pull-out and swimming hole. This is one of only two places in the park (Boiling River on the North Entrance Road is the other) where you can safely and legally swim in the park's thermally heated waters. Also, look carefully for osprey and other raptors, plus animal bones in a small cave on the opposite bank of the river. ⊠ *1 mi (2 km) south of Madison on Grand Loop Rd., Madison.*

HISTORIC SIGHTS

Some of the most visible evidence of the park's many Indian tribes is located in this section of the park. Roadside displays mark the influence of the Nez Perce and Sheepeater Indians. For frontier history, don't miss the Museum of the National Park Ranger.

Museum of the National Park Ranger. The former Norris Soldier Station housed soldiers who guarded the park from 1886 to 1916. It is now a museum where you can see a movie telling the history of the National Park Service. Other exhibits relate to army service in Yellowstone and early park rangers. ⊠*Grand Loop Rd. at Norris, Norris* ☉*Late May–Sept., daily 9–5.*

Roaring Mountain. On this barren hillside many steam vents have obliterated the vegetation. Try dawn or dusk for the best show. ⊠ *4 mi (6 km) north of Norris on Grand Loop Rd., Norris.*

Sheepeater Cliff. These 500,000-year-old lava cliffs are named for members of the Shoshone tribe who were the park's most consistent inhabitants in the late 18th and early 19th century. Bighorn sheep were a prized portion of their diet. Whereas the Bannock and Crow migrated through the park over vast stretches of the western and northern plains, Sheepeater were much more localized hunters and root gatherers who camped in this area of the park.

According to Joel Janetski's *Indians in Yellowstone National Park,* the first park superintendent Philetus W. Norris obtained agreements with all three tribes to ban them permanently from the park—shortly after Yellowstone's declaration as the national park in 1872. Notwith-

The Nez Perce in Yellowstone

The flight of the Nez Perce Indians during the summer of 1877 took them through Yellowstone for about two weeks. The desperate tribe started out as a group 800 men, women, and children, plus almost 2,000 horses, traveling from their homeland in present-day Oregon and Idaho. Many were killed, however, by the U.S. Army at Big Hole, Montana, in early August. On August 23, the remainder of the group entered the park, following the present-day Mary Mountain Trail (Nez Perce Creek) from the Firehole River to the Yellowstone River. They departed the park through the Absaroka Mountains before surrendering on October 5 just 40 mi from the Canadian border. Upon surrendering, it is believed that Chief Joseph uttered the famous statement, "From where the sun now stands, I will fight no more forever."

standing the storied escape attempt to Canada of the Nez Perce in the summer of 1877 (which took them directly through the heart of the park), hundreds of years of Native American inhabitation, hunting, and migration here ended in less than one decade. ⊠*Grand Loop road 10 mi (16 km) north of Norris Ranger Station, Norris.*

SCENIC STOPS

Gibbon Falls. Water rushes over the caldera rim in this 84-foot waterfall on the Gibbon River. ⊠*4 mi (6 km) east of Madison on Grand Loop Rd. Madison.*

☾ **Norris Geyser Basin.** From the Norris Ranger Station, choose
★ either Porcelain Basin or Back Basin, or both. The volatile thermal features are constantly changing, although you can expect to find a variety of geysers and springs here at any time. The area is accessible via an extensive system of boardwalks, some of them suitable for people with disabilities. ⊠*Grand Loop Rd. at Norris, Norris.*

The trail through **Back Basin** is a 1.5-mi loop guiding you past dozens of features highlighted by Steamboat Geyser. When it erupts fully (most recently in 1985), it's the world's largest, climbing 400 feet above the basin. More often, Steamboat growls and spits constantly, sending clouds of steam high above the basin. Kids will love the Puff 'n' Stuff Geyser and the mysterious cave-like Green Dragon Spring. Ask the Norris ranger for an anticipated schedule of geyser eruptions—you might catch the Echinus Geyser, which erupts almost hourly. ⊠ *Grand Loop Rd. at Norris, Norris*. The **Porcelain Basin** in the eastern portion of the Norris Geyser Basin is reached by a 0.75-mi, partially boardwalked loop from Norris Geyser Basin Museum. In this geothermal field of whitish geyserite stone, the earth bulges and belches from the underground pressure. You'll find bubbling pools, some milky white and others ringed in orange because of the minerals in the water, as well as small geysers such as extremely active Whirligig. ⊠ *Grand Loop Rd., Norris*.

OLD FAITHFUL AREA

Old Faithful is 16 mi (26 km) south of Madison.

The world's most famous geyser is the centerpiece of **Old Faithful** village, a destination almost all visitors include in their itinerary. Upper Geyser Basin has expansive boardwalks throughout, and the most extensive visitor services in the park are found in this area. The historic Old Faithful Inn is the most prominent lodging and dining facility in Yellowstone (if not the entire National Park System). The adjacent Old Faithful Snow Lodge and Old Faithful Lodge give you the same feeling of sleeping adjacent to a national icon, though they both pale compared to "the old house."

This crowded village also offers you multiple dining and shopping options, plus a gas station, medical clinic, post office, and more. Be advised, however, that the temporary visitor center is extremely limited in size and in the services that it offers. A new signature visitor center is slated to open in 2010.

Old Faithful Snow Lodge is one of just two lodgings open in the winter (Mammoth Hot Springs Hotel is the other). You can dine and stay in this area and cross-country ski or snowshoe throughout the Geyser Basin from your base here.

VISITOR CENTERS

Old Faithful Visitor Center. Unfortunately, the most visited place in the park does not have an adequate visitor center at this writing. A temporary trailer has housed an information center and Yellowstone Association bookstore since 2006. Park officials hope to open a new visitor center in 2010, but construction had not yet begun as of January

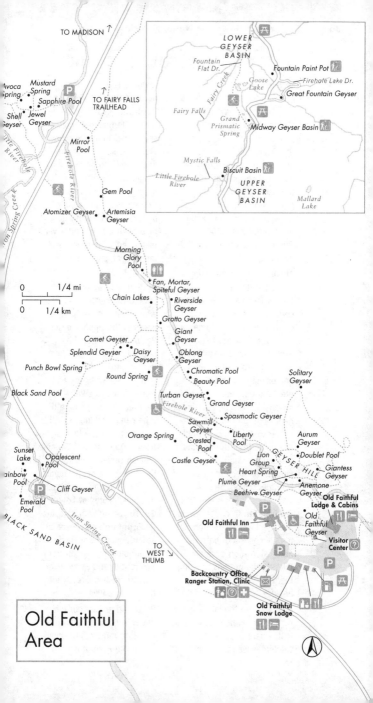

Old Faithful Area

TO MADISON ↑

Avoca Spring
Mustard Spring
Sapphire Pool
Shell Geyser
Jewel Geyser

↑ TO FAIRY FALLS TRAILHEAD

Mirror Pool

Firehole River

Little Firehole River

Iron Spring Creek

Gem Pool
Atomizer Geyser
Artemisia Geyser

Morning Glory Pool

0   1/4 mi
0   1/4 km

Fan, Mortar, Spiteful Geyser
Chain Lakes
Riverside Geyser
Grotto Geyser
Giant Geyser
Comet Geyser
Splendid Geyser
Daisy Geyser
Oblong Geyser
Punch Bowl Spring
Round Spring
Chromatic Pool
Beauty Pool
Black Sand Pool
Turban Geyser
Firehole River
Grand Geyser
Spasmodic Geyser
Orange Spring
Sawmill Geyser
Liberty Pool
Crested Pool
Castle Geyser
Sunset Lake
Opalescent Pool
Rainbow Pool
Cliff Geyser
Emerald Pool

BLACK SAND BASIN

Iron Spring Creek

Solitary Geyser

Aurum Geyser
Lion Group
Heart Spring
Plume Geyser
Beehive Geyser
Doublet Pool
Giantess Geyser
Anemone Geyser

GEYSER HILL

TO WEST THUMB ↓

Old Faithful Lodge & Cabins

Old Faithful Inn

Old Faithful Geyser

Visitor Center

Backcountry Office, Ranger Station, Clinic

Old Faithful Snow Lodge

Inset: Lower & Upper Geyser Basins

LOWER GEYSER BASIN

Fountain Flat Dr.
Fountain Paint Pot
Firehole Lake Dr.
Great Fountain Geyser

Fairy Creek
Goose Lake

Fairy Falls

Grand Prismatic Spring
Midway Geyser Basin

Mystic Falls

Little Firehole River

Biscuit Basin

UPPER GEYSER BASIN

Mallard Lake

A GOOD TOUR: OLD FAITHFUL

Serious exploration of the Old Faithful area takes a full day. Begin your morning at **Old Faithful Visitor Center,** where you should pick up the Old Faithful Area trail guide (suggested donation: 50¢) and check a board with the latest predictions for six geyser eruptions. (Predictions are approximate; for example, even in the case of Old Faithful, it's plus or minus 20 minutes.)

At Old Faithful Village you're in the heart of the Upper Geyser Basin, the densest concentration of geysers on earth, with about 140 geysers in 1 square mi. Start your exploration at **Old Faithful,** which spouts 130 to 180 feet approximately every 94 minutes. You don't need to jostle for position on the boardwalk directly in front of the visitor center to enjoy Old Faithful— any angle from the boardwalk surrounding the geyser is impressive. Depending on Old Faithful's timing, be sure to walk to the century-old **Old Faithful Inn** to check out its massive log construction. The Inn's second-floor balcony and observation deck are two shaded options to catch the geyser's eruption on a hot day.

Next, explore the larger basin with a hike around **Geyser Hill,** where you may see wildlife as well as thermal features. Follow the trail north to the **Morning Glory Pool,** with its unique flower shape. On this trail you will see Castle, Grand, and Riverside geysers, which are monitored and predicted by rangers at the visitor center. If you're short on time, return to the Village and continue by car to **Black Sand Basin** or **Biscuit Basin.** Better yet, hike to either and have a member of your party pick you up there.

At Biscuit Basin, boardwalks lead to the Mystic Falls Trail, where you can get good views of the Upper Geyser Basin. After a short hike, return to your car and head farther north. Take a break from geyser watching and picnic at the Nez Perce Picnic Area, close to where the tribe camped during its 1877 journey to escape federal troops. Don't neglect Firehole Canyon Drive (enter from the north); the deep canyon is impressive though often overlooked. Stop at **Lower Geyser Basin** with its colorful **Fountain Paint Pots,** or at **Midway Geyser Basin** where steaming runoff from 370-foot **Grand Prismatic Spring** crashes directly into the Firehole River.

Relax and revisit your long day with dinner (advance reservations required) or drinks at the Old Faithful Inn.

2008. Even with its limitations, this is the best place to inquire about geyser eruption predictions. Backcountry and fishing permits are handled out of the ranger station adjacent to the Old Faithful Snow Lodge. ⊠*Old Faithful Bypass Rd., Old Faithful* ☎*307/545–2750* ☉*Late Apr.– May, 9–5; June–Aug., 8–7; Sept., 8–6; Oct.–mid-Nov., 9–5; late Dec.–early March, 9–5.*

SCENIC DRIVES

Firehole Lake Drive. Eight miles north of Old Faithful, this one-way, 3-mi-long road takes you past **Great Fountain Geyser,** which shoots out jets of water reaching as high as 200 feet about twice a day. Rangers' predictions have a two-hour window of opportunity. Should you witness it, however, you'll be rewarded with a view of waves of water cascading down the terraces that form the edges of the geyser. Watch for bison, particularly in the winter. ⊠*Firehole Lake Dr., 8 mi (13 km) north of Old Faithful Old Faithful.*

HISTORIC SIGHTS

Old Faithful Inn. It's hard to imagine how any work could be accomplished when snow and ice blanket the region, but this historic hotel was constructed over the course of a single winter in 1903. Serving as a lodging establishment since 1904, this massive log structure is an attraction in its own right. Even if you don't spend a night at the Old Faithful Inn, walk through or take the free 45-minute guided tour to admire its massive open-beam lobby and rock fireplace (where tours begin). There are antique writing desks on the second-floor balcony, and during evening hours a pianist plays there as well. You can watch Old Faithful geyser from two second-floor outdoor decks. ⊠*Old Faithful Bypass Rd., Old Faithful* ☎*307/344–7901* ☉*May–mid-Oct.; tours daily, times vary.*

NEED A BREAK? Late afternoon is a good time to relax with a cool drink in the lobby or on the second-floor balcony of the **Old Faithful Inn** (⊠*Old Faithful Bypass Rd., Old Faithful*). You'll hear piano music floating around the massive log walls and stone fireplace, and witness the hustle and bustle of visitors from around the world.

SCENIC STOPS

Black Sand Basin. There are a dozen hot springs and geysers near the cloverleaf entrance from Grand Loop Road to Old Faithful. Emerald Pool is one of the prettiest. ⊠*North of Old Faithful on Grand Loop Rd., Old Faithful.*

Biscuit Basin. North of Old Faithful, this basin is also the trailhead for the Mystic Falls Trail. The namesake "biscuit" formations were reduced to crumbs when Sapphire Pool erupted following the 1959 Hebgen Lake Earthquake. Now, Sapphire is a calm, beautiful blue pool again, but that could change at any moment. ⊠*3 mi (5 km) north of Old Faithful on Grand Loop Rd., Old Faithful.*

☾ **Geyser Hill Loop.** Along the 1.3-mi Geyser Hill Loop boardwalk you will see active thermal features such as violent Giantess Geyser. Normally erupting only a few times each year, Giantess spouts 100 to 250 feet in the air for five to eight minutes once or twice hourly for 12 to 43 hours. Nearby Doublet Pool's two adjacent springs have complex ledges and deep blue waters, which are highly photogenic. Starting as a gentle pool, Anemone Geyser overflows, bubbles, and finally erupts 10 feet or more, every three to eight minutes. The loop boardwalk brings you close to the action, making it especially appealing to children intrigued with the sights and sounds of the basin. Also keep a lookout for elk and buffalo in this area. To reach Geyser Hill, head counterclockwise around the Old Faithful boardwalk 0.3 mi from the visitor center, crossing the Firehole River and entering Upper Geyser Basin. ⊠*Old Faithful, 0.3 mi (0.5 km) from the Old Faithful Visitor Center, Old Faithful.*

Lower Geyser Basin. Shooting more than 150 feet in the air, the Great Fountain Geyser is the most spectacular sight in this basin. Less impressive but more regular is White Dome Geyser, which shoots from a 20-foot-tall cone. You'll also find pink mud pots and blue pools at the basin's Fountain Paint Pots. ⊠*Midway between Old Faithful and Madison on Grand Loop Rd.*

Midway Geyser Basin. Called "Hell's Half Acre" by writer Rudyard Kipling, Midway Geyser Basin is a more interesting stop than Lower Geyser Basin. A series of boardwalks wind their way to the Excelsior Geyser, which deposits 4,000 gallons of vivid blue water per minute into the Firehole river. Just above Excelsior is Yellowstone's largest hot spring, Grand Prismatic Spring. Measuring 370

Old Faithful Inn

If you love architecture, crafts-manship, and history, the daily 45-minute tour of Old Faithful Inn is a don't-miss event. The hotel, which was constructed in just 13 months and opened in 1904, has been faithfully updated and restored over the years. It has survived more than 100 inhospitable winters, a 7.5-magnitude earthquake, and the fires of 1988, which burned several adjacent cab-ins but almost miraculously spared this National Historic Landmark.

Architect Robert Reamer de-signed and built the Inn when he was 29 years old. He con-structed the "Old House" out of local materials—lodgepole pine is the basis for the struc-ture, and rhyolite stone from nearby Black Sand Basin com-prises the mammoth fireplace and chimney that draw your attention to the ceiling, 76 feet above the lobby floor.

Note the "treehouse," a maze-like network of stairs and catwalks leading into the rafters above the lobby. The third story accesses bellhop's quarters (to this day, still the only hotel where employees are entitled to live inside the building). Additional stairs lead to dormer windows, a fourth-floor platform to reset the gigantic clock, the uppermost platform where musicians once performed regularly, and the "Widow's Walk" on the roof. Visitors can only ascend to the second floor, but you can listen to piano, collect your thoughts at antique writing desks, peer into the dining room from a balcony, or venture onto the veranda to watch Old Faithful erupt.

Reamer wasn't the only crafts-man to contribute to the inn, and you can see the work of several other artisans through-out the structure. For example, blacksmith George Colpitts' iron work is larger-than-life. Note the locks and hinges on the bright, red front door; the clock on the fireplace, the five-foot long fireplace tools (in-cluding popcorn popper), light fixtures, and much more, which he designed.

Artist Walter Oehrle created the "Bear Pit" panels originally of Douglas fir. Commissioned in 1933 by Reamer to cel-ebrate the end of Prohibition, cartoon character wildlife are depicted celebrating the end of Prohibition. In 1988, they were re-created as sandblasted glass panels, which now separate the Dining Room and the Bear Pit Tavern.

The late Western artist Paco Young created the painting of Old Faithful for the dining room fireplace in 2000. He passed away just a few years later of leukemia.

feet in diameter, it's deep blue in color with yellow and orange rings formed by bacteria that give it the effect of a prism. ⊠*Between Old Faithful and Madison on Grand Loop Rd.*

Morning Glory Pool. Shaped somewhat like a morning glory flower, this pool once was a deep blue, but tourists dropping coins and other debris into it clogged the natural plumbing vent. At one point the pool had turned a sickly green color. Though it has been cleaned and people are warned not to throw anything into it, the Morning Glory Pool has never regained its pristine color. To reach the pool, follow the boardwalk past Geyser Hill Loop and stately Castle Geyser, which has the biggest cone in Yellowstone. It erupts every 10 to 12 hours, to heights of 90 feet, for as much as an hour at a time. From Morning Glory Pool, it's almost 3 mi back to the visitor center. ⊠*At the north end of Upper Geyser Basin, Old Faithful.*

DID YOU KNOW? An Inspirational Geyser Morning Glory Pool is the inspiration for award-winning Jan Brett's popular children's book Hedgie Blasts Off!, in which a hedgehog goes to another planet to unclog a geyser clogged by space tourists' debris.

★ Fodor'sChoice **Old Faithful.** Almost every visitor includes the world's most famous geyser on his or her itinerary. Yellowstone's most predictable big geyser—although not its largest or most regular—sometimes reaches 180 feet, but it averages 130 feet. Sometimes it doesn't shoot as high, but in those cases the eruptions usually last longer. The mysterious plumbing of Yellowstone has lengthened Old Faithful's cycle somewhat in recent years, to every 94 minutes or so. To find out when Old Faithful is likely to erupt, check at the visitor center, or at any of the lodging properties in the area. You can view the eruption from a bench just yards away, from the dining room at the lodge cafeteria, or from a guest room at the spectacular Old Faithful Inn (assuming you are lucky enough to spend the night there). The 1-mi hike to Observation Point yields yet another view—from above—of the geyser and its surrounding basin. ⊠*Southwest segment, Grand Loop Rd., Old Faithful.*

YELLOWSTONE LAKE

West Thumb is 17 mi (27 km) east of Old Faithful; Grant Village is 2 mi (3 km) south of West Thumb; Bridge Bay is

*18 mi (29 km) north of West Thumb; Lake Village is 4 mi
(6.5 km) northeast of Bridge Bay; Fishing Bridge is 1.5 mi
(2.5 km) northeast of Lake Village.*

The soul and lifeline of Yellowstone National Park, this
132-square mi ice-cold lake is not as dramatic as the park's
peaks nor as sublime as its valleys. Nonetheless, the frigid
expanse of water sustains much of the park and—as has
recently been revealed—may hold important secrets of the
park's geological history in its depths.

The northern and western shores of Yellowstone Lake
are accessible to the public. Lodging, restaurants, campgrounds, and services are available at a cluster of villages
in the north, at Lake Village, Fishing Bridge, and Bridge
Bay; Grant Village has the only lodging in the entire southern third of the park. Each village has departure points for
boating, fishing, and hiking. If you base yourself in one of
the lake villages, you will be in easy striking distance of the
unique geyser basin of West Thumb, great wildlife-viewing
spots in the Pelican Valley, and good hiking trails to small
peaks like Elephant Back and Lake Overlook.

Except for the four developed areas, the remainder of the
lake and its coastline lie inaccessible except to boaters and
backcountry hikers. In fact, the Thorofare Ranger Station in the southeast corner of the park is the most remote
inhabited spot in the lower 48 states. It's more than 30 mi
(48 km) in any direction to a paved road. It's beautiful,
rugged forest, but only for the well-prepared. In the winter
months, the lake freezes over completely with ice ranging
in depth from a few inches to several feet.

Grant Village, on the western shore of Lake Yellowstone, is
the first community on the road from the South Entrance.
It has basic lodging and dining facilities and provides easy
access to the West Thumb Geyser Basin. It takes about two
hours to hike to Lake Overlook and explore West Thumb
Geyser Basin.

VISITOR CENTERS

Grant Village Visitor Center. Each visitor center in the park
tells a small piece of the park's history. This one tells the
story of fire in the park. A seminal moment in Yellowstone's
historical record, the 1988 fire burned 36% of the total
acreage of the park and forced multiple federal agencies to
re-evaluate their fire control policies. Watch an informative

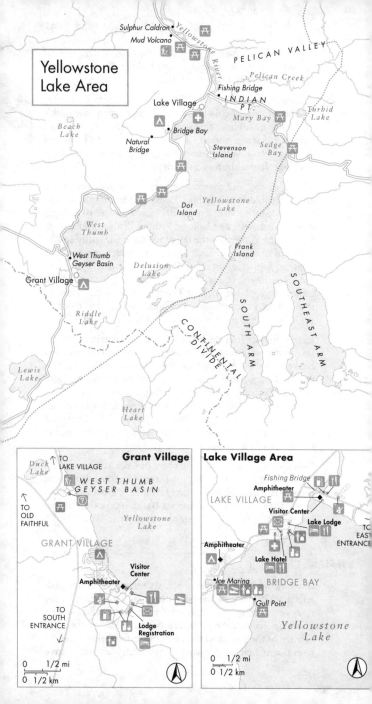

Yellowstone Lake Area

Sulphur Caldron
Mud Volcano
Yellowstone River
PELICAN VALLEY
Pelican Creek
Fishing Bridge
INDIAN PT.
Lake Village
Mary Bay
Turbid Lake
Beach Lake
Bridge Bay
Natural Bridge
Stevenson Island
Sedge Bay
Dot Island
Yellowstone Lake
Frank Island
West Thumb
West Thumb Geyser Basin
Grant Village
Delusion Lake
Riddle Lake
CONTINENTAL DIVIDE
SOUTH ARM
SOUTHEAST ARM
Lewis Lake
Heart Lake

Grant Village

Duck Lake
TO LAKE VILLAGE
WEST THUMB GEYSER BASIN
TO OLD FAITHFUL
Yellowstone Lake
GRANT VILLAGE
Visitor Center
Amphitheater
TO SOUTH ENTRANCE
Lodge Registration

0   1/2 mi
0   1/2 km

Lake Village Area

Fishing Bridge
Amphitheater
LAKE VILLAGE
Visitor Center
Lake Lodge
TO EAST ENTRANCE
Amphitheater
Lake Hotel
Ice Marina
BRIDGE BAY
Gull Point
Yellowstone Lake

0   1/2 mi
0   1/2 km

video, purchase maps or books, and learn more about the 25,000 firefighters from across America who fought the 1988 fire. There's no coffee available here. ⊠*Grant Village* ☎*307/242-2650* ⊙*Late May–Labor Day daily 8–7; Labor Day–Sept. 30, daily 9–6.*

West Thumb Information Station. This historic log cabin houses a Yellowstone Association bookstore and doubles as a warming hut in the winter. There are restrooms in the parking area. Check for informal ranger-led discussions "beneath the old Sequoia tree" in the summer. There's no coffee available here. ⊠*West Thumb* ⊙*Late May–Sept., daily 9–5.*

☙ **Fishing Bridge Visitor Center.** This distinctive stone-and-log building, which was built in 1931, has been designated a National Historic Landmark. If you can't distinguish between a Clark's nut hatch and an ermine (note: one's a bird, the other a rodent), check out the extensive exhibits on park wildlife. Step out the back door to find yourself on one of the beautiful black obsidian beaches of Yellowstone Lake. The Yellowstone Association bookstore here features books, guides, and other educational materials, but you can't buy coffee. ⊠*East Entrance Rd., 1 mi (2 km) from Grand Loop Rd.* ☎*307/242-2450* ⊙*Memorial Day–Labor Day, daily 8–7; Sept. (after Labor Day), daily 9–6.*

SCENIC DRIVES

East Entrance Road. Crossing the Absaroka Range, this 16-mi (26-km) drive descends from the 8,530-foot Sylvan Pass to idyllic views of Yellowstone Lake. The road hugs the lake shoreline between Lake Butte and Fishing Bridge where some vistas may remind you of the northern California coast. ⊠*Begin drive at East Entrance gate.*

South Entrance Road. The sheer black lava walls of the Lewis River canyon make this a memorable drive. Turn into the parking area at the highway bridge for a close-up view of the spectacular Lewis River Falls, one of the park's most-photographed sights. ⊠*Begin drive at South Entrance gate.*

HISTORIC SIGHTS

★ Fodor'sChoice **Lake Yellowstone Hotel.** Completed in 1891, this structure on the National Register of Historic Places is the oldest lodging in any national park. Spiffed up for its cen-

CLOSE UP

Geological Cheat Sheet

These four definitions will help keep you out of hot water as you navigate the park's myriad geothermal features:

■ "Hot Springs" occur when visible hot water is circulating at the surface.

■ "Fumaroles" occur when water turns to vapor before reaching surface and exits cracks in the earth as steam.

■ "Geysers" occur when underground water is trapped and comes to surface periodically only when the pressure "bursts through" the impediment and shoots into the air.

■ "Mudpots" occur when hot springs of water combine with sulfuric acid to dissolve surrounding rock into clay, forming "boiling" mud.

tennial in 1991, it now feels fresh and new. Casual daytime visitors can lounge in white wicker chairs in the sunroom and watch the waters of Yellowstone Lake through massive windows. Robert Reamer, the architect of the Old Faithful Inn, added its columned entrance in 1903 to enhance the original facade. ⊠*Lake Village Rd., Lake Village* ☎*307/344–7901* ⊘*Mid-May–early Oct.*

★ **Lake Yellowstone Lodge.** More rustic and homey than the elegant Lake Yellowstone Hotel, this lodge features a 140-foot big-timber foyer and a view of the sunrise from its eastern porch that is unparalleled. Completed in 1926, this Robert Reamer structure has registration for adjacent cabins, a restaurant, bar, gift shop, two dramatic fireplaces, and plenty of space to catch up with fellow travelers or the latest newspaper. ⊠*Lake Village Rd., Lake Village* ☎*307/344–7901* ⊘*Early June–late Sept.*

Lake Ranger Station. Completed in 1923, this eight-sided cabin with a central fireplace is one of the niftiest little structures in the park. It's also the oldest continuously used ranger station in the 397-unit National Park System. ⊠*Adjacent to Lake General Store, behind Lake Hotel, Lake Village.*

SCENIC STOPS

Lake Overlook. From this hilltop northwest of West Thumb and Grant Village you get an expansive view of the southwest portion of Yellowstone. You reach the promontory by taking a 1.5-mi hiking trail through forest still recovering from the massive fires of 1988; the clearing caused by the fire makes this a prime area for sighting elk. ⊠ *1.5 mi (2.5 km) northwest of Grant Village.*

☙ **West Thumb Geyser Basin.** The primary Yellowstone caldera was created by a volcanic eruption 640,000 years ago, but West Thumb came about much more recently—"only" 150,000 years ago—as the result of a another volcanic eruption. This unique geyser basin is the only place to see active geothermal features in Lake Yellowstone. Two boardwalk loops are offered; take the longer one to see features like "Fishing Cone," where fishermen used to catch fish, pivot, and drop their fish straight into boiling water for cooking without ever taking if off the hook. This area is particularly popular for winter visitors, who take advantage of the nearby warming hut and a stroll around the geyser basin before continuing their trip via snow coach or snowmobile. ⊠ *Grand Loop Rd., 22 mi (35 km) north of South Entrance, West Thumb.*

Lake Butte. Reached by a spur road off the East Entrance Road, this wooded promontory rising 615 feet above Yellowstone Lake is a prime spot for watching the sun set over the lake. ⊠ *Approx. 8.5 mi (13.5 km) east of Fishing Bridge on East Entrance Rd., Fishing Bridge.*

LeHardy Rapids. Witness one of nature's epic battles as cutthroat trout migrate upstream to spawn in spring by catapulting themselves out of the water to get by, over, and around rocks and rapids here on the Yellowstone River. The quarter-mile forested loop takes you to the river's edge. Also keep an eye out for waterfowl and bears, which feed on the trout. ⊠ *3 mi (5 km) north of Fishing Bridge, Fishing Bridge.*

☙ **Mud Volcano.** The 0.75-mi round-trip Mud Volcano Interpretive Trail loops gently around seething, sulfuric mud pots with names such as Black Dragon's Cauldron and Sizzling Basin before making its way around Mud Volcano itself, a boiling pot of brown goo. ⊠ *10 mi (16 mi) south of Canyon; 4 mi (6 km) north of Fishing Bridge on Grand Loop Rd., Fishing Bridge.*

Natural Bridge. You can take an easy 1-mi hike or bicycle ride from Bridge Bay Campground to Natural Bridge, which was formed by erosion of a rhyolite outcrop by Bridge Creek. The top of the bridge is about 50 feet above the creek, and there is a trail to its top, though travel over the bridge itself is prohibited. ⊠ *1 mi (2 km) west of Bridge Bay Campground, Bridge Bay.*

Pelican Valley. The long valley following Pelican Creek is some of the best wildlife habitat in the lower 48 states. If you take a hike here, you are likely to see bison, elk, moose, osprey, eagles, sandhill cranes, and possibly grizzly bears. There are a variety of trails in the valley, ranging from the 3.4-mi trail to Pelican Creek Bridge, to the 16-mi trail that takes you clear across the broad meadow and forest ecosystem. Because this area is so widely used by grizzly bears, there are certain restrictions, including no trail hiking during evening and night hours. For backcountry users, campsites are established outside the valley itself. The trailhead for Pelican Valley is east of Fishing Bridge; inquire at the visitor center there for trail conditions and restrictions. ⊠ *3 mi (5 km) east of Fishing Bridge, Fishing Bridge* ☉ *Closed Apr.–early July due to bear activity.*

Sulphur Caldron. You can smell the sulphur before you even leave your vehicle to walk to the overlook of Sulphur Caldron, where hissing steam escapes from a moonscape-like surface as superheated bubbling mud. ⊠ *9.5 mi (15 km) south of Canyon; 4.5 mi north of Fishing Bridge on Grand Loop Rd., Fishing Bridge.*

★ Fodor'sChoice**Yellowstone Lake.** One of the world's largest ☪ alpine lakes, encompassing 132 square mi, Yellowstone Lake was formed when glaciers that once covered the region melted into a caldera—a crater formed by a volcano. The lake has 141 mi (227 km) of shoreline, less than one-third of it followed by the East Entrance Road and Grand Loop Road, along which you will often see moose, elk, waterfowl, and other wildlife. In winter you can sometimes see otters and coyotes stepping gingerly on the ice at the lake's edge. Many visitors head here for the excellent fishing— streams flowing into the lake give it an abundant supply of trout. ⊠ *Intersection of East Entrance Rd. and Grand Loop Rd., between Fishing Bridge and Grant Village.*

MAMMOTH HOT SPRINGS AREA

Mammoth Hot Springs is 33 mi (53 km) northwest of Canyon Junction, 5 mi (8 km) south of the North Entrance, 18 mi (29 km) northwest of Tower Falls, and 21 mi (34 km) north of Norris.

Mammoth Hot Springs is known for its massive natural terraces, where mineral water flows continuously, building an ever-changing display. You will almost always see elk grazing in the area. Mammoth Hot Springs is also headquarters for Yellowstone National Park. In the early days of the park, it was the site of Fort Yellowstone, and the brick buildings constructed during that era are still used for various park activities. The Albright Visitor Center has information and displays about the park history, including reproductions of original Thomas Moran paintings, created on an 1871 government expedition to the area, that made the broader public aware of Yellowstone's beauty and helped lead to its establishment as a national park. There is a complete range of visitor services here as well. Schedule about half a day for exploration. There are lots of steps on the lower terrace boardwalks, so plan to take your time there.

VISITOR CENTERS

↻ **Albright Visitor Center.** Serving as bachelor quarters for cavalry officers from 1886 to 1918, this red-roof building now holds a museum with exhibits on the early inhabitants of the region and a theater showing films about the history of the park. There are original Thomas Moran paintings of the park on display here as well. Kids and taxidermists will love extensive displays of park wildlife, including bears and wolves. ✉*Mammoth Hot Springs* ☎*307/344–2263* ☉*Late May–Aug., daily 8–7; Sept., daily 8–5; Oct.–May, daily 9–5.*

SCENIC DRIVES

Blacktail Deer Plateau Drive. Keep an eye out for coyotes on this dirt road that traverses sagebrush-covered hills and forests of lodgepole pines. ✉*10 mi (16 km) east of Mammoth Hot Springs.*

Upper Terrace Drive. Limber pines as old as 500 years line this 1.5-mi loop near Mammoth Hot Springs. You'll also spot a variety of mosses growing through white travertine, composed of lime deposited here by the area's hot springs. ✉*Approx. 2 mi by car from Mammoth Hot Springs Hotel*

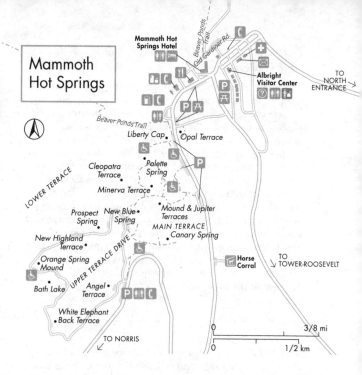

Mammoth Hot Springs

Mammoth Hot Springs Hotel

Beaver Ponds Trail

Old Gardiner Rd.

Albright Visitor Center

TO NORTH ENTRANCE

Beaver Ponds Trail

Liberty Cap • Opal Terrace

Cleopatra Terrace

Palette Spring

Minerva Terrace

Prospect Spring

New Blue Spring

Mound & Jupiter Terraces

MAIN TERRACE

Canary Spring

New Highland Terrace

Orange Spring Mound

Bath Lake

Angel Terrace

Horse Corral

TO TOWER-ROOSEVELT

White Elephant • Back Terrace

UPPER TERRACE DRIVE

LOWER TERRACE

TO NORRIS

| 0 | | 3/8 mi |
| 0 | | 1/2 km |

on Grand Loop Rd. Reachable by foot from Lower Terrace Dr., Mammoth Hot Springs.

HISTORIC SIGHTS

Fort Yellowstone. The oldest buildings at Mammoth Hot Springs served as Fort Yellowstone from 1886 to 1916, the period when the U.S. Army managed the park. The redbrick buildings cluster around an open area reminiscent of a frontier-era fort parade ground. You can pick up a self-guided tour map of the area to make your way around the historic fort structures. ⊠*Mammoth Hot Springs.*

SCENIC STOPS

★ **Fodor's**Choice **Mammoth Hot Springs Terraces.** Multicolored travertine terraces formed by slowly escaping hot mineral water mark this unusual geological formation. It constantly changes as a result of shifts in water flow. You can explore the terraces via an elaborate network of boardwalks. The best is the Lower Terrace Interpretive Trail. If you start at

CLOSE UP

Ever-Changing Yellowstone

Yellowstone is definitely not a sleepy world of natural wonders. The park truly feels alive when you see mud pots, steam vents, fumaroles, and paint pots—all different aspects of the park's geyser basins, and all intriguing. Beyond the geyser activity, seasonal changes in wildlife and vegetation make Yellowstone fascinating to visit over and over again.

The force and nature of the various geysers depend on several factors, including the complex underground geology at Yellowstone. Rangers say the greatest threats to the geyser basin activity are earthquakes (which occur regularly in the region, though they are usually very small tremors) and the impact caused by people. The fate of Morning Glory Pool is a particularly troubling cautionary tale (see ⇨ Morning Glory Pool in Old Faithful Area, above).

The ongoing ecological development of the region draws widespread interest. The efforts to control the movement of bison, the lingering effects of the 1988 fire, and reintroduction of wolves to the ecosystem and are just three examples of issues that divide opinions on the management of Yellowstone.

Bison leave the park in winter—mainly through the North and West entrances—in part because of overpopulation and the need to find adequate feed. Their movements are sometimes made easier by the winter grooming of Yellowstone roads for use by over-snow vehicles.

When massive wildfires tore through Yellowstone in 1988, some believed it would take generations for the park to recover. Already, the park has begun to renew itself. Certainly, when you visit Yellowstone now you will see reminders of fires from 1988 and more recent fires, but you will also see the new growth. Lodgepole-pine forests need fire to release their seeds, and once seeds get a start, trees grow quickly.

Wolves were brought back to Yellowstone in 1995. They acclimated so well that they quickly formed several packs, some of which have ventured outside the park's boundaries, and their presence has had a lasting effect on wildlife populations. The wolves feed on both elk and buffalo, and researchers have noted a significant decline in elk calf survival throughout the region. Park rangers have also reported a significant decline in Yellowstone's coyote population. Since the wolves are bigger and stronger than coyotes, they kill coyotes or force them to find a new range.

2

Liberty Cap, at the area's north end, and head uphill on the boardwalks, you'll pass bright and ornately terraced Minerva Spring. It's about an hour walk. Along the way you may spy elk, as they graze nearby. Alternatively, you can drive up to the Lower Terrace Overlook on Upper Terrace Drive and take the boardwalks down past New Blue Springs to the Lower Terrace. This route, which also takes an hour, works especially well if you can park a second vehicle at the foot of Lower Terrace. ⊠*Northwest corner of Grand Loop Rd., Mammoth Hot Springs.*

★ **Roosevelt Arch.** One of the enduring symbols of the park, Roosevelt Arch has greeted visitors on the north entrance road since President Theodore Roosevelt helped set the giant cornerstone in April 1903. The 50-foot arch was designed by Old Faithful Inn architect Robert Reamer. Its simple, noble inscription reads: FOR THE BENEFIT AND ENJOY- MENT OF THE PEOPLE, the words taken from a Theodore Roosevelt speech on the day the cornerstone was set. ⊠*North Entrance Rd., just south of Gardiner, Mont.*

YELLOWSTONE CANYON AREA

The Yellowstone River's source is in the Absaroka mountains in the extreme southeast corner of the park. It winds its way through the heart of the park, entering Yellowstone Lake at the Southeast Arm and heading northward under Fishing Bridge through Hayden Valley. It cuts through the multicolored Grand Canyon of the Yellowstone near Canyon Village, is joined by the Lamar River at Tower Fall, then flows north of the Grand Loop Road through the gateway community of Gardiner, Montana, on its 676-mi journey to the Missouri River in North Dakota. The lands surrounding the river range from peaceful meadows, such as the Hayden Valley, to the 1,000-foot Grand Canyon walls with its two major falls. For fishermen, hikers, or sightseers, the river offers something from everyone.

The Canyon Area is one of the most spectacular places in Yellowstone, but it attracts an almost unmanageable number of tourists as well. Here in the central part of the park, near the eastern meeting point of the Upper and Lower loops, you will find all types of visitors' services and lots of hiking opportunities.

⚠ **Construction will wreak havoc on visitors to the canyon's north rim for the entire 2008 season, however, as the North**

Rim Road is scheduled to be closed. Popular north rim scenic stops Grand View, Lookout Point, Inspiration Point, and Brink of the Lower Falls may be reachable only by foot, if at all. Check with park officials for the latest updates.

North of Canyon lie more peaceful areas of the park. At nearly 9,000 feet, Dunraven Pass, along the road from Canyon to Tower-Roosevelt, is the highest pass on the Grand Loop Road, and as a result, it's the last road to open each summer. Head east at the Tower-Roosevelt junction on the Northeast Entrance Road for a remote, 29-mi stretch of road to tiny Cooke City, Montana. It bisects the wildlife-rich Lamar Valley, with its wolf packs, grizzly bears, and bison, before following Soda Butte Creek under the shadow of the most beautiful peaks in the park.

Hiking and horseback riding are the best means to see many of the sights in the area, such as a petrified forest, trout-filled streams, and high ridges that offer broad vistas. It will take you a couple of hours to drive through this area and a full day if you decide to explore on foot.

VISITOR CENTERS

☼ **Canyon Visitor Center.** This gleaming new Visitor Center is
★ the pride of the park service with elaborate, interactive exhibits for adults and kids. The focus here is volcanoes and earthquakes, but there are also exhibits on Native Americans and park wildlife, including bison and wolves. The video entitled *Water, Heat & Rock* is a riveting look at the geo- and hydrothermal basis for the park. As at all visitor centers, you can obtain park information, backcountry camping permits, etc. The adjacent bookstore, operated by the Yellowstone Association, is the best in the park, with guidebooks, trail maps, gifts, and hundreds of books on the park, its history, and the science surrounding it. ⊠ *Canyon Village, Canyon Area* ☎ *307/242–2552* ☼ *Late May–Aug., daily 8–7; Sept., daily 8–6; Oct. 1–14, daily 9–5.*

SCENIC DRIVES

Northeastern Grand Loop. A 19-mi segment of Grand Loop Road running between Canyon Village and Roosevelt Falls, this byway passes some of the park's finest scenery, twisting beneath a series of leaning basalt towers 40 to 50 feet high. That behemoth to the east is 10,243-foot

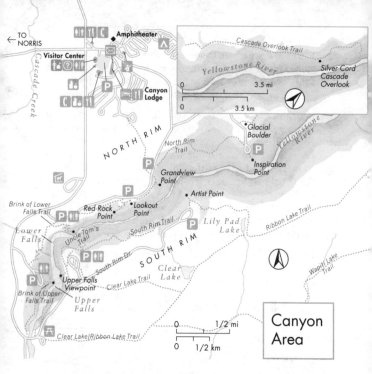

Mount Washburn. ⊠*Between Canyon Village and Roosevelt Falls, Canyon Area.*

★ Fodor's Choice **Northeast Entrance Road and Lamar Valley.** The 29-mi road features the richest diversity of landscape of the five entrance roads. Just after you enter the park from the northeast, you'll cut between 10,928-foot Abiathar Peak and the 10,404-foot Barronette Peak. You'll pass the extinct geothermal cone called Soda Butte as well as the two nicest campgrounds in the park, Pebble Creek and Slough Creek. Lamar Valley is the melancholy home to hundreds of bison, while the rugged peaks and ridges adjacent to it are home to some of the park's most famous wolf packs (reintroduced in 1995). The main wolf-watching activities in the park occur here during early-morning and late-evening hours year-round. As you exit Lamar Valley, the road crosses the Yellowstone River before leading you to the rustic Roosevelt Lodge. ⊠*From Northeast Entrance near Cooke City to junction with Grand Loop Rd. at Roosevelt Lodge, Tower-Roosevelt.*

A GOOD TOUR: GRAND CANYON

Most Canyon visitors catch their first view of the **Grand Canyon of the Yellowstone** from **Artist Point,** where there are two viewing levels, but only the lower one is accessible to wheelchairs. After you have peered into the canyon, take at least a short hike along the rim; then return to your vehicle and backtrack along **South Rim Drive** to the Uncle Tom's parking area. If your schedule allows, park there and hike along the **South Rim Trail,** which offers impressive views of the yellow walls above the river.

After your explorations from the South Canyon rim, return to the Grand Loop Road and proceed to the Canyon Village, where you should begin explorations at the park's impressive new **Canyon Visitor Center,** where park rangers can give you specific details about hikes, and where you can learn more about bison, geology, volcanic activity, and Native Americans in the park. If you enjoyed the South Canyon rim, skip the crowded **North Rim Drive** (closed throughout 2008), except for **Brink of the Lower Falls** (if it's open), where you can feel as much as 60,000 gallons of water per second race by you on its way to a 308-foot plunge.

For a great early-morning or late-evening side trip with opportunities to see a variety of wildlife, travel south of Canyon and into the open meadows of the **Hayden Valley,** which is home to hundreds of bison, water birds, and other wildlife.

Depending on how much hiking you want to do, it can take you anywhere from half a day to a couple of days to explore the Grand Canyon of the Yellowstone.

Hayden Valley. Bison, bears, coyotes, wolves, and birds of prey all call Hayden Valley home—almost year-round. Once part of Yellowstone Lake, the broad valley now features peaceful meadows, rolling hills, and the placid Yellowstone River. There are multiple turnouts and picnic areas on the 16-mi drive, many with uniquely enjoyable views of the river and valley. Ask a ranger about "Grizzly Overlook," where wildlife watchers, including Park Service rangers with spotting scopes for the public to use, congregate in the summer. The overlook is three turnouts north of Mud Volcano—look for the timber railings. ⊠*Between Canyon and Fishing Bridge on Grand Loop Rd.*

Wolf Reintroduction

Amid great controversy and highly charged emotions, the National Park Service reintroduced wolves to the park in 1995. A native predator when the park was founded in the 19th century, wolves had been completely eradicated from the park for 70 years. However, when the gray wolf was listed as an endangered species in 1974, it triggered a movement to bring wolves back to their natural habitat.

In January 1995 and 1996, 31 wolves were released in the park after being captured in Canada. Elaborate preparations were made to minimize the wolves' interaction with humans, to select animals from the same social group, and to acclimatize the wolves to the park. Although five years of relocations had been planned, the original wolves thrived—growing in a decade to 48 packs and nearly 400 wolves in the Yellowstone ecosystem.

NPS documents suggest that the wolf recovery has been an unqualified success, leading to greater biodiversity in the ecosystem. Incidents between wolves and humans or wolves and livestock outside the park have occurred less frequently than expected. The flourishing of the wolves has even led to the proposed delisting of wolves from endangered species list.

Private citizen "wolf watchers" visit the park on a daily basis now. They can often be found at roadside turnouts in Lamar Valley monitoring packs through their spotting scopes.

HISTORIC SIGHTS

Lamar Buffalo Ranch. For the first half of the 20th century, park employees managed the park's near-extinct bison population from this ranch. It is thought that hundreds of thousands of bison once roamed the park, but the herds were systematically winnowed to less than 100 animals by the turn of the 20th century. There are no public services available here, except to participants in the natural and cultural history courses taught here by the Yellowstone Association. An informative roadside marker provides more details and helps visitors picture thousands upon thousands of bison in the valley before them. ⊠ *Grand Loop Rd., at Norris* ☎ *No phone* ⊗ *June–Sept., daily 10–5.*

SCENIC STOPS

★ FodorsChoice **Grand Canyon of the Yellowstone.** This stunning canyon is 23 mi (37 km) long, but there is only one trail from rim to base. As a result, a majority of Park visitors clog the north and south rims to see Upper and Lower Falls. To compound problems, the North Rim Road has been closed for the 2008 season for construction, leaving many popular viewpoints reachable only by foot, if at all. Unless you're up for the six-hour strenuous hike called Seven Mile Hole, you have no choice but to join the crowds on the rims to see this natural wonder. ⊠*Canyon.*

★ **Artist Point.** The most spectacular view of the Lower Falls of the Yellowstone River is seen from this point, which has two different viewing levels, one of which is accessible to wheelchairs. The South Rim Trail goes right past this point, and there is a nearby parking area open in both summer and winter. ⊠*East end of South Rim Rd., Canyon.*

Brink of the Lower Falls Trail. The best viewpoint of the Lower Falls (and a glimpse of the Upper Falls) is on the North Rim Trail. It's a steep descent on a paved switchback trail that deposits you on a viewing platform just a few feet from the top of the 308-foot falls, where you can feel and hear the spray of water. ■TIP→ **This trail may be affected, or closed, by the closure of the North Rim road for all of 2008, so check with park rangers.** ⊠*0.75 mi south of Canyon, off Grand Loop Rd.*

Brink of the Upper Falls Trail. A spur road off Grand Loop Road south of Canyon gives you access to the west end of the North Rim Trail and takes you down a fairly steep trail for a view of Upper Falls from almost directly above. ■TIP→ **This trail may be affected, or closed, by the closure of the North Rim road for all of 2008, so check with park rangers.** ⊠*0.75 mi south of Canyon, off Grand Loop Rd., Canyon.*

Grand View Point. With four viewpoints from the North Rim Trail, you can easily skip this one and proceed to Lookout Point and/or Brink of the Lower Falls Trail. ■TIP→ **This trail may be affected, or closed, by the closure of the North Rim road for all of 2008, so check with park rangers.** ⊠*Off North Rim Dr., Canyon.*

Inspiration Point. The only inspiration here comes from the information panel that reminds visitors that 100 feet of the observation deck plunged into the canyon during a 1965 earthquake. As a result, there is no inspiring view of the

Lower Falls from here, just busloads of disappointed tourists and a logjam of cars. Skip this stop. Reached via a spur road off North Rim Road at Canyon, this is also a starting or ending point on the North Rim Trail, so the real reason to come here is the hike, not the view. ■TIP→ **This trail may be affected, or closed, by the closure of the North Rim Dr. for all of 2008, so check with park rangers.** ⊠*Off Spur Rd. and North Rim Dr., Canyon.*

Lookout Point. Located midway on the North Rim Trail—or accessible via the one-way North Rim Drive—Lookout Point gives you a view of the Grand Canyon of the Yellowstone from above the falls. Follow the right-hand fork in the path to descend a steep trail (approximately 500-foot elevation change) for an "eye-to-eye" view of the falls from a half-mile downstream. The best time to hike the trail is early morning, when sunlight reflects off the mist from the falls to create a rainbow. ■TIP→ **This trail may be affected, or closed, by the closure of the North Rim road for all of 2008, so check with park rangers.** ⊠*Off North Rim Dr., Canyon.*

Petrified Tree. If you enjoy seeing bears in zoo pens, you'll get the same level of satisfaction as you look at this geological landmark surrounded on all four sides by high wrought-iron gates. Unfortunately, a century of vandalism has forced park officials to completely enclose this 45 million-year-old redwood tree. ⊠*Grand Loop Rd., 1 mi (2 km) west of Tower-Roosevelt, Tower.*

Tower Fall. This is one of the easiest waterfalls to see from the roadside; you can also view volcanic pinnacles here. Tower Creek plunges 132 feet to join the Yellowstone River. A trail runs to the base of the falls, but it is closed at this writing due to erosion problems several hundred yards before you reach the bottom of the canyon; thus, there is no view of Tower Fall from this trail at present. ⊠*2 mi south of Roosevelt on Grand Loop Rd.*

Yellowstone Picnic Area. One of nearly 50 picnic areas in the park, this one is situated less than 2 mi (3 km) east of the Tower Junction, just east of the bridge where the Northeast Entrance Road crosses the Yellowstone River. A trailhead takes you by a volcanic boulder and to the Specimen Ridge Trail. Even if you choose not to hike along the ridge top, at least walk the half-mile from the picnic area to the ridge for a spectacular view. ⊠*2 mi (3 km) east of Tower Junction on Northeast Entrance Rd.*

Yellowstone Hikes & Other Activities

WORD OF MOUTH

"I was up in Yellowstone/Tetons the first week of September. I hiked partway into Cascade Canyon but turned around before completing the hike because of weather. I took some awesome photos . . . this trip took me back to the serenity and the beauty."

—sjk 9/2007

By Steve Pastorino

SOMEWHAT OVERLOOKED in the clamor of cars driving to geyser basins and in search of "bear jam" roadside wildlife sightings is some of America's most rewarding wilderness. The 1,000-mi network of trails offers 10,000-foot peaks to climb, waterfalls by the dozen to view, tranquil streams to fish, and, by the way, plenty of geysers and bears. Closed to motorized vehicles and, in most cases, bicycles, the park's trails are the most direct paths to many hidden treasures. In the winter, the landscape is snow-covered and frigid, perfect for spotting the park's wildlife and geothermal features via snowshoe or cross-country skis. Yellowstone Lake and Lewis Lake are popular destinations for paddlers in canoes and kayaks, but be wary of afternoon storms. Boating is prohibited on all of the park's rivers, except for the Lewis Channel, which connects Lewis Lake and Shoshone Lake.

DAY HIKES

Your most memorable Yellowstone moments will likely take place along a park hiking trail. Encountering a gang of elk in the woods is unquestionably more exciting than watching them graze on the grasses of Mammoth Hot Springs Hotel. Hearing the creak of lodgepole pines on a breezy afternoon feels more authentic than listening to idle tourist chatter as you jostle for the best view of Old Faithful on a recycled plastic boardwalk for 94 minutes or so.

Even a one-day visitor to Yellowstone can—and should—get off the roads and into the "wilderness." Since the park is a wild place, however, even a half-mile walk on a trail puts you at the mercy of nature, so be sure to prepare yourself accordingly. As a guide on an Old Yellow Bus Tour said, "You don't have to fear the animals—just respect them."

HIKING BASICS
"Where do I start?" you ask. Along the Grand Loop Road lie dozens of geyser basins and nature trails. Ranging from all-boardwalk loops (the only places where bear spray is probably not an absolute requirement) to self-guided trails. Many noteworthy sights are just yards from your car door. For example, several geyser basins (Biscuit, West Thumb, Upper, Midway, Lower, and Norris), several overlooks at Grand Canyon of the Yellowstone, Tower Fall, Mud Vol-

cano, and the Mammoth Hot Springs Terraces can all be seen on short walks of less than 1 mi.

Every visitor center has a one-page handout describing day hikes in the immediate area. These handouts are extraordinarily useful, listing five to six hikes per area along with the distance, estimated hiking time, level of difficulty, directions to trailhead, and, in most cases, a simple map.

If you plan to spend a more extended time in the park or if you just seek longer hikes and/or want more detailed information, the park's many bookstores and visitor centers sell several different hiking guides. *Yellowstone Trails* by Mark Marschall is particularly recommended.

National Geographic publishes five maps for Yellowstone. One covers the entire park, lists 20 top hikes, and shows the locations of some major trails and trailheads. The other four subdivide the park into four quadrants geographically. Each of these more detailed maps provides much more information than the park overview map, including all major trails and backcountry campsites.

★ **Fodor's Choice** If you are interested in having a park expert, whether a naturalist, geologist or wildlife specialist accompany you, the **Yellowstone Association Institute** offers daylong hiking excursions; multiday "Lodging and Learning" trips geared around hikes, some of them designed for families (there are age restrictions on some trips); and full-blown backcountry backpacking trips. The Lodging and Learning trips include nightly accommodations at park facilities, but for the hikes you bring your own personal gear; they provide group gear and instruction plus permits as needed and some meals. The association also offers courses on topics ranging from nature writing to wolf biology. Taught by college professors or other experts, most courses are for people age 18 and older. ✉*Box 117, Yellowstone National Park, WY82190* ☎*307/344–2293* 🖷*307/344–2486* ⊕*www.yellowstoneassociation.org* 💲*From $80 for one-day trips to $1,000+ for 5-night trips including lodging.*

HIKES TO LOOK OUT FOR
To experience trees, wildflowers, fewer people (often almost none), and the possibility of encountering wildlife on their terms (carry bear spray!), try to carve out time for some of these hikes.

What to Take on a Hike

CLOSE UP

No matter how short the hike, the following items are essential, not discretionary:

Bear spray. At $40 a can and available for sale in the park, it's not cheap, but it's a critical deterrent if you run into one. Know how to use it, too. Be aware that sometimes supplies are sold out.

Food and water. Your "meal" can be as simple as a protein bar and a bottle of water, but the properly prepared hiker has an energy-boosting snack, and it's just foolish to head out without some drinking water.

Appropriate clothing. Watch the forecast closely (available at every lodging office and visitor center). Bring a layer of clothing for the opposite extreme if you're hiking at least half the day. Yellowstone is known for fierce afternoon storms, so be ready with gloves, hat, and waterproof clothing.

Altitude awareness. Yes, this is rather intangible, but much of Yellowstone lies more than 7,500 feet above sea level, significantly higher than Denver. The most frequent incidents requiring medical attention are respiratory problems, not animal attacks. Be aware of your physical limitations—as well as your young children or elderly companions if they are with you.

Very short hikes (under two hours): Trout Lake, Storm Point, Elephant Back, Old Faithful Observation Point, Harlequin Lake, Mystic Falls.

Half-day hikes: Hellroaring Creek (turn around at the creek), Riddle Lake, Lone Star Geyser, Fairy Falls, Mt. Washburn, Canyon Rim, Bunsen Peak, Avalanche Peak.

Full-day hikes: Shoshone Lake, Heart Lake, Seven Mile Hole, Slough Creek, Pebble Creek, Pelican Valley/Creek.

GRANT VILLAGE

Lacking an iconic natural attraction or signature hotel, the Grant Village area is a somewhat bland assemblage of visitor services that serves three principal needs for the park—campsites, affordable accommodations, and boat launches. As a result, it attracts many families, campers, and boaters, especially as other areas fill up. There's plenty to enjoy just the same in this area, from short walks around the nearby West Thumb geyser basin to some of the park's best backcountry wilderness. You can also go boating on either Yellowstone or Lewis lake.

Riddle Lake. Rangers recommend this easy trail for an enjoyable 5-mi (round-trip) loop if you're in the southern third of the park. Cross the Continental Divide, hike through small meadows, and arrive at a picturesque little lake. Due to bear activity, the trail is closed annually until July 15, and rangers discourage hiking here alone at any time. ✉ *2.1 mi (3.4 km) south of Grant Village intersection on South Entrance Rd.* ⏱ *Easy.*

Dogshead Trail. A favorite half-day hike off the south entrance road takes you to Shoshone Lake; if you return via the **Lewis Channel Trail** you will see both the second- and third-largest lakes in the park. Pick up the trailhead about 5 mi south of Grant Village on the west side of the road. The 11-mi round-trip crosses several miles of lodgepole pine forest where the contrast between 20-year-old trees (post-1988 fire) and century-old ones is stark and telling. The first 4.5 mi along the Dogshead leads you to Shoshone Lake, and your only company will likely be elk, deer, grouse, and various other animals.

There is a great backcountry campsite (and a summer ranger station) where the trail intersects Shoshone Lake, and if you choose, this would make a very manageable overnight wilderness experience. (Be sure to get a backcountry camping permit from any ranger station before you depart.)

Long-distance backcountry trekkers can cross the Lewis River (named for famed explorer Meriwether Lewis of Lewis & Clark) just to the west of Shoshone Lake and continue for 8 mi to Shoshone Geyser Basin. It's active, remote, and unseen by 99.5% of Yellowstone visitors.

But day hikers follow the trail markers from Shoshone Lake for the Lewis River Channel Trail for their return trip to the parking area. The lava rock beach where the Lewis River empties into Shoshone Lake is sheltered from wind, making it a great place to stop for rest or lunch before tackling the 6.5-mi trek back to the road. The trail back parallels the Lewis River, which is popular with anglers looking for brown trout. An overhang of volcanic boulders 2 mi upstream from the mouth marks a lazy bend in the river, where you should look for beavers among the lily pads. When you arrive at Lewis Lake's northwest corner,

Art in the Park

During the 1871 Washburn Expedition, it was the paintings of Thomas Moran and the photographs of William Henry Jackson that sold a curious nation on the virtues of Yellowstone as a national park. The artistic tradition flourishes today.

Enter the Old Faithful Inn lobby most days (Tuesday through Saturday) and you'll find painter Jim Reed tending his canvases. Selected as the artist-in-residence in 2003, he abruptly ended his 25-year career as a Caspar, Wyoming firefighter to turn his lifelong hobby into an avocation. His work integrates the park's wildlife into the dramatic scenery.

Hitch a ride at the Xanterra stables and you might meet Les Kollerup, mountain woman, cowgirl, and photographer. Raised in Colorado upstairs from the family bar and restaurant, Kollerup knew she'd follow the cowboy life when she grew up. Recently, she turned her endearing shots of Xanterra's stock of 200+ horses into postcards and prints that are available at Roosevelt Ranch.

you may see Mt. Sheridan and the red mountains to the east. On a clear day, look to the south when you reach a clearing on the north side of Lewis Lake for a view of the Grand Tetons. ⊠*Trailhead approximately 5 mi south of Grant Village on the west side of South Entrance Rd.* ⌖*Moderate.*

OLD FAITHFUL AREA

Since it has multiple hotels, stores, employee housing, and every other service you might imagine, it's sometimes easy to forget that Old Faithful Village is a great starting point for some great hiking. Besides the well-traveled boardwalks and paths between the Upper, Midway, and Lower geyser basins, there are geothermal features, overlooks, and rivers to explore. Portions of long, multiday trails, such as the Continental Divide Trail and Howard Eaton Trail, are also accessible here.

SPOTLIGHT HIKE: FAIRY FALLS & IMPERIAL GEYSER

☉ You'll hear rushing water before you round a bend and finally see the 197-foot Fairy Falls. It's a great payoff for the anticipation that has built in your 2.6-mi one-way hike (about two hours round-trip) from the south trailhead in this easy, almost entirely flat hike. You could go home content, but a noisy backcountry geyser, steaming river, and broad meadow still await if you have the energy. You'll travel 5.8 mi round-trip (three hours) if you turn around at Imperial Geyser. If you continue on through Imperial Meadows to Goose Lake, it's 8.5 mi (five hours) round-trip. ⊠ *1 mi south of Midway Basin Grand Loop Rd. Old Faithful* ☞ *Easy.*

0 MI: FAIRY FALLS TRAILHEAD

Start your hike at the Fairy Falls trailhead, 1 mi south of Midway Basin on the Grand Loop Road. In your first mile you'll pass several small hydrothermal springs adjacent to the gravel road, before you begin to parallel steamy Midway Basin and the park's largest hot spring, Grand Prismatic Spring. Climb the steep hill on your left for 100 yards (no trail, just pick a spot), and you'll be rewarded with a great view of the basin and Grand Prismatic.

1.1 MI: TRAIL LEAVES FOUNTAIN FREIGHT ROAD FOR FOREST

Having passed the Midway Geyser Basin and briefly walked along Fountain Freight Road, look for the bike rack (you can ride to this point if you like) and the FAIRY FALLS sign on your left. Follow the trail into the trees and enjoy a peaceful walk through 1.5 mi of lodgepole pine forest, where you'll witness the devastation—and rebirth—caused by the 1988 fire. Want to know what it's like to camp in the backcountry? Look for the OD1 sign, and follow the path to see a clearing for pitching a tent; 100 yards away is a bear pole for hanging food. (This is one of the most accessible backcountry camping sites in the park.)

2.6 MI: FAIRY FALLS

About 2.6 mi into your hike, you'll come upon Fairy Falls, which cuts through black and grey volcanic rock towers and clatters to a small pool before you. The volume of water isn't huge, but it's the fourth-highest named waterfall in the park. You can rest here and turn around for a total of 5.2 mi.

2.9 MI: IMPERIAL GEYSER

If you cross Fairy Creek and follow the trail another 0.3 mi you will come to Imperial Geyser. You'll encounter its steaming runoff first, flowing hot over tiny rusty red, dark green, and mustard-yellow terraces. Ascend the small slope to the geyser, which tends to shoot steam and noisy

TRAIL TIPS

There is little shade on this hike, so bring sunscreen and plenty of water if it's hot, or expect a chilly wind in Imperial Meadows if it's cold.

A good third of this hike is along Fountain Freight Road, which is the antithesis of backcountry hiking. Still, Fairy Falls, as well as the wildlife-watching at Goose Lake and Firehole River, make it worth the trip.

You can also access this hike from the north. Park at the end of Fountain Flat Drive and walk (or bike) along the gravel road until you reach Fairy Falls, which you'll be able to see and hear for a mile before you get there; there's no suspense.

rushes of water 5 to 20 feet in the air almost constantly. Note a mud pot and spring in the clearing above the geyser—but tread carefully because you are in an active geothermal area. Again, you have the option to turn around and retrace your steps back, or continue north to Imperial Meadows.

5 MI: FOUNTAIN FREIGHT ROAD

If you choose to forge ahead, you will cross broad Imperial Meadows, which is bisected by Fairy Creek. Look for springs, bison bones, and wildlife. Check out another backcountry campsite (OD4) if you wish, but after 2 mi you will reconnect with Fountain Freight Road. The 2-mi walk back along the gravel road passes Goose Lake (look for waterfowl) and the Firehole River before you find yourself back at the bike rack. Retrace your steps the last mile to the parking area where you began.

OTHER OLD FAITHFUL HIKES

Biscuit Basin Trail. This easy 2.5-mi round-trip trail goes via a boardwalk across the Firehole River to colorful Sapphire Pool. ⊠ *3 mi north of Old Faithful Village off Grand Loop Rd., Old Faithful* ☞ *Easy.*

Mystic Falls Trail. From the Biscuit Basin boardwalk's west end, this trail gently climbs 1 mi (3.5 mi round-trip from Biscuit Basin parking area) through heavily burned forest to the lava-rock base of 70-foot Mystic Falls. It then switchbacks up Madison Plateau to a lookout with the park's least-crowded view of Old Faithful and the Upper Geyser Basin. ⊠*3 mi north of Old Faithful Village off Grand Loop Rd., Old Faithful* ⚐*Moderate.*

Observation Point Loop. A 2-mi round-trip from the temporary Old Faithful Visitor Center leaves Geyser Hill Loop boardwalk and becomes a trail shortly after the boardwalk crosses the Firehole River; it circles a picturesque overview of Geyser Hill with Old Faithful Inn as a backdrop. You may also see Castle Geyser erupting as well. Even when 1,000+ people are crowded on the boardwalk to watch Old Faithful, expect to find fewer than a dozen here. ⊠*Old Faithful Village, Old Faithful* ⚐*Moderate.*

Old Faithful Geyser Loop. Old Faithful and its environs in the Upper Geyser Basin are rich in short-walk options, starting with three connected loops that depart from Old Faithful visitor center. The 0.75-mi loop simply circles the benches around Old Faithful, filled nearly all day long in summer with tourists. Currently erupting approximately every 92 minutes, Yellowstone's most frequently erupting big geyser—although not its largest or most regular—reaches heights of 100 to 180 feet, averaging 130 feet. ⊠*Old Faithful Village, Old Faithful* ⚐*Easy.*

🕭 **Lone Star Geyser.** Escape the crowds at Old Faithful by visiting one of the largest active geyser cones in the park. Lone Star erupts with startling regularity—about every three hours, year after year. The geyser shoots water as high as 40 feet in the air. It's about a 9-mi round trip from the bike rental shop at Old Faithful Snow Lodge, so you must plan on two to three hours by bike or twice that on foot. Pack a picnic and time it right, and you'll be glad you got off the beaten path.

If you are going by bicycle, head toward Grant Village along the South Loop Road for 1.5 mi. It's a steady climb over the first half-mile, but the road will level out. You should now look for the Kepler Cascades pullout and take a short rest, rewarding your climb with a view of a small waterfall in a narrow ravine. Find the Lone Star Trailhead at the south end of the parking lot, and follow an old road (now gravel) for about 2.5 mi until the trail forks. Follow the right fork (the left takes you on the Spring Creek Trail) and follow the signs for another 0.5 mi to the geyser. The gravel road is flat and parallels Kepler Creek; for this part of the ride keep your eyes open for elk and other wildlife and your ears tuned to the plentiful birds in the area. Return via the same path.

If you're on foot, you can reach the geyser by following the Howard Eaton Trail, which you can access near the Ranger Station south of Old Faithful. It's 2.9 mi through lodgepole pine forest before you'll turn left to the geyser. Retrace your steps for the shortest route back—or follow the gravel road the parallels Kepler Creek. ⊠*Lone Star Trailhead is about 2.0 mi by bicycle south of Old Faithful Snow Lodge on Grand Loop Rd. at Kepler Cascades parking area; trailhead is 1.1 mi on foot from Old Faithful Snow Lodge (via foot trail, where bikes are not allowed). Geyser is then 5 mi (round-trip) on foot from Kepler Cascades parking area. Old Faithful ☞Easy.*

Fountain Paint Pots Nature Trail. Take the easy 0.5-mi loop boardwalk of Fountain Paint Pot Nature Trail to see fumaroles (steam vents), blue pools, pink mud pots, and minigeysers in this thermal area. It's popular in both summer and winter because it's right next to Grand Loop Road. ⊠*Lower Geyster Basin, between Old Faithful and Madison ☞Easy.*

NORRIS

In addition to a teeming, bubbling geyser basin, the Norris area has several trailheads to interesting hikes on the west side of the Washburn Range. On the northwest rim of the Yellowstone caldera, a variety of volcanic formations, river cascades, and valleys beckon. Rangers at the campground or geyser basin can point you in the right direction.

Back Basin Trail. A 1.5-mi loop passes Emerald Spring, Steamboat Geyser, Cistern Spring (which drains when Steamboat erupts), and Echinus Geyser. The latter erupts 50 to 100 feet every 35 to 75 minutes, making it Norris's most dependable big geyser. ⊠*Grand Loop Rd., Norris ☞Easy.*

Porcelain Basin Trail. At Norris Geyser Basin, this 0.75-mi, partial-boardwalk loop leads from the north end of Norris Museum through whitish geyserite stone and past extremely active Whirligig and other small geysers. ⊠*Grand Loop Rd., Norris ☞Easy.*

MAMMOTH HOT SPRINGS

The Mammoth area is many visitors' favorite for the multitude of year-round activities. The geothermal terraces are accessible by foot or car in the summer and on skis or snowshoes in the winter. Trails extend in every direction, ranging from easy half-day loops like the Beaver Ponds Trail to serious day hikes like the trek to Electric Peak. Dedicated hikers can follow the historic Bannock Indian Trail, which crisscrosses the park, following the modern-day Fawn Pass Trail in this region.

Beaver Ponds Loop Trail. The hike to Beaver Ponds is a 2.5-hour, 5-mi round-trip starting at Liberty Cap in the busy Lower Terrace of Mammoth Hot Springs. You enter Yellowstone backcountry within minutes as you climb 400 feet through spruce and fir, passing several ponds and dams, as well as a glacier-carved moraine, before emerging on a wind-swept plain overlooking the 45th parallel (Montana/Wyoming border), Boiling River, and the north entrance. Look up to see Everts Peak to the East, Bunsen Peak to the South, and Sepulcher Mountain to the West. Bear, elk, bighorn sheep, coyote, and fox may frequent the area. Your final descent into Mammoth Springs offers great views of Mammoth Springs. ⊠*Grand Loop Rd. at Old Gardiner Rd., Mammoth Hot Springs* ☞*Moderate.*

Bunsen Peak Trail. Past the entrance to Bunsen Peak Road, the moderately difficult trail is a 4-mi, three-hour round-trip that climbs 1,300 feet to Bunsen Peak for a panoramic view of Blacktail Plateau, Swan Lake Flats, the Gallatin Mountains, and the Yellowstone River valley. (Use a topographical map to find these landmarks.) ⊠*Grand Loop Rd., 1.5 mi (2.5 km) south of Mammoth Hot Springs* ☞*Moderate.*

Osprey Falls Trail, The 4-mi, two-hour round-trip starts near the entrance to Bunsen Peak Road. A series of switchbacks drops 800 feet to the bottom of Sheepeater Canyon and the base of the Gardner River's 151-foot Osprey Falls. As at Tower Fall, the canyon walls are basalt columns formed by ancient lava flow. ⊠*Bunsen Peak Rd., 3 mi (5 km) south of Mammoth Hot Springs* ☞*Difficult.*

Skyline Trail. In the park's northwest corner, the extremely difficult 16.5-mi, 10-hour hike is a combination trail that climbs up and over numerous peaks whose ridgelines mark the park's northwest boundary before looping sharply back

Bannock Trail

Information about park anthropological history is not as prevalent as geologic and contemporary events, but the centuries-old Bannock Indian Trail in Yellowstone's north section is an example of the park's long history. Much of this trail, originally mapped by the Washburn Expedition, can be followed today as it follows these modern-day routes from West to East: the Fawn Pass Trail from the park's western boundary at Gallatin River to Mammoth Hot Springs; the Yellowstone River Trail from Gardiner to Lamar Valley; and the Northeast Entrance Road through Soda Butte Canyon to Cooke City. An intrepid trekker could probably hike this 80+ mile journey in about a week.

down via Black Butte Creek. For much of its length the trail follows the ridgetops, with steep drop-offs on either side. ⊠ *U.S. 191, 25 mi (40 km) north of West Yellowstone* ☞ *Difficult.*

TOWER-ROOSEVELT

Like an old trading post, Tower Store and nearby Roosevelt Lodge are ideally situated for guests circumnavigating the north loop of the Grand Loop Road, or as last spots for hikers to stock up on supplies before heading into the park's northernmost reaches. Tower Falls marks the northern end of the Grand Canyon of the Yellowstone River, which along with the Lamar River define this area of the park.

Hellroaring Creek. This famous backcountry, overnight trail is primarily frequented by anglers and hunters (it's illegal to hunt in Yellowstone, but the trail continues on Forest Service land across the park boundary). Day hikers shouldn't dismiss it, however, because the first 2 mi (to the creek) and back makes for a rewarding half-day hike in itself. One highlight is a suspension bridge 1 mi from the trailhead. Built in the 1960s, the steel suspension bridge carries hikers and horses across the Yellowstone River high above the rapids.

The elevation change of about 600 feet in the first mile is steep but short. Assess as you go, but it shouldn't cause any more than some huffing-and-puffing on the climb back up for the reasonably healthy walker/hiker. After the bridge, continue through a cluster of trees with volcanic boulders strewn about. You emerge in a pretty meadow surrounding a pond. Veer right to follow Coyote Creek (5.6 mi until the park boundary), or bear left and follow the trail a few hundred yards to Hellroaring Creek, which is a tranquil brook here and an ideal spot for lunch.

To the left, the trail continues for 1.3 mi to the junction of Hellroaring Creek and the Yellowstone River. You may also ford the river to continue on the Hellroaring Creek trail—a favorite for anglers—for approximately 5 mi before you will reach the park's northern boundary. Buffalo, coyote, pronged sheep and bear may be spotted here. ⊠ *3 mi (6.5 km) west of Roosevelt Lodge on Grand Loop Rd.* ☞ *Moderate.*

★ Fodor'sChoice **Slough Creek Trail** Starting at Slough Creek Campground, this trail climbs steeply along a historic wagon trail for the first 1.5 mi before reaching expansive meadows and prime fishing spots, where moose are common and grizzlies occasionally wander. From this point the trail, now mostly level, meanders another 9.5 mi to the park's northern boundary. Anglers absolutely rave about this trail. ⊠ *7 mi (11 km) east of Tower-Roosevelt off Northeast Entrance Rd.* ☞ *Moderate.*

CANYON AREA

Thomas Moran's paintings of Grand Canyon of the Yellowstone bolstered public and political support for the naming of Yellowstone as the first U.S. national park. The canyon he saw remains largely unchanged and, for good reason, is probably the second-most visited spot in the park after Old Faithful. Construction will wreak havoc on visitors to the canyon for the entire 2008 season, however, as the North Rim Road is scheduled to be closed. Popular north rim scenic stops Grand View, Lookout Point, Inspiration Point, and Brink of the Lower Falls may be reachable only by foot, if at all. Check with park officials for the latest updates. Artist Point and Uncle Tom's Trail should be unaffected. To truly experience, hear, and feel the Yellowstone River's power, trek the strenuous Seven Mile Hole trail down the canyon wall to the river's bank.

SPOTLIGHT HIKE: SEVEN MILE HOLE

★ Fodor'sChoice A challenging half-day hike, Seven Mile Hole is the most direct way to the base of Yellowstone Canyon. You'll pass unmapped thermal features and gain an appreciation of the depth and immensity of the canyon. Take a lunch and plan to sit on the boulders alongside the Yellowstone River. Plan on five to six hours for this 11-mi hike. *⊠2 mi (3 km) from Canyon Village. Take North Rim Drive to the Inspiration Point road. Look for trailhead marker at Glacial Boulder. ☞Difficult.*

0 MI: GLACIAL BOULDER/SEVEN MILE HOLE TRAILHEAD

Parking is available at the trailhead adjacent to Glacial Boulder on the one-way road from Canyon along the North Rim. You can also hike to the trailhead from Canyon Campground in Canyon Village. The trail beings with 3 mi of rolling hills—don't miss the canyon overlooks on the right or the broad meadow on your left.

3 MI: MT. WASHBURN SPUR TRAIL

Just after the trail split to Mt. Washburn (stay right), you begin a steep, almost treacherous descent with loose footing due to limestone, gravel, and tricky tree roots. It's 1,100 feet to the canyon bottom, so be careful and conserve your water and energy.

4 MI: HOT SPRINGS

You'll pass through a thermal area with hot springs, including an inactive stand-alone geyser cone about 8 feet high, at mile 4, and then a field with numerous features including a "martini glass" spring and several steaming, gurgling vents.

4.5 MI: TWO THERMAL CONES

Follow the sign for campsite 4C1 (about 100 yards off the trail) to see an inactive thermal feature, two cones side-by-side, the larger one towering about 12 feet in the air.

5.5 MI: YELLOWSTONE RIVER

You are rewarded with the blissful sound of the rushing Yellowstone River at the base of this dead-end trail. Look for streams and small waterfalls on the far bank emptying into the river. Enjoy, eat, rest, and prepare for your ascent (there is no other way out!). Do not attempt to ford the river as it flows very quickly here. Rough terrain makes it difficult to follow the shoreline very far in either direction.

SEVEN MILE HOLE TIPS

■ Yellowstone hikers are urged to keep their distance from all thermal features, but in this case, the trail runs right through an active, albeit smaller, area. Tread lightly around multiple thin crusts, steaming vents, and scalding water.

■ Bears are often spotted in this area (the nearby Mt. Washburn trail was closed throughout late summer 2007 due to bear activity), so carry bear spray and make noise so you don't surprise one.

■ The water in the small creek you will step across at mile 5 of the hike was measured to be exponentially more acidic that battery acid. Do not drink it under any circumstances and avoid contact with bare skin.

■ Backcountry campsites 4C1, 4C2, and 4C3 are on this trail—examples of relatively accessible, quiet, private campsites if you want to get away from the campgrounds.

OTHER CANYON TRAILS

★ **Brink of the Lower Falls Trail.** Especially scenic, this trail is accessed from the one-way North Rim Dr. The steep 0.5-mi one-way trail switchbacks 600 feet down to within a few yards of the top of the Yellowstone River's Lower Falls. △ **CAUTION** This trail may be affected, or closed, by the closure of the North Rim road for all of 2008. Check with park rangers. ✛ *0.2 mi. east of Grand Loop Rd. on south end of North Rim Dr.* ☞ *Moderate.*

Mud Volcano Interpretive Trail. This 0.75-mi round-trip trail loops gently around seething, sulfuric mud pots with such names as Sizzling Basin and Black Dragon's Cauldron and around Mud Volcano itself. ✉ *10 mi south of Canyon Village on Grand Loop Rd., Canyon* ☞ *Easy.*

★ **North Rim Trail.** Offering great views of the Grand Canyon of the Yellowstone, the 1.75-mi North Rim Trail runs from Inspiration Point to Chittenden Bridge. You can wander along small sections of the trail, or combine it with the South Rim Trail. Especially scenic is the 0.5-mi section of the North Rim Trail from the Brink of the Upper Falls parking area to Chittenden Bridge that hugs the rushing Yellowstone River as it approaches the canyon. ■ **TIP→** **Portions of this trail may be affected, or closed, by the closure of the North Rim road for all of 2008, so check with park rangers.** ✉ *1 mi south of Canyon Village, Canyon* ☞ *Moderate.*

South Rim Trail. Partly paved and fairly flat, this 4.5-mi loop along the south rim of the Grand Canyon of the Yellowstone affords impressive views and photo opportunities of the canyon and falls of the Yellowstone River. It starts at Chittenden Bridge. Along the way you can take a break for a snack or a picnic, but you'll need to sit on the ground, as there are no picnic tables. Beyond Artist Point, the trail crosses a high plateau and meanders through high mountain meadows, where you're likely to see bison grazing. ⊠*Chittenden Bridge, off South Rim Dr., Canyon* ☞*Moderate.*

Uncle Tom's Trail. The spectacular and very strenuous 700-step trail (⊠*South Rim Dr., about 0.5 mi east of Chittenden Bridge*) descends 500 feet from the Uncle Tom's parking area to the roaring base of the Lower Falls of the Yellowstone. ■TIP➔ **Much of this walk is on steel sheeting, which can have a film of ice on early summer mornings or anytime in spring and fall.** ⊠*1 mi south of Canyon Village, Canyon* ☞*Difficult.*

★ **Mt. Washburn.** The 10,243-foot peak of Mt. Washburn is accessible from three trailheads. The first two depart from the Grand Loop Road between Tower-Roosevelt and Canyon. You can approach from the north via the Chittenden Road Trail parking area or from the south from the Dunraven Pass Trail. In these two cases, you have a 3-mi (one-way) hike that climbs about 1,400 feet in elevation. You may see bighorn sheep, rodents, or bears along the way—and you're guaranteed to see some of the most spectacular panoramic views of the park if it's a clear day. At the top, you're invited to sign a guestbook in the shelter inside the fire lookout. Maps and interpretive exhibits here help orient you.

If you are looking for something more strenuous, hike the 8.5-mi (one-way) on the Seven Mile Hole Trail that begins at the Glacial Boulder Trailhead (*see* ➯*Spotlight Hike: Seven Mile Hole, above for more information on this trail*) outside Canyon village. You'll follow the rolling Seven Mile Hole trail for about 3 mi before passing Washburn Hot Springs and embarking on some much steeper climbing than the other more common trails. ■TIP➔**This area can be very active bear territory. Check with a ranger before embarking. Hiking from Dunraven was prohibited in late summer 2007 due to the bear activity.** ⊠*Chittenden Road Trailhead is 10.3 mi (16.6 km) north of Canyon Junction. Dunraven*

Pass Trailhead is 4.5 mi (7.2 km) north of Canyon Junction. Glacial Boulder Trailhead is on the road from Canyon to Inspiration Point.

YELLOWSTONE LAKE

The lake beckons to boaters of all types. Kayakers hug the shoreline. Anglers put in at Bridge Bay or Grant Village marinas. But hikers can also enjoy this pristine body of water. Long hikes descend from the East Entrance Road into the remote Thorofare region. Several more accessible trails start from the lake's north side—and offer incomparable panoramic views or up-close encounters with some of the lake's 141 mi of shoreline.

★ Fodor'sChoice **Avalanche Peak.** On a busy day in the summer, maybe six parties will fill out the trail register at the Avalanche Peak trailhead, so you won't have a lot of company on this hike. Yet many say it's one of the best-kept secrets in the park. Starting across from a parking area on the East Entrance Road, the difficult 4-mi, 4-hour round-trip climbs 2,150 feet to the peak's 10,566-foot summit, from which you'll see the rugged Absaroka Mountains running north and south. Some of these peaks have patches of snow year-round. Look around the talus and tundra near the top of Avalanche Peak for alpine wildflowers and butterflies. Don't try this trail before late June or after early September—it may be covered in deep snow. Also, rangers discourage hikers from attempting this hike in September or October due to bear activity. Whenever you decide to go, carry a jacket: the winds at the top are strong. ⊠*2 mi east of Sylvan Lake on the north side of East Entrance Rd., Fishing Bridge* ☞*Difficult.*

☾ **Storm Point Trail.** Well marked and mostly flat, this 1.5-mi
★ loop leaves the south side of the road for a perfect beginner's hike out to Yellowstone Lake. The trail rounds the western edge of Indian Pond, then passes moose habitat on its way to Yellowstone Lake's Storm Point, named for its frequent afternoon windstorms and crashing waves. Heading west along the shore, you're likely to hear the shrill chirping of yellow-bellied marmots, rodents that grow as long as two feet. Also look for ducks, pelicans, and trumpeter swans. You will pass several small beaches where kids can explore on warm summer mornings. ⊠*3 mi east of Lake Junction on East Entrance Rd., Fishing Bridge.*

Elephant Back. For a relaxing walk in the woods and a rewarding view of Yellowstone Lake, this moderate trail offers an enjoyable 3.6-mi loop. Hit the trail early enough and enjoy a stunning sunrise. Start from Lake Lodge, or pick up the trailhead 1 mi south of Fishing Bridge Junction. The trail climbs 800 feet through dense lodgepole forest to a southeast-facing overlook. Halfway up you will come to a fork giving you two choices to reach the hilltop; go left for the slightly easier incline. The circular path will return you to this same spot on the way down. Listen for the bugle calls of elk—and be alert for bears. ✉ *1 mi southwest of Fishing Bridge Junction on Grand Loop Rd., Lake Village* ☞ *Moderate.*

SUMMER SPORTS & ACTIVITIES

BICYCLING

Park management does not encourage bicycling in the park. It considers the vast majority of the park's roads "unimproved" and unsafe for bicyclists. A brochure entitled *Bicycling in Yellowstone National Park* is available at some visitor's centers and at the park Web site (⊕*www. nps.gov/yell*), but is not widely promoted or disseminated. Still, many long-distance cyclists do ride in Yellowstone, despite heavy traffic and narrow roads. If you choose to ride the Grand Loop Road or entrance roads, be safe, ride single file, and wear helmet and reflective gear. Be cautious in May and June as high snow banks can make riding the park's narrow roads particularly dangerous. Remember that some routes, such as those over Craig Pass, Sylvan Pass, and Dunraven Pass, are especially challenging because of their steep climbs.

The brochure recommends 13 secondary roads (many are gravel) that are open to bicycles, but they comprise a total riding distance of a scant 33 mi (53 km), with no trail longer than 6 mi (10 km). Bikes are prohibited on virtually all hiking trails except for a few that are converted roads or railroad lines.

The most ideal time to cycle Yellowstone is from mid-March to the third Thursday in April. Weather permitting, this early in the season the park is open to bicycles, but not cars (other than some park administrative vehicles) between the West Entrance and Mammoth Hot Springs (approximately 49 mi [79 km]). Expect to ride alongside significant roadside snow pack.

You may also register in advance for the Fall Cycle Tour (usually the first Saturday in October) organized by the Free Heel and Wheel bike shop in West Yellowstone. Complete with aid stations and sag wagons, you will share the road with cars and a maximum of 300 riders

Since 2006, Xanterra has operated a bike-rental shop at the gift shop at **Old Faithful Snow Lodge** (✉ *Old Faithful Village, far end of Old Faithful Bypass Rd.* ☎ *307/545–4824*). The shop carries a fleet of three dozen Trek hybrid mountain bikes in adult and child sizes. They have a limited number of trailers (for small children), cargo bags, gloves, and windbreakers. Rates for rentals are $8 per hour, $25 per half-day, and $35 per day including helmet and bike lock; there are discounts for children.

Free Heel and Wheel (✉ *40 Yellowstone Ave., West Yellowstone, MT* ☎ *406/646–7744* ⊕ *www.freeheelandwheel. com*), just outside the West Entrance, rents bikes, dispenses advice, and sells hiking and cross-country skiing gear. The staff here can also recommend road cycling routes outside the park. Rates are $8 per hour, or $25 per day, including helmet and water bottle.

BEST PLACES TO RIDE BICYCLES

OLD FAITHFUL
Old Faithful to Morning Glory Pool. This paved 2-mi trail starts at the General Store at Old Faithful Village, loops near Old Faithful geyser, and ends at Morning Glory Pool. The entire route is through a geyser basin, so stay on the trail. Watch for pedestrians, elk, and buffalo. ✉ *Trailhead begins at Old Faithful Basin Store, Old Faithful Village.*

MADISON
Fountain Freight Road. Fountain Flat Drive departs the Grand Loop Road south of the Nez Perce picnic area and follows the Firehole River to a trailhead 1.5 mi away. From there, the Fountain Freight Road continues along the old roadbed, giving bikers access to the Sentinel Meadows Trail and the Fairy Falls Trail. The total length of the route is 5.5 mi. Mountain bikes are recommended; you'll share Fountain Flat Drive with one-way automobile traffic and the freight road with hikers. ✉ *Exit Grand Loop Rd. at Fountain Flat Rd., 5 mi (8 km) south of Madison. Fountain Flat*

Paco Young

The single most prominent piece of artwork in Yellowstone National Park hangs above the 104-year-old dining room fireplace in the Old Faithful Inn Dining Room. It is an image of Old Faithful surrounded by three bison, painted by Paco Young in 2001 (the National Park Service commissioned the painting). It seemed odd to me that such a recent piece of artwork would hang in one of the most iconic places in America. So, I asked. "He died recently, that's all I know," said the tour guide.

Paco Young painted for 20 years, earning renown for his works depicting the landscapes and animals of Montana, Glacier National Park, Yellowstone, and other western destinations. The National Park Service commissioned Young to paint Old Faithful. On December 3, 2004, he was diagnosed with leukemia and passed away just 363 days later, on December 1, 2005, holding the hand of his wife, Toni.

Rd. dead-ends at a parking lot, where you can pick up the Fountain Freight Rd. trailhead, Madison.

MAMMOTH HOT SPRINGS

Old Gardiner Road. Automobiles and bicycles share this gravel road that runs parallel to U.S. 89 between Mammoth Hot Springs and the "gateway" town of Gardiner. Cars can travel only north, but bikes are allowed in both directions. The 5-mi route has views of the Gardner River. It's downhill from Mammoth Hot Springs to Gardiner. Mountain bikes are recommended. ⊠*From Mammoth, pick up Old Gardiner Rd. directly behind Mammoth Hot Spring Hotel, Mammoth Hot Springs.*

TOWER-ROOSEVELT

Blacktail Plateau Drive. Running parallel to Grand Loop Road, this gravel road is one-way traffic for cars traveling east, but bicycles are allowed in both directions. The strenuous ride climbs and dips through forest where you might see deer, coyotes, or elk. Start at the western entrance to the road, 9 mi east of Mammoth Hot Springs, and head east. Once you arrive at the eastern entrance, 2 mi west of Tower-Roosevelt, take the Grand Loop Road back. This is one place to see great autumn colors as the trees turn in late September or early October. Mountain bikes are recommended. ⊠*10 mi (16 km) east of Mammoth Hot Springs on Grand Loop Rd., Tower-Roosevelt.*

Mt. Washburn. Climbing 1,400 feet in elevation to the 10,243-foot summit of Mt. Washburn, this may be the most strenuous short (3-mi) ride in the park. Park your car at the parking lot on the north side of Mt. Washburn. This trail starts as a long, steady incline that becomes switchbacks near the top. The road is plenty wide, as it also serves as a service road for the ranger lookout at the top, but its steepness can be a problem, especially if you're not used to climbing on an uneven surface at nearly 2 mi above sea level. The view of Dunraven Peak to the West, Yellowstone Lake and the Grand Tetons to the south (on a clear day) make all the work worthwhile. Bring plenty of water and an extra windbreaker, and make sure your brakes are in order for the rib-rattling descent. Mountain bikes are recommended. ⚠**CAUTION** Bicycles are *not* allowed on the south end of the Mt. Washburn Trail, which descends to Grand Canyon of the Yellowstone and Canyon Village. ⊠*9 mi north of Canyon on Grand Loop Rd., Tower-Roosevelt.*

YELLOWSTONE LAKE

Natural Bridge Road. An excellent diversion with children if you're camping at Bridge Bay, this 1-mi bike loop briefly follows the western shore of Yellowstone Lake. The easy ride leads to Natural Bridge, a 50-foot cliff cut through by Bridge Creek. ⊠*0.2 mi south of Bridge Bay on Grand Loop Rd., Bridge Bay.*

BIRD-WATCHING

Raptors are the main attraction for bird-watchers in Yellowstone, but you will see many of the park's 209 species. Bald eagles, golden eagles, ospreys, and red-tailed hawks are common sights if you know where to look. Along the West Entrance road, look for signs indicating PROTECTED EAGLE HABITAT. Stopping in cars is prohibited in this area, but look for a large bald eagle nest on the south side of the road. There is also a nest near Bridge Bay Marina. Charter a boat or take the one-hour cruise aboard the *Lake Queen II* from Bridge Bay out to Stephenson Island, the majority of which is a protected bird habitat. The best place to see ospreys is the Grand Canyon of the Yellowstone; the best

CLOSE UP

Lake Trout Crisis

Park officials are panicked over the discovery of lake (Mackinaw) trout in Yellowstone Lake, which first occurred in 1994. This nonnative fish spawns and spends significant amount of time in deep water (Yellowstone Lake is more than 300 feet deep in places) and out of reach of most predators. It preys on the native Yellowstone cutthroat trout, which live in shallow water and spawn in dozens of small streams surrounding the lake. A severe reduction in cutthroat trout may have catastrophic impact on the ospreys, bears, pelicans, and otters, all of which eat them. If you catch a lake trout anywhere in the park, you *must* kill it.

place to see hawks is the Hayden Valley; and the best place to see eagles is Madison Valley.

BOATING

Motorized boats are allowed only on Lewis Lake and Yellowstone Lake. Kayaking or canoeing is allowed on all park lakes except Sylvan Lake, Eleanor Lake, Twin Lakes, and Beach Springs Lagoon; however, most lakes are inaccessible by car, so accessing the park's lakes requires long portages. Boating is not allowed on any park river, except for the Lewis River between Lewis Lake and Shoshone Lake, where nonmotorized boats are permitted.

You must purchase a seven-day, $5 permit for boats and floatables, or a $10 permit for motorized boats at Bridge Bay Ranger Station, South Entrance Ranger Station, Grant Village Backcountry Office, or, occasionally, at Lewis Lake Ranger Station (at the campground). Nonmotorized permits are available at the Northeast and West entrances, backcountry offices at Mammoth, Old Faithful, and Canyon; Bechler Ranger Station; West Yellowstone Chamber of Commerce; and locations where motorized permits are sold. Annual permits are also available.

PLACES TO RENT BOATS

Watercraft from rowboats to powerboats are available at **Bridge Bay Marina** by the hour or by the day for trips on Yellowstone Lake. You can even rent 22- and 34-foot cabin cruisers. ⊠ *Grand Loop Rd., 2 mi south of Lake Vil-*

Fishing Details You Need to Know

CLOSE UP

■ **Barbless Hooks Only.**
Park Service officials decided
in 2006 that barbless hooks
would allow caught and released fish to return to the
water more quickly and safely.

■ **Fishing Season Excep-
tions.** There are numerous
exceptions to the Memorial
Day–November schedule. Yellowstone Lake opens for fishing on June 15, and July 15
for streams flowing into the
lake. Heart, Sylvan, and Eleanor
lakes, in addition to Clear and
Cub creeks, open in July or August due to bear activity.

■ **Trout Conservation and
Enhancement Areas.** Catch-

and-release policies vary in the
park's two regulation areas.
Know the rules. Remember
that fishing is never allowed in
a portion of Hayden Valley, nor
in streams that feed the Yellowstone River.

■ **Know Your Fish.** If it has
a red slash, put it back. If it's
a lake trout, you're prohibited
from throwing it back.

■ **Kids and Bait.** In the Gardner River, as well as in Obsidian, Indian, and Panther creeks,
plus Joffe Lake, children 11
years of age or younger may
fish with worms as bait. Otherwise, no live bait is allowed in
the park.

3

lage, Bridge Bay ☎*307/344–7311* 💲*$70–$90 per hour for
guided sightseeing or fishing boats; $9.50 per hour for row-
boat; $45 per hour for small boat with outboard motor.*
⊙*June–mid-Aug., daily 8–8; mid-Aug.–mid-Sept, daily
8–5:30* PM.

🅒 **Yellowstone Lake Scenic Cruises,** run by Xanterra Parks &
★ Resorts, operates the *Lake Queen II* from out of Bridge
Bay Marina on Yellowstone Lake. The one-hour cruises
make their way to Stevenson Island and then return to
Bridge Bay. Boats depart throughout the day. ✉*Bridge Bay
Marina, Bridge Bay* ☎*307/344–7311* 💲*$11.25* ⊙*June–
mid-Sept., daily.*

FISHING

Anglers flock to Yellowstone beginning the Saturday of
Memorial Day weekend, when fishing season begins. By
the time the season ends in November, thousands have
found a favorite spot along the park's rivers and streams.
Native cutthroat trout are one of the prize catches, but four
other varieties—brown, brook, lake, and rainbow—along
with grayling and mountain whitefish inhabit Yellow-

stone's waters. Popular sportfishing opportunities include the Gardner and Yellowstone rivers as well as Soda Butte Creek, but the top fishing area in the region is Madison River, known to fly fishermen throughout the country.

Every angler, outfitter, and fishing blogger has his or her own opinion about the best places to fish in Yellowstone. Bob Sadrakula, author of *Frugal Fly-Fisherman,* concurs with many who suggest the Madison and Yellowstone rivers offer the some of the best trout fishing in the country. To avoid crowds however, he heads down a hiking trail: "Three million people visit the park each year . . . take a short hike [and you can] have a large section of stream to yourself." The Firehole, Gardner, and Gibbon rivers each attract fishermen on the west side of the park (as well as Nez Perce Creek). Slough Creek and the Lamar River are popular favorites on the east side of the park.

Some of the best fishing lies deep in the backcountry but requires chartering a boat, hiking great distances, and backcountry camping. Ask a backcountry ranger if you're interested.

Catch and release is the general policy, with the exception of the nonnative lake trout. If you catch a nonnative trout, you cannot throw it back alive. You can get a copy of the fishing regulations at any visitor center. Fishing supplies are available at general stores found throughout the park; the biggest selection is at Bridge Bay.

Yellowstone fishing permits are required for people over age 16. Montana and Wyoming fishing permits are NOT valid in the park. Yellowstone fishing permits cost $15 for a three-day permit, $20 for a seven-day permit, or $35 for a season permit. Anglers ages 12 to 15 must have a non-fee permit or fish under direct supervision of an adult with a permit. Anglers younger than 12 don't need a permit but must be with an adult who knows the regulations. Permits are available at all ranger stations, visitor centers, and Yellowstone general stores.

FISHING CHARTERS

The park concessionaire **Xanterra Parks & Resorts** offers guided Yellowstone Lake fishing charters on boats large enough for as many as six guests. The cost of a charter includes your guide plus fishing gear. Charters are on 22- and 34-foot cabin cruisers that accommodate as many as three people fishing at one time. ⊠*Grand Loop Rd.,*

2 mi south of Lake Village, Bridge Bay ☎*307/344–7311*
🖃*$70–$90 per hour* ⊙*Mid-June–early Sept.*

HORSEBACK RIDING

Xanterra Parks & Resorts offers horseback rides of one and two hours in length at Mammoth, Tower-Roosevelt, and Canyon. Advance reservations are recommended. Guides (and horses) are catered toward beginning riders (they estimate 90% of riders have not been on a horse in at least 10 years), but let them know if you're an experienced rider and would like a more challenging pace or ride.

From Mammoth, you will cross sagebrush plateaus, have a dramatic view of the Lava Creek Bridge, and may see deer, elk, or bison. From Canyon, rides almost always include bison sightings.

Roosevelt Lodge stables offer the greatest variety of wildlife—you may see bears, moose, and antelope—in addition to bison. Roosevelt also hosts extremely popular summer cookouts. Travel via horseback or wagon rides to a frontier cookout for a steak dinner. (*For more information, see* ⇨*Roosevelt Lodge Dining Room in Chapter 6; advance reservations are required.*)

Private stock can be brought into the park. Horses are not allowed in frontcountry campgrounds but are permitted in certain backcountry campsites. For information on planning a backcountry trip with stock, call the Backcountry Office (*see* ⇨*Exploring the Backcountry, below*).

About 50 area outfitters lead horse-packing trips and trail rides into Yellowstone. Expect to pay about $250 to $400 per day for a backcountry trip, including meals, accommodations, and guides. A guide must accompany all horseback-riding trips.

HORSEBACK OUTFITTERS

Since 1968, **Gunsel Horse Adventures** has provided four-day pack trips into the Yellowstone backcountry. The trips are a great way to see moose, bear, deer, elk, and wolves in Yellowstone's forests. Bring only your sleeping bag and personal effects. ⑩*Box 1575, Rapid City, SD 57709* ☎*605/343–7608* ⊕*www.gunselhorseadventures.com* 🖃*$325 per day.*

♋ Mike and Erin Thompson at **Wilderness Pack Trips** have led small-group trips exclusively in Yellowstone National Park for 15 years. Trips from one to nine days are available.

Popular destinations include the spectacular remote waterfalls of the Bechler area (southwest corner of the park) and Mirror Plateau bear management area, which accesses a wildlife-rich region closed to the general public 11 months a year. Families welcome. ⌖*172 E. River Rd. Emigrant, MT59027* ☎*406/848–9953* ⊕*www.wildernesspacktrips. com* ⌖*From $240 per person for day trips to $3,100 per person for multiday trips.*

One- and two-hour horseback trail rides run by **Xanterra Parks & Resorts** leave from three sites in the park: Mammoth Hot Springs, Roosevelt Lodge, and Canyon Village. Children must be at least eight years old and 48 inches tall; kids 8–11 must be accompanied by someone age 16 or older. In order not to spook horses or wildlife, guests are prohibited from bringing cameras or cell phones. ⌖*Box 165, Mammoth Hot Springs, Yellowstone, WY82190* ☎*307/344–7311* ⊕*www.travelyellowstone.com* ⌖*$35–$54.*

Yellowstone Wilderness Outfitters is exclusively dedicated to trips inside Yellowstone National Park (no elk-hunting trips here). Multi-talented guide Jett Hitt (he has a doctorate in music composition and wrote the violin concerto *Yellowstone for Violin and Orchestra*) leads trips ranging from half- and full-day family rides to three- to 10-day pack trips in every area of the park. Trips may feature wildlife biologists and lecturers. ⌖*Box 745, Yellowstone NP, WY82190* ☎*406/223–3300* ⊕*www.yellowstone.ws* ⌖*From $110 for half-day trips up to $2,400 for multiday trips.*

SWIMMING

☾ There are numerous lakes and streams that kids can enjoy,
★ the largest being Yellowstone Lake. Most visitors, except those during the warmest days of July and August, forego swimming due to the extremely cold water. Streams and lakes seldom have an opportunity to warm up in this climate, where nights can be fairly cool, if not cold, even in the summer months. But even when the waters are "warm," the unacclimated may find a quick dip to be bone-chilling even in the summer. The two exceptions are Boiling River and Firehole River. Along the North entrance road, follow a trailhead off the east parking lot at the 45th parallel to **Boiling River,** one of two spots in the park where you can swim in thermally heated waters. The Gardner River here is fed by hot springs water that is believed to originate in Mammoth. Lounge in the water within 10 feet of the banks

any time of year for a Jacuzzi-like experience. Multiple signs advise visitors not to walk on the delicate geothermal features adjacent to the river and to avoid direct contact with the boiling water that comes directly from the ground. ⊠ *2.5 mi south of Gardiner, MT, on the North Entrance Rd., Mammoth Hot Springs.*

☼ **Firehole River** is reached by driving south on Firehole Canyon
★ Road, a 2-mi bypass off the Grand Loop Road, just south of Madison Junction. Park in designated spots and follow signs to descend to the river bank. The water temperature here is just under 70°F—refreshing on a hot summer day, but probably a bit cool any other time. ⊠ *1 mi south of Grand Loop Rd. on Firehole Canyon Dr., Madison.*

WINTER SPORTS & ACTIVITIES

SKIING, SNOWSHOEING & SNOWMOBILING

Yellowstone can be the coldest place in the continental U.S. in winter, with temperatures of -30 degrees not uncommon. Still, winter sports enthusiasts flock here when the park opens for its winter season the last week of December. Until early March, the park's roads teem with oversnow vehicles like snowmobiles and snow coaches. Its trails bristle with cross-country skiers and snowshoers.

Snowmobiling is an exhilarating way to experience Yellowstone. It's also controversial: there's heated debate about the pollution and disruption to animal habitats. The number of riders per day is limited, and you must have a reservation, a guide, and a four-stroke engine (which is less polluting than the more common two-stroke variety). About a dozen companies have been authorized to lead snowmobile excursions into the park from the North, West, South, and East entrances. Prices vary as do itineraries and inclusions—be sure to ask about insurance, guides, taxes, park entrance fees, clothing, helmets, and meals. Regulations are subject to change.

SKI TRAILS

A list of 34 ski trails is available at the Xanterra Web site (*see* ⇨ Nordic Skiing Outfitters, *below*). When you need a break from the cold, you can stop at a strategically located hut. Warming huts at Canyon Village, West Thumb, and Madison are intermittently staffed; huts at Indian Creek,

Fishing Bridge, and Old Faithful Village are unstaffed. All are open 24 hours.

Lone Star Geyser Trail is an easy 2.3-mi ski to the Lone Star Geyser, starting south of Keppler Cascades. You can ski back to the Old Faithful area. ⊠*Shuttle at Old Faithful Snow Lodge; trailhead 3.5 mi west of Old Faithful Village, Old Faithful.*

Five ski trails begin at the **Madison River Bridge** trailhead. The shortest is 4 mi and the longest is 14 mi. ⊠ *West Entrance Rd., 6 mi west of Madison, Madison.*

NORDIC SKIING OUTFITTERS

Free Heel and Wheel (⊠*40 Yellowstone Ave., West Yellowstone, MT* ☎*406/646–7744* ⊕*www.freeheelandwheel. com*) outside the West Yellowstone entrance gate, is a source for cross-country ski gear and advice. Expect to pay $20 to $30 per day for ski rentals.

The **Yellowstone Association Institute** (✏*Box 117, Yellowstone National Park, WY82190* ☎*307/344–2293* ⊕*www. yellowstoneassociation.org*)offers everything from daylong cross-country skiing excursions to multiday "Lodging and Learning" trips geared around hiking, skiing, and snowshoeing treks. Ski instruction is available. Expect to pay $120 to $500 for excursions; $545 to $1,000+ for Lodging and Learning trips.

At Mammoth Hot Springs Hotel and Old Faithful Snow Lodge, **Xanterra Parks & Resorts** (☎*307/344–7901* ⊕*www. travelyellowstone.com*) rents skis and snowshoes. Ski rentals (including skis, poles, gloves, gaiters) are $11 per half day, $16 per full day. Snowshoes rentals are $9 per half day, $12 per full day. Shuttle service is $13.50 from Snow Lodge, $14.50 from Mammoth. Group and private lessons available. Skier shuttles run from Mammoth Hotel to Indian Creek and from Old Faithful Snow Lodge to Fairy Falls.

SNOWMOBILING OUTFITTERS

Jackson-based **National Park Adventures** (⊠*650 W Broadway, Jackson, WY* ☎*307/733–1572 or 800/255–1572* ⊕*www.anpatours.com*)specializes in one-, two-, and multiday guided snowmobile trips into Yellowstone, centering on Canyon and Old Faithful. Lodging is sometimes within the park, sometimes just outside. No riders under six years old are allowed. Day trips including meals cost $235 per driver, $110 per passenger to Old Faithful; $250 per driver,

$110 per passenger to Canyon; approximately $425 per person for multiday trips including meals and lodging. Park admission fees are not included.

Xanterra Parks & Resorts (☎307/344–7311 or 866/439–7375 ⊕*www.travelyellowstone.com*)rents snowmobiles from Mammoth Hotel and Old Faithful Snow Lodge and leads tours through the park from Mammoth Hot Springs. Rentals cost $230 to $250 per day.

Yellowstone Tour & Travel (✉*211 Yellowstone Ave., West Yellowstone, MT* ☎*406/646–9310 or 800/221–1151* ⊕*www.yellowstone-travel.com*)rents snowmobiles and leads trips into the park from West Yellowstone. Longer packages may include lodging in West Yellowstone. Rentals cost $164 to $239 per day with guide.

Yellowstone Vacations (✉*415 Yellowstone Ave., West Yellowstone, MT* ☎*406/646–9564 or 800/426–7669* ⊕*www.yellowstonevacations.com*) offers snowmobile rentals and snow coach tours from West Yellowstone. Rentals start at $189 per day for a single sled and $214 per day for a double sled, including guide, clothing rental, and park entrance fee.

SNOWCOACH TOURS

Visiting the park via these oversnow coaches (converted vans or mini-buses) is an increasingly popular way to see the natural beauty of Yellowstone in winter. A dozen concessionaires offer services, including Xanterra Parks & Resorts, which offers round-trips between Old Faithful, Mammoth, Flagg Ranch (South of the park), and West Yellowstone for $51 to $64 per person. Day-trips from West Yellowstone through one of a dozen licensed private companies start at approximately $99.

From December through March, a quieter way than snowmobiling to sight buffalo herds, trophy-size bull elk, moose, and other winter wildlife is within a comfortable snow coach of the **Yellowstone Alpen Guides Co.** (✉*555 Yellowstone Ave., West Yellowstone, MT* ☎*406/646–9591 or 800/858–3502* ⊕*www.yellowstoneguides.com*). You'll pay $99 per person (not including tax, gratuity, lunch, or park entrance fee) for a day-trip into the park. Cross-country ski and snowshoe rentals are also available for $16 in case you want to get out in the snow.

EXPLORING THE BACKCOUNTRY

If you are more ambitious than 98% of park visitors, even one night of camping in the Yellowstone backcountry will be rewarding. In 2005, less than 40,000 backcountry use nights were recorded out of more than 2.8 million park visitors. Although backcountry campsites consist of nothing more than a pole to protect your food and gear from bears, a fire pit (not in all cases), and a level sleeping area, the lack of amenities is balanced by utter peace and quiet. It's not for everyone—failure to take personal responsibility for your own water, food, tent, animal safety, and first aid can be dangerous or fatal. Because of that, Yellowstone rangers insist that anyone camping in backcountry obtain a permit (which is free, but advance reservations cost $20), provide an itinerary, and review a 15-point checklist of backcounty regulations and safety.

ABOUT BACKCOUNTRY RESERVATIONS

Yellowstone issues reservations for each summer beginning on April 1. All reservation requests received prior to April 1 are booked in random order. After April 1, requests are on a first-come, first-served basis. The nonrefundable reservation fee is $20 per itinerary, regardless of the number of nights or number of people. However, it's important to remember that a reservation confirmation *is not* a backcountry permit. For prime campsites during high season (July and August), reservations are highly recommended. Also, if you have a complicated backcountry itinerary with the intention (or necessity) of staying in particular sites in certain nights (especially in areas where campsites are miles apart), advance reservations are wise.

Permits are *only* issued 48 hours prior to your departure—in order to provide you with the latest conditions (including bear activity, weather, water levels, etc.). Permits must be picked up by 10 AM on the day of your trip, or your reservation will be released.

ABOUT BACKCOUNTRY PERMITS

In general, you should obtain your backcountry permit from the ranger station or visitor center closest to where the backcountry portion of your trip begins. Permits are available seven days a week between 8 AM and 4:30 PM, but rangers may close the backcountry desk at lunchtime. The process takes about 30 to 60 minutes minimum.

You can get backcountry permits at the following range stations and visitor centers:

1. Bechler Ranger Station 2. Canyon Ranger Station/Visitor Center 3. Mammoth Visitor Center 4. Old Faithful Ranger Station 5. Tower Ranger Station 6. West Entrance Ranger Station 7. Grant Village Backcountry Office* 8. South Entrance Ranger Station* 9. Bridge Bay Ranger Station* *If you are boating as part of your backcountry trip, you must obtain a boating permit from one of these three offices.

Bridge Bay Ranger Station has the most complete information about water-related activities, including motorized boating, kayaking, or canoeing; lake and river conditions; and fishing. Grant Village Backcountry office has the most complete information about trails, regulations, and backcountry campsites.

BACKCOUNTRY TIPS

Many of Yellowstone's trails were originally created—and are currently maintained—for stock use. This is particularly important if your backcountry hike crosses water; there are relatively few bridges on trails, so you may have to ford water on foot.

Yellowstone has a complex calendar due to snowpack, elevation, bear management activity, water levels, and more, so the opening and closing dates of various areas in the park vary greatly. There are 16 different bear management areas, each with its own peculiarities. For example, the popular Firehole region (including Firehole Freight Road and Firehole Lake Road) is closed from March 10 through the Friday of Memorial Day Weekend; Pelican Valley is closed from April 1 through July 3, and restricted to day use from July 4 through November 10. Yellowstone's **Backcountry Office** (☎*307/344–7381* ⊕*www.nps.gov/yell*) is an essential resource early in your planning process; you can brush up on Yellowstone's backcountry regulations before you arrive by reading the "Backcountry Trip Planner," available by mail or as a download. The Backcountry Office can also inform you of the complex opening dates for many popular backcountry areas.

RECOMMENDED TRAILS

Heart Lake–Mt. Sheridan Trail. This very difficult 24-mi, 13-hour round-trip provides one of the park's top overnight backcountry experiences. After traversing 5.5 mi of

The Backcountry Checklist

Once you arrive and meet with a ranger, you'll have to watch a 20-minute video about the Yellowstone backcountry, and then you must complete the following checklist with a ranger:

■ Bear safety, including avoidance, food security, and repellents

■ Trash and sanitation

■ Fires and firewood (It is permissible to use down, dead firewood in the backcountry, but be aware that fires are prohibited at some sites, and they may be prohibited at all sites during times of high fire danger.)

■ Precautions for thermal features

■ Precautions for wildlife

■ Natural features (It is illegal to remove antlers, bones, rocks, artifacts, etc.)

■ Banned items (including pets, weapons, traps, nets, motor- and wheeled vehicles; some service dogs and wheelchairs are allowed)

■ Potable water advice

■ Weather, hypothermia, and fatigue

■ Vehicle security

■ River fords and latest trail conditions

■ Stock use (horses and/or pack animals such as burros)

■ Boating permits

■ Fishing permits and regulations

partly burned lodgepole-pine forest, the trail descends into Heart Lake Geyser Basin, reaching Heart Lake at the 8-mi mark. This is one of Yellowstone's most active thermal areas; the biggest geyser here is Rustic Geyser, which erupts to a height of 25 to 30 feet about every 15 minutes. Circle around the northern tip of Heart Lake and camp at one of five designated backcountry sites on the western shore (remember to get your permit beforehand). Leave all but the essentials here as you take on the 3-mi, 2,700-foot climb to the top of 10,308-foot Mt. Sheridan. To the south, if you look carefully, you can see the Tetons. ⊠ *1 mi north of Lewis Lake on the east side of South Entrance Rd., Grant Village* ☞ *Difficult.*

Shoshone Lake–Shoshone Geyser Basin Trail. A 22-mi, 11-hour, moderately difficult overnight trip combines several shorter trails. The trail starts at the DeLacy Creek Trail, gently descending 3 mi to the north shore of Shoshone Lake. On the way, look for sandhill cranes and browsing moose. At the lake turn right and follow the North

Shore Trail 8 mi, first along the beach and then through lodgepole-pine forest. Make sure you've reserved one of the several good backcountry campsites (reservations can be made at any ranger station in the park). Take time to explore the Shoshone Geyser Basin, reached by turning left at the fork at the end of the trail and walking about 0.25 mi before bedding down for the night. On your second morning, turn right at the fork, follow Shoshone Creek for 2 mi, and make the gradual climb over Grant's Pass. At the 17-mi mark the trail crosses the Firehole River and divides; take a right onto Lone Star Geyser Trail and continue past this fine coned geyser through Upper Geyser Basin backcountry to Lone Star Geyser Trailhead. ⊠*8 mi (13 km) east of Old Faithful Village on north side of Grand Loop Rd., Old Faithful* ☞*Moderate.*

Specimen Creek Trail. Starting at Specimen Creek Trailhead, follow the 2.5 mi trail and turn left at the junction; you'll pass petrified trees to your left. At the 6.5-mi mark, turn left again at the fork and start climbing 1,400 feet for 2 mi up to Shelf Lake, one of the park's highest bodies of water, at an altitude of 9,200 feet. Stay at one of the pair of designated backcountry campsites, which you can reserve at any ranger station in the park. Just past the lake is the trailhead for Skyline Trail. Watch for bighorn sheep as you approach Bighorn Peak's summit. The trail's most treacherous section is just past the summit, where it drops 2,300 feet in the first 2.5 mi of descent; make sure you take a left where the trail forks at the big meadow just past the summit to reach Black Butte Creek Trail. Moose and elk can be seen along this last 2.5-mi stretch. ⊠*U.S. 191, 27 mi (43 km) north of West Yellowstone* ☞*Moderate.*

EDUCATIONAL PROGRAMS

CLASSES & SEMINARS

In 1985, a Ranger-led program available at the Buffalo Ranch in the Lamar Valley called "Expedition: Yellowstone!" was set up for students grades four to eight. The four- to five-day residential program runs from September through mid-December and again from mid-December through May. Through hikes, talks, and other outdoor activities, "Expedition: Yellowstone!" teaches groups of students about the natural and cultural history of Yellowstone National Park, investigates current issues affecting the Greater Yellowstone Ecosystem, and promotes stewardship and preservation in the park and in home communities. ⌂ *Box 168, Yellowstone National Park, WY82190-0168* ☏ *307/344–2256 for information* ☉ *Sept.–May by advance arrangement* ⚑ *$35 per person per night.*

The not-for-profit **Yellowstone Institute,** based at the Buffalo Ranch in Lamar Valley, offers a wide range of summer and winter courses about the ecology, history, and wildlife of Yellowstone. Search with a historian for the trail the Nez Perce Indians took in their flee from the U.S. Army a century ago, or get tips from professional photographers on how to get the perfect shot of a trumpeter swan. Some programs are specifically designed for young people and families. ✉ *North Park Rd., between Tower-Roosevelt and Northeast Entrance* ☏ *307/344–2294* ⊕ *www.yellowstoneassociation.org/institute* ☉ *Year-round, programs vary with season.*

RANGER PROGRAMS

Ranger-led programs are available at all visitor centers, some during the day and some at night.

☾ **Evening Ranger Programs** are held both day and night all
★ year long. Yellowstone's interpretive rangers are accessible and approachable. The quickest way to learn about the park, its wildlife, geology, and history is to attend a ranger-led program. Most are free, intimate, and geared to families. Ask for the *Ranger Programs* newspaper when you enter the park or at any visitor center. Certain programs are geared primarily to children; others will be of more interest to people interested in the park's natural environment. Summer programs are held primarily at outdoor amphitheaters at the following campgrounds: Bridge Bay, Canyon, Fishing Bridge RV Park, Grant Village, Madison, Mammoth, and Norris. Old Faithful area ranger talks are held either on the benches in front of Old Faithful, or outside the temporary visitor center. The Norris programs have an old-fashioned "campfire" feel. There are also limited talks outside the park in West Yellowstone, at the Visitor Information Center (corner of Yellowstone Ave. and Canyon St.) or the Grizzly and Wolf Discovery Center (201 S. Canyon St.). Winter programs are held at West Yellowstone, Old Faithful, and Mammoth. If you want more details about the types of programs that will be available during your

CLOSE UP

Yellowstone Association

Celebrating 75 years of service in 2008, the Yellowstone Association can be an invaluable learning resource to any park visitor, as resident instructor MacNeil Lyons says. "Interpretive rangers don't have the time and resources to provide the in-depth education that some park visitors would like. That's where we come in."

The not-for-profit organization underwrites publications such as *Yellowstone Today*, the park newspaper you receive when you enter the park, and the free self-guiding trail leaflets available throughout the park. Through its teaching arm, the Yellowstone Association Institute, visitors can participate in educational programs in the park ranging from one to four days in length.

More than 50 hiking-based field seminars are offered every summer, allowing participants to get up close and personal with wildlife, geological features, or flora. Some are hosted at the historic Lamar Buffalo Ranch field campus in the quiet northeast section of the park, while others take place at various park locations. Multi-night backpacking courses teach group participants about minimum-impact camping, bear safety, and backcountry orientation. Finally, "Lodging and Learning" courses offer three- to five-day courses

throughout the year with meals and accommodations provided by Xanterra, which operates all of the hotels inside the park.

More than 60 instructors bring decades of experience to the program. They include some of the most accomplished and internationally regarded scientists in the world. For example, bear management specialist Kelly Gunther has worked in the park almost 25 years; Doug Smith has guided the controversial wolf reintroduction program in the park since the early 1990s and coauthored the award-winning *Decade of the Wolf.*

"Yellowstone for Families" is a four-day "learning adventure" for families with children from eight to 12 years old. In the program, families explore, hike, and learn together—under the attentive leadership of an Institute instructor. "A lot of people feel [an affinity for] national parks and wild places and want to introduce their kids to that . . . but they aren't sure where to start," says Jeff Brown, Yellowstone Association director of education. "[We offer] high-quality, structured, age-appropriate activities . . . that allow one generation to connect with another and share something that's important to them."

3

Junior Ranger Program

With two levels, one for children five to seven years old and the other for children eight to 12, the Junior Ranger program is flourishing. For $3, children may register at any ranger station or visitor center.

Children receive a 12-page newspaper with games, activities, and assignments, such as finishing activity pages in the paper, hiking at least one trail, understanding park rules, and attending one program hosted by a ranger.

Upon completing the requirements, children receive a Junior Ranger patch presented by a park ranger.

trip, contact these locations for additional information, as the schedule of talks changes frequently.

GUIDED TOURS

Grub Steak Expeditions & Tours. These tours, ranging from a half-day to several days in length, focus on photography, geology, history, wildlife, and other topics. They're led by a former Yellowstone park ranger, who is a professional photographer and retired teacher. ⌀*Box 1013, Cody, WY 82414* ☎*307/527–6316 or 800/527–6316* ⊕*www. grubsteaktours.com* ⌑*From $325.*

During the summer, the National Park Service offers a series of half-day hikes with park rangers. **Ranger Adventure Hikes** range from easy (Lone Star Geyser) to strenuous (Avalanche Peak); and from meadows (Hayden Valley) to forested backcountry (Shoshone Lake). Starting dates and times vary, but they are scheduled in various locations inside the park. These hikes are not free (they cost $15 for adults and $5 for children 7–15), but they are an inexpensive way to get in-depth knowledge from a ranger in a small-group setting. They are not widely publicized—check the bulletin boards at campgrounds or visitor centers, find a copy of the newspaper *Ranger Programs*, or ask a ranger.

Xanterra Parks & Resorts, the company that runs most of the concessions in the park, offers bus, boat, horseback, and stagecoach tours of Yellowstone in summer and skiing, snowmobiling, and snowshoeing treks in winter. ⌀*Box 165,*

Mammoth Hot Springs, Yellowstone, WY82190 ☎*307/ 344–7901* ⊕*www.travelyellowstone.com.*

★ Fodor'sChoice Operated by Xanterra, **Historic Yellow Bus Tours** ☾ on White Motors' 14-passenger buses are the most elegant way to see and learn about the park. Eight of the 70-year-old vehicles were restored at a cost of more of than $2 million and were reintroduced to rave reviews in 2007. The soft-top convertibles allow you to bask in the sun if it's warm enough—and keep you plenty warm when it's not. Well-trained guides amuse and educate you through more than a dozen itineraries ranging from one hour to the entire day. Reservations are essential during peak summer season but can usually be made a few days in advance. ☎*307/344– 7901* ⊕*www.travelyellowstone.com* ᎒*$12.50–$87* ☉*Late May–late Sept., but schedules for specific tours vary.* Operated by Xanterra, the *Lake Queen* offers one-hour tours of Lake Yellowstone. Guided by an NPS ranger, you'll learn about a submarine currently mapping geothermal features in the lake, see the remnants of the *E.C. Waters* steamship that sailed for less than one season before being grounded, and skirt the bird sanctuary on Stephenson Island. Advance reservations are recommended. ☎*866/439–7375 for reservations* ⊕*www.travelyellowstone.com* ᎒*$12.25* ☉*Early June–mid-Sept. .*

SHOPPING

Xanterra operates gift shops at or near its lodging facilities at Canyon, Grant, Lake Hotel, Lake Lodge, Mammoth, and all three Old Faithful properties. You'll find daily newspapers, snacks, and park souvenirs—but generally not as much variety as at the Yellowstone General Stores.

A dozen **Yellowstone General Stores** (☎*406/585–7593* ⊕*www. yellowstonegeneralstores.com*) are located throughout the park. Each offers basic souvenirs and snacks, but several are destinations unto themselves. The 1950s-inspired Canyon General Store, the 100-year-old "Hamilton's Store" at Old Faithful, and the Fishing Bridge Store (you can't miss the massive fireplace) are three of the largest, combining architectural significance with a broad variety of groceries, books, apparel, outdoor equipment, and soda fountain–style food service. All stores except the Canyon General Store offer Yellowstone fishing permits. Bridge Bay Marina Store (fishing and boating essentials) and Canyon Village's

Yellowstone Adventures (sporting goods and outdoor gear) are particularly helpful. Hours vary seasonally, but most stores are open from 7:30 AM to 9:30 PM from late May through September. All stores close for winter, except for Mammoth General Store, and all stores accept major credit cards, including Discover and Amex.

Bridge Bay Marina Store (⊠*Bridge Bay Marina, Bridge Bay* ☎*307/242–7326*) has the best selection in the park for fishing and boating needs, including poles, flies, line, and life vests (required for every passenger on any boat). Built in the 1950s, **Canyon General Store** (⊠*Canyon Village* ☎*307/242–7377*) is a throwback to that decade. A kitsch hunter's paradise, it carries every conceivable Yellowstone souvenir. It also has one of the larger grocery sections, including fruits, vegetables, dairy, meat, alcohol, and packaged goods—just don't expect too many choices or bargains. A grill and soda fountain offer hot foods and ice cream treats. Stop inside **Fishing Bridge General Store** (⊠*Fishing Bridge* ☎*307/242–7200*) to see the giant fireplace that has anchored this landmark building since it was built in 1924. One of the largest stores in the park, it has a vast selection of souvenirs, outdoor gear, jewelry, and groceries. The media center offers photo processing, downloading camera cards to disk, and blank media. Groceries include fruits, vegetables, dairy products, meat, alcohol, and packaged goods—at the usual inflated Yellowstone prices. **Grant Village General Store** (⊠*Grant Village* ☎*307/242–7266*)offers a wide selection of apparel, souvenirs, and jewelry; there's also a grocery section, sandwich shop, and ice cream counter.

Grant Village Mini Store (⊠*Grant Village* ☎*307/242–7390*), adjacent to the Backcountry office and gas station, opens about two weeks earlier than the Grant Village General Store and closes about two weeks later. It offers an extremely limited supply of souvenirs, snacks, and beverages.

The historic **Lake General Store** (⊠*Lake Village* ☎*307/242–7563*) has an eight-sided, 30-foot-high atrium and the typical assortment of souvenirs and outdoor gear. It has a small grocery section and a soda fountain, where the affable staff serves up hot panini, cold sandwiches, and ubiquitous ice cream. **Mammoth General Store** (⊠*Mammoth Hot Springs* ☎*307/344–7702*) offers the typical assortment of souvenirs, apparel, and basic outdoor needs. Recognize the **Old Faithful Basin Store** (⊠*Old Faithful Village, Old Faithful* ☎*307/545–7237*) by the wooden sign labeled HAMILTON'S

STORE over the entrance; this is the second-oldest building in the park. It swarms with tourists seeking souvenirs, a seat at the lunch counter, groceries, photo processing, and hand-dipped ice cream. Adjacent to the Old Faithful Inn, the busy **Old Faithful General Store** (⊠ *Old Faithful Village, Old Faithful* ☎ *307/545–7282*) offers a wide selection of apparel, in addition to souvenirs, snacks, and food service. The small **Roosevelt Store** (⊠ *Tower-Roosevelt* ☎ *307/344–7779*) is adjacent to Roosevelt Lodge, offering last-minute needs if you're going on a horseback or stagecoach ride from the Roosevelt stables. **Tower Fall Store** (⊠ *Tower Fall, 2 mi south of Roosevelt on Grand Loop Rd.* ☎ *307/344–7786*), conveniently located adjacent to the Tower Fall trailhead just south of Tower Junction, offers basic camping and hiking gear in addition to jewelry, souvenirs, and snacks. You've come a long way to hike or camp. If you left the camp stove, warm jacket, or other essential in your driveway, **Yellowstone Adventures** (⊠ *Canyon Village* ☎ *307/242–7377*) should be able to fill your outdoor needs. Apparel, hiking, and camping gear are all on offer.

There are eight **Yellowstone Association Park Stores** (☎ *307 /242–2293* ⊕ *www.yellowstoneassociation.org*) located throughout the park. These "bookstores" have the most complete collection of educational books, videos, and maps relating to Yellowstone that you are likely to find anywhere. From geology to wildlife to history, if it's about Yellowstone, this bookstore has it. The largest—the flagship store—is at Canyon Visitor Center. Other locations can be found at the Fishing Bridge Visitor Center, Grant Visitor Center, Mammoth (Albright) Visitor Center, Madison Information Station, Norris, Old Faithful Temporary Visitor Center, and West Thumb Information Station. Most books are also available for purchase via the Association's Web site. Proceeds from this not-for-profit association benefit Yellowstone National Park.

Exploring Grand Teton National Park

WORD OF MOUTH

"Driving around the Teton[s] is easy, and there are many [scenic] stops for your convenience . . . September—especially the first half of the month—is a great time to go there. The fall foliage makes for some magnificent views and the animals are ever-present and relatively easy to spot at mating season."
—HowardR 3/2007

By Gil
Brady

BEFORE EURO-AMERICANS ARRIVED in the early 19th century, native peoples roamed alone among the shadows of the striking Teton Mountains for more than 11,000 years. The prehistory of the Yellowstone plateau—and the surrounding area—has been dated to the Paleo-Indian period (11,500 to 8,000 BC), when hunters and gatherers passed through in search of game and edible plants, most likely between spring and fall, in what is now Grand Teton and Yellowstone national parks.

Today hikers, travelers and visitors can stop by Jackson Lake, where in the 1930s ranch foreman W. C. "Slim" Lawrence began to collect artifacts along its northern shore. For the next 30 years, Lawrence's trove of relics, in combination with those of professional archeologists, aided in chronicling 110 centuries of human activity here. Like the European and American fur trappers, mountain men, and explorers who began to flock into the greater Jackson Hole region as early as John Colter did in 1807, your jaw will probably drop the first time you see the Teton Range jabbing up from the valley floor, high above the rich variety of wildlife, plants, and natural minerals that flourish here.

These glacial mountains provide an unforgettable testament to the complexity, beauty, and raw power of 2.5 billion years of subterranean geological forces. The Tetons resulted from uplift along the Teton Fault, which is still seismically active, beginning 9 million years ago. The fault runs north to south and parallels the eastern side of the range. Thanks to the park's many admirers, and the Rockefeller family's undying commitment to preserving and expanding this lesser known of two neighboring national treasurers, Grand Teton National Park remains an unspoiled source for recreation, just as John D. Rockefeller first imagined back in 1929.

According to legend, "Le Trois Teton" (or "The Three Teats"), were christened in the 18th century by lonely French fur trappers. Some historians claim the range's controversial name derives from the Teton Sioux tribe. What is known more definitively is that "Jackson's Hole" acquired its moniker in 1829, when William Sublette named the 50-mi long, 8- to 15-mi-wide valley after his partner in the fur trade, David E. Jackson. Today the area makes up Teton County, Wyoming.

Approaching from either the North or the South along U.S. Hwy. 191/89/26, without any foothills to soften the

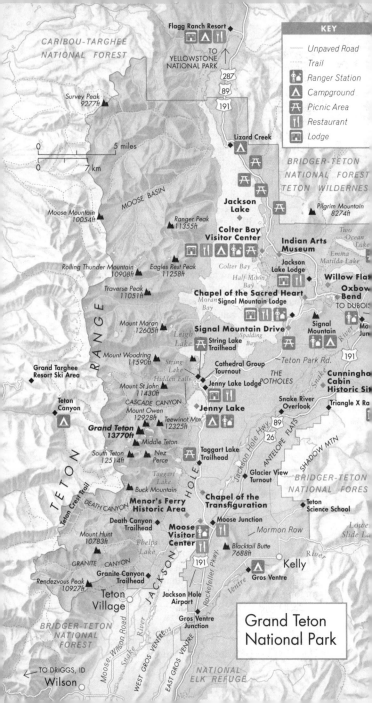

Grand Teton National Park

KEY

— Unpaved Road
······ Trail
Ranger Station
Campground
Picnic Area
Restaurant
Lodge

CARIBOU-TARGHEE NATIONAL FOREST

Flagg Ranch Resort

TO YELLOWSTONE NATIONAL PARK

287
89
191

Survey Peak 9277ft

BRIDGER-TETON NATIONAL FOREST TETON WILDERNESS

Lizard Creek

MOOSE BASIN

Moose Mountain 10054ft

Pilgrim Mountain 8274ft

Jackson Lake

Ranger Peak 11355ft

Colter Bay Visitor Center

Indian Arts Museum

Two Ocean Lake

Emma Matilda Lake

Rolling Thunder Mountain 10908ft

Eagles Rest Peak 11258ft

Colter Bay

Jackson Lake Lodge

Willow Flat

Half Moon Bay

Oxbow Bend

TO DUBOIS

Traverse Peak 11051ft

Moran Bay

Chapel of the Sacred Heart
Signal Mountain Lodge

Signal Mountain Drive

Signal Mountain

Mo Jun

Mount Moran 12605ft

Leigh Lake

Spalding Bay

89
191
26

Grand Targhee Resort Ski Area

String Lake Trailhead

Mount Woodring 11590ft

String Lake

Hidden Falls

Cathedral Group Tournout

Teton Park Rd.

THE POTHOLES

Cunningha Cabin Historic Sit

Teton Canyon

Mount St John 11430ft

CASCADE CANYON

Jenny Lake Lodge

Snake River Overlook

Triangle X Ra

Mount Owen 12928ft

Jenny Lake

Teewinot Mtn 12325ft

R A N G E

Grand Teton 13770ft

Middle Teton

South Teton 12514ft

Nez Perce

Taggart Lake Trailhead

ANTELOPE FLATS

SHADOW MTN

Taggart Lake

Glacier View Turnout

BRIDGER-TETON NATIONAL FORES

Buck Mountain

Menor's Ferry Historic Area

Chapel of the Transfiguration

Teton Science School

Teton Crest Trail

DEATH CANYON

Death Canyon Trailhead

Moose Visitor Center

Moose Junction

Mormon Row

Lowe Slide La

Mount Hunt 10783ft

Phelps Lake

Blacktail Butte 7688ft

Kelly

River

GRANITE CANYON

191

Granite Canyon Trailhead

Gros Ventre

Rendezvous Peak 10927ft

Teton Village

Jackson Hole Airport

Gros Ventre Junction

JACKSON HOLE

Rockefeller Pkwy

BRIDGER-TETON NATIONAL FOREST

Moose-Wilson Road

Snake River

WEST GROS VENTRE

EAST GROS VENTRE

Gros Ventre

NATIONAL ELK REFUGE

TO DRIGGS, ID

Wilson

0 — 5 miles
0 — 7 km

blow, the sight of the Tetons' glacier-scoured crags and snowcapped peaks makes for an overwhelming close-up. This massif is long on natural beauty. Before your eyes, mountain glaciers creep imperceptibly down 12,605-foot Mt. Moran. Large and small alpine lakes gleam along the range's base. And many of the West's most iconic animals (elk, bear, moose, and bald eagle) call this park home.

Try visiting Grand Teton National Park in the off-season (September through April) if you can. For you'll be doubly rewarded by experiencing a world in transition. Huckleberries bloom in spring, attracting foraging bears and their cubs. In fall, the park's vast meadows and aspen groves turn brilliant colors and behold migrating wildlife such as elk and trumpeter swans. During either season, you'll have more of the park to yourself and will avoid much of the congestion accompanying Grand Teton's and Yellowstone's noisy and crowded summers.

Two main roads run through the 311,000-acre park; U.S. Hwy. 191/89/26 curves along the eastern side, while Teton Park Road runs closer to the mountain range.

The winding Snake River cuts south along the eastern side of the park. The northern portion of the park is premiere wildlife-watching territory—you can see everything from rare birds to lumbering moose to the big predators (mountain lions, and black and grizzly bears). But don't feed the bears! In 2007 alone, officials had to put down at least nine bears in the area. Summer droughts and human carelessness can cause bears to wander closer to homes, cabins, and campsites. Bears and their cubs are easily habituated to improperly stored food and can become unexpectedly aggressive toward people. Caution and common sense apply to approaching all large animals and predators, too.

All too often, the lethal mix of attractive wildlife and unassuming tourist ends in the unnecessary deaths of both. A great rule of thumb while exploring these wild parts is to keep a safe distance from all animals and store your food in well-designed containers as you look at and enjoy—but never feed or touch—the wildlife. Pets on leashes are allowed inside the park but not on trails or inside any facilities.

Grand Teton National Park visitors have several new options for 2008, ranging from two brand-new attractions: a groundbreaking trail at Phelps Lake and a cell-phone based self-guided tour at Menor's Ferry (dial 408/794–3828, and follow the instructions). Inquire at any park visitor center—or at the Menor's Ferry landing—for an accompanying map and more information on the six, 2- to 3-minute cell-phone messages that detail the history and significance of various points-of-interest within the park. The service is free, except for the cell-phone minutes used. ■ TIP→ Listen to message 4.

PARK INFORMATION. When you are in Grand Teton, the park's newspaper *Teewinot* is an up-to-date summary of all the latest details you may need to know (road conditions, rules, etc.). The official Web site for **Grand Teton National Park** (☎ 307/739–3300, 307/739–3682 for road conditions ⊕ www.nps.gov/grte) is the most comprehensive source for park information before your visit. Most of the National Park Service brochures and maps are given out in the park itself or they can be downloaded in PDF form from the Web site.

MOOSE

Moose Junction is 13 mi (20.9 km) north of Jackson, 8.6 mi (13.8 km) northeast of Teton Village.

Made up of longtime Wyoming family inholdings, the small community of Moose is actually located completely within the boundaries of Grand Teton National Park. Besides serving as one of the park's main gateways, Moose is also host to Grand Teton National Park's headquarters. You'll find the Moose Junction/GTNP Entrance and rest area 13 mi (21 km) north of Jackson and 19 mi (30 km) south of Moran Junction, about 0.5 mi off U.S. 26/89/191. For those looking to recharge their batteries or mail a postcard, there's a post office, gas station, float-trip outfitter, and general store, where you can stock up on supplies. You can even catch a solid dinner at Dornan's restaurant and chuck wagon. Nearby, you'll also find the brand-new Craig Thomas Discovery & Visitor's Center. From here, every corner of the park is easily accessible. For those heading to Teton Village, take the 8.5-mi scenic short cut through the park, southwest along the paved and unpaved Moose–Wilson Rd.

This historic community is also home to the Chapel of the Transfiguration, and was once the stomping grounds of early settlers at Menor's Ferry. Today, the ferry, originally

GRAND TETON TOP 5

Heavenward hikes: Trek where grizzled frontiersmen roamed. Jackson Hole got its name from mountain man David Jackson; now there are dozens of trails for you to explore.

Wildlife big and small: Keep an eye out for little fellows like short-tailed weasels and beaver, as well as bison, elk, wolves, and both black and grizzly bears.

Waves to make: Float the Snake River or take a canoe or motorboat onto Jackson Lake or Jenny Lake.

Homesteader history: Visit the 1890s barns and ranch buildings of Mormon Row or Menor's Ferry.

Rare bird-watching: Raise the binoculars—or just your head—to see more than 300 species of birds, including trumpeter swans, bald eagles, and osprey.

built in 1894, has been re-created to demonstrate how it once provided transport across the Snake River before there were bridges. Menor's Ferry served as a vital crossing for Jackson Hole's earliest settlers. Due to the harsh climate and isolation of this mountain hamlet, Jackson Hole was one of the last regions in the lower 48 states to be settled when homesteaders, mainly from Idaho, began to arrive in the late 1880s.

VISITOR CENTERS

Craig Thomas Discovery & Visitor Center. This attractively designed building covers nearly 22,000-square-feet that's architecturally inspired by the Teton Range, which looms on the horizon. It's named after the late U.S. Senator Craig Thomas of Wyoming, a devoted national parks advocate and three-term Republican from Cody. The center opened its doors to the public in August 2007, replacing an older and smaller nearby structure. The brand-new center has interactive and interpretive exhibits dedicated to themes of preservation, mountaineering, and local wildlife. There's also a 3-D map of the park and streaming video along a footpath showing the area's intricate natural features. At this writing an auditorium was slated to be added in 2009. Before becoming a U.S. senator in 1994, Thomas replaced fellow Wyomingite Vice President Dick Cheney in 1989 as the Cowboy state's lone congressman in the U.S. House of Representatives. Thomas died in 2007 after winning

GREAT ITINERARIES

GRAND TETON IN ONE DAY

Begin the day by packing a picnic lunch or picking one up at a Jackson eatery. Arrive at **Moose Visitor Center** in time for a 9 AM, two-hour, guided Snake River float trip (make reservations in advance with one of the dozen or so outfitters that offer the trip). When you're back on dry ground, drive north on Teton Park Road, stopping at scenic turnouts—don't miss Teton Glacier—until you reach Jenny Lake Road, which is one-way headed south. After a brief stop at **Cathedral Group Turnout,** park at the Jenny Lake ranger station and take the 20-minute boat ride to **Cascade Canyon** trailhead for a short hike. Return to your car by mid-afternoon, drive back to Teton Park Road, and head north to Signal Mountain Road to catch a top-of-the-park view of the Tetons. In late afternoon descend the mountain and continue north on Teton Park Road. At Jackson Lake Junction, you can go east to **Oxbow Bend** or north to **Willow Flats,** both excellent spots for wildlife viewing before you head to **Jackson Lake Lodge** for dinner and an evening watching the sun set over the Tetons. Or if you'd like to get back on the water, drive to **Colter Bay Marina,** where you can board a 1.5-hour sunset cruise across Jackson Lake to Waterfalls Canyon. You can reverse this route if you're heading south from Yellowstone: start the day with a 7:30 AM breakfast cruise from Colter Bay and end it with a sunset float down the Snake River.

GRAND TETON IN THREE DAYS

Spend one day as suggested above, then spend your second day further exploring the park. Take an all-day hike, a white-water raft trip, a horseback trail ride, or a gentle meander around Jenny Lake. Have dinner at a chuck wagon, either by taking a horseback or wagon ride at Colter Bay or Jackson Lake Lodge, or dining in the teepees at Dornans.

On your third day explore some of Grand Teton's human history by visiting the **Indian Arts Museum** at Colter Bay Visitor Center, **Menor's Ferry, Chapel of the Transfiguration, Cunningham Cabin,** and **Mormon Row.** Cap off the day with dinner in the elegant dining room of **Jenny Lake Lodge.** If you still have energy to spare, you can spend the night whooping it up at a cowboy bar in Jackson.

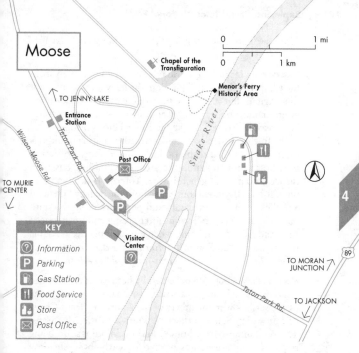

Moose

0 .... 1 mi
0 .... 1 km

↑ TO JENNY LAKE

Chapel of the Transfiguration

Menor's Ferry Historic Area

Entrance Station

Wilson–Moose Rd.

Teton Park Rd.

Snake River

Post Office

P

P

P

TO MURIE CENTER ↙

KEY

ⓘ Information
P Parking
⛽ Gas Station
🍴 Food Service
🏪 Store
✉ Post Office

Visitor Center
ⓘ

TO MORAN JUNCTION ↗

89

Teton Park Rd.

TO JACKSON ↙

4

reelection and battling leukemia. ⊠ *0.5 mi west of Moose Junction, Moose* ⊙ *Early June–early Sept., 8–7; early Sept.–early June, 8–5.*

SCENIC DRIVES

Jackson Hole Highway (U.S. 191/26/89). Slicing through the middle of Jackson Hole, this busy highway passes views of the Teton Range along most of its distance, with a turnout at the Snake River Overlook and another picturesque Snake River view at Oxbow Bend.

HISTORIC & CULTURAL SITES

★ FodorsChoice **Chapel of the Transfiguration.** This tiny chapel built in 1925 on land donated by Maud Noble is still a functioning Episcopal church. Couples come here to exchange vows with the Tetons as a backdrop, and tourists come to take photos of the small church with its awe-inspiring view. ⊠ *Turn off Teton Park Rd. onto Chapel of the Transfiguration Rd., 1.1 mi north of Moose Junction,*

Moose ⊗ *Late May–late Sept., Sun.: Eucharist 8* AM, *service 10* AM.

★ Fodor'sChoice **Menor's Ferry Historic Area.** Down a path from the Chapel of the Transfiguration, the ferry on display is not the original, but it's an accurate re-creation of the double-pontoon craft built by Bill Menor in 1894. It demonstrates how people crossed the Snake River before bridges were built. In the cluster of turn-of-the-20th-century buildings there are historical displays, including a photo collection of historic shots taken in the area; one building has been turned into a small general store. You can pick up a pamphlet for a self-guided tour. Check out the nearby "General Supplies" store where candy and pop are sold in the summer. The ferry typically runs after spring runoff, between June and August, and only when a park ranger is available to operate it. ⊠*0.5 mi off Teton Park Rd., 1 mi north of Moose Junction, Moose* ⊗ *Year-round, dawn–dusk.*

Mormon Row Historic Area. Settled by homesteaders between 1896 and 1907, this area received its name because many of the settlers were members of the Church of Jesus Christ of Latter-day Saints, otherwise known as the Mormons. The remaining barns, homes, and outbuildings are being restored and are representative of early homesteading in the West. You can wander among the buildings, hike the row, and take photographs of the aging structures or herds of buffalo and their calves that frequently graze here. ⊠*Take Antelope Flats Rd., 2 mi north of Moose Junction off Hwy. 191/89/26, and go right at Mormon Row Road for 0.5 mi until you see buildings.* ⊗ *Year-round.*

SCENIC STOPS

Laurance S. Rockefeller Preserve & Center. In November 2007, the Rockefeller family continued their legendary commitment to preserving Jackson Hole's unique character and natural wonders that began over a half-century earlier with the expansive philanthropic vision of family patriarch, John D. Rockefeller. And in 2008, a preserve and visitor's center are scheduled to open for the public to contemplate the role of stewardship and philanthropy as originally conceived in 2001 by John's son, the late Laurance S. Rockefeller. Before his death in 2004, Laurance initiated the process of donating and transitioning a 1,106-acre family retreat, once known as the JY Ranch, to the National Park Service. The ranch was founded in 1906 by Lewis Joy and is widely believed to have been Jackson's first dude ranch when the

Rockefellers bought it in 1932. The 30 or so original ranch buildings have been relocated. Some were converted into employee housing throughout the park, thus restoring the landscape to its original state with the hope of inspiring collective reverence for biodiversity among all conservation-minded visitors. This new preserve also includes a green-designed, 7,000-plus square-foot interpretive center and 8 mi of trails. You can access the preserve via the Valley Trail, 1.75 mi (2.8 km) north of the Granite Canyon trailhead and 0.5 mi (0.8 km) south of the Death Canyon turnoff. For the first time, hikers can now admire the new public view from the south–southwestern shore of Phelps Lake. ☒*Located on the east side of the Moose–Wilson Rd., about 4 mi (7 km) south of park headquarters and 3 mi (5 km) north of the Granite Canyon Entrance Station, Moose.*

JENNY LAKE

Jenny Lake is 14 mi (22.5 km) north of Moose Junction, 15 mi (24 km) southwest of Oxbow Bend.

Nestled south of String and Leigh lakes, Jenny Lake is at the base of the "Cathedral Group" and Grand Teton peak, which at 13,770 feet above sea level is the highest point in the park. This notable summit, standing out from nearby Mt. Owen (at 12,928 feet) and Teewinot (12,325), is affectionately known as "The Grand" by locals. Jenny Lake, below, is a microcosm of the park and, like the peaks above, was the result of ancient glacial movements. In this developed area, you can visit a museum, purchase supplies, or talk to a ranger—plus ride a boat across the lake, hike around it, have a picnic, or camp nearby.

VISITOR CENTERS

Jenny Lake Visitor Center. Geology exhibits, including a relief model of the Teton Range, are on display here. ☒*S. Jenny Lake Junction, 8 mi north of Moose Junction on the Teton Park Rd., Jenny Lake* ☎*307/739–3392* ☉*Early June–early Sept., daily 8–4:30; early Sept.–late Sept., daily 8–4:30; early June–early Sept., daily 8–7.*

SCENIC DRIVES

★ **Fodor's**Choice **Jenny Lake Scenic Drive.** This 4-mi one-way loop provides the park's best roadside close-ups of the Tetons as

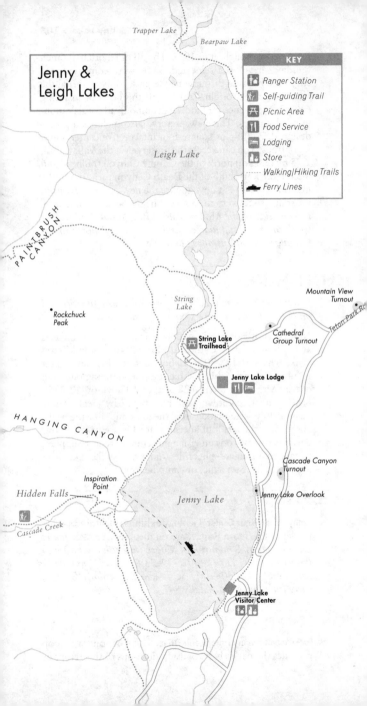

Jenny & Leigh Lakes

KEY

- 🚹 Ranger Station
- 🚶 Self-guiding Trail
- 🌲 Picnic Area
- 🍴 Food Service
- 🛏 Lodging
- 🏪 Store
- ⋯⋯ Walking/Hiking Trails
- 🚢 Ferry Lines

Trapper Lake

Bearpaw Lake

Leigh Lake

P A I N T B R U S H   C A N Y O N

String Lake

Mountain View Turnout

Teton Park Rd.

Rockchuck Peak

Cathedral Group Turnout

🌲 **String Lake Trailhead**

🍴🛏 **Jenny Lake Lodge**

H A N G I N G   C A N Y O N

Cascade Canyon Turnout

Inspiration Point

Hidden Falls

🚶
Cascade Creek

Jenny Lake

Jenny Lake Overlook

🚢

🚹🏪🍴 **Jenny Lake Visitor Center**

it winds south through groves of lodgepole pine and open meadows. Roughly 1.5 mi off Teton Park Rd., the Cathedral Group Turnout faces 13,770-foot Grand Teton (the range's highest peak), flanked by 12,928-foot Mt. Owen and 12,325-foot Mt. Teewinot. ⊠*Jenny Lake.*

Teton Park Road. Linking Moose Junction with Jackson Lake Junction, this 20-mi drive is the closest to the Teton Range and it ties in with the Jenny Lake Scenic Drive. The main road skirts Jackson Lake, with Signal Mountain looming to the east. Farther south, turnouts give you excellent views of Mt. Moran and the Cathedral Group (the three highest peaks in the Teton Range).

SCENIC STOPS

★ **Jenny Lake.** Named for the Native American wife of mountain man Beaver Dick Leigh, this alpine lake south of Jackson Lake draws paddle-sports enthusiasts to its pristine waters and hikers to its tree-shaded trails. ⊠*Off Teton Park Rd. midway between Moose and Jackson Lake, Jenny Lake.*

ANTELOPE FLATS

Antelope Flats is about 2 mi (3.2 km) north of Moose Junction, 16.7 mi (26.9 km) southwest of Moran Junction.

You will find the turnoff for Antelope Flats Road 2 mi north of Moose Junction, on U.S. 26/89/191. Popular with bikers in the summer, the road cuts through a sagebrush and wildflower migration corridor for moose, buffalo, elk, and antelope, all of whom frequently roam the sagebrush meadows and roads as if they own the place (which they do), so drive carefully and take time to enjoy the scenery. Depending on the time of year, you might spend 15 minutes or endless hours here contemplating the marvelous wildlife, mountain views, and rustic buildings still standing the test of time. If you turn right at Mormon Row Road and travel for 0.5 mi, you can visit Mormon Row; if you continue on Antelope Flats Road, you will merge into Gros Ventre Road before reaching the charming town of Kelly. At Kelly, you can travel Gros Ventre Road into the backcountry for a trip or picnic to Slide Lake in the belly of the Gros Ventre (pronounced *grow vont*). Slide Lake was the site of two disasters—in 1925 and 1927—when 50 million cubic yards of Sheep Mountain slid after heavy rainstorms in 1925. Two years later, the natural dam the slide created in the Gros Ventre River failed, flooding the old town of Kelly, which once stood downstream, and killing six people. Today, you can still see the scar the landslide formed on the north face of Sheep Mountain.

SCENIC DRIVES

☼ **Antelope Flats Road.** Off U.S. 191/89/26, about 2 mi north of Moose Junction, this narrow road wanders eastward over rolling plains, rising buttes and sagebrush flats. The road intersects Mormon Row, where you can turn off to see abandoned homesteaders' barns and houses from the turn of the 20th century. Less than 2 mi past Mormon Row is a four-way intersection where you can turn right to loop around past the town of Kelly and Gros Ventre campground and rejoin U.S. 191/26/89 at Gros Ventre Junction. Keep an eye out for pronghorn, bison, moose, and mountain bikers.

HISTORIC & CULTURAL SITES

Cunningham Cabin Historic Site. At the end of a gravel spur road, an easy 0.75-mi trail runs through sagebrush around Pierce Cunningham's 1890 log cabin homestead. Although you can peer inside, the building has no furnishings or displays. Watch for badgers, coyotes, and Uinta ground squirrels in the area. ⊠ *0.5 mi off Jackson Hole Hwy., 5 mi south of Moran Junction, Antelope Flats* ⊗ *Year-round.*

★ Fodor's Choice **Mormon Row Historic Area.** Settled by homestead-
☼ ers from 1896–1907, this area received its name because many of them were members of the Church of Jesus Christ of Latter-day Saints, otherwise known as the Mormons. The remaining barns, homes, and outbuildings frequented by buffalo herds are representative of early homesteading in the West. You can wander among the buildings, hike the row, and take photographs. ⊠ *Just off Antelope Flats Rd., 2 mi north of Moose Junction, Antelope Flats* ⊗ *Year-round.*

SCENIC STOPS

Glacier View Turnout. When the light is right, you're likely to see photographers here eyeing the play of light and clouds over the jagged, white-powder peaks and their receding glaciers in the distance, waiting for the perfect shot. You might spot a bald eagle or osprey searching for trout while soaring over the Snake River, or a buffalo herd idly grazing among the vast open plains and rolling buttes. Occasionally, handsomely marked black-and-tan pronghorn antelopes can be seen springing around the sagebrush flats. Those with road fatigue will enjoy stretching their legs here knowing they've finally arrived in Jackson Hole. ✉ *14.6 mi (23.5 km) south of Moran Junction, Antelope Flats.*

Snake River Overlook. If you are entering or leaving Jackson Hole via U.S. 191/89/26, you will pass by Snake River Overlook, between Deadman's Bar Road and Lost Creek Ranch Road. Stopping here will give you a good idea of the depth and breadth of northwestern Wyoming's raw geography and wildlife. Here, the majestic Cathedral Group of Tetons towers above the long and winding Snake River while Jenny and Leigh lakes form a backdrop in the distance framed by Grand Teton to the south and Mt. Moran to the north. ✉ *Off U.S. 191/89/26, 9.5 mi (15.3 km) south of Moran Junction, Antelope Flats.*

4

OXBOW BEND

Oxbow Bend is about 13 mi (21 km) northeast of Jenny Lake, 7 mi (11.3 km) southeast of Colter Bay.

Located 2.5 mi west of the Moran Junction entrance off U.S. 191/89/26, Oxbow Bend is one of the most photographed panoramas within the park. As you approach Oxbow Bend, Signal Mountain will rise to the southwest across the Snake River, and Jackson Lake and the Cathedral Group of the Tetons will often appear to rise through layers of soft white clouds, like frozen tidal waves in the horizon. This is a must-see for those visiting Jackson Hole in the fall, when the bright orange and red aspen leaves can reflect off the glassy, slow-moving river for an effect much-admired by painters. This is also a ripe spot for observing the Snake River and its inhabitants, especially in early morning or near dusk. You are likely to see moose feeding in willows, elk grazing in aspen stands, and birds such as bald eagles, osprey, sandhill cranes, ducks, and American white pelicans.

VISITOR CENTERS

★ **Colter Bay Visitor Center.** The auditorium here hosts several free daily programs about Native American culture and natural history. Also, at 11 and 3 daily, a 30-minute "Teton

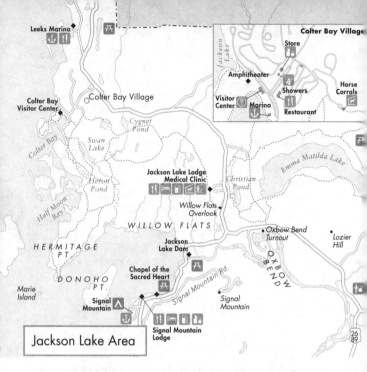

Jackson Lake Area

Highlights" ranger lecture provides tips on park activities.
✉*Colter Bay, 0.5 mi west of Colter Bay Junction on Hwy.
89/191/287, Oxbow Bend* ☎307/739–3594 ☉*Mid-May–
early June, daily 8–5; early June–early Sept., daily 8—7,
Sept.–early Oct., daily 8–5.*

SCENIC DRIVES

★ **Fodor'sChoice Signal Mountain Road.** This exciting drive climbs
☉ Signal Mountain's 1,040-foot prominence along a 5-mi
stretch of switchbacks. As you travel through forest you
can catch glimpses of Jackson Lake and Mt. Moran. The
trip ends with a sweeping view—from 7,720 feet above sea
level—of Jackson Hole and the entire 40-mi Teton Range.
Sunset is the best time to make the climb up Signal Mountain. The road is not appropriate for long trailers and is
closed in winter. ✉*Oxbow Bend.*

HISTORIC & CULTURAL SITES

☉ **Indian Arts Museum.** This collection's standout exhibits
include Plains Indian weapons and clothing. You will see

CLOSE UP

Good Reads

You can purchase excellent park-related books at Grand Teton visitor center bookstores, run by the **Grand Teton Natural History Association** (☎307/739–3403 ⊕www.grandtetonpark.org). Among them are the following:

■ *Grand Teton Wild and Beautiful* by Fred Pflughoft and Henry H. Holdsworth

■ *A Naturalists Guide to*

Grand Teton and Yellowstone National Parks by Frank Craighead

■ *Interpreting the Landscape: Recent and Ongoing Geology of Grand Teton and Yellowstone National Parks* by J.M.M. Good and Kenneth L. Pierce

■ *Legacy of the Tetons: Homesteading in Jackson Hole* by Candy Moulton

4

Crow blanket strips with elegant beadwork, sashes from the Shawnee and Hopi tribes, and various weapons, games and toys, flutes and drums, and a large collection of moccasins from many tribes. From June through early September, you can see crafts demonstrations by tribal members, take ranger-led tours of the museum, and listen to a daily 45-minute ranger program on Native American culture. ✉*2 mi off U.S. 89/191/287, 5 mi north of Jackson Lake Junction inside the Colter Bay Visitor Center, Oxbow Bend* ☎*307/739–3594* ✆*Free* ☉*Mid-May–mid-June and Sept., daily 8–5; mid-June–Labor Day, daily 8–7.*

SCENIC STOPS

Chapel of the Sacred Heart. This small log chapel sits in the pine forest with a view of Jackson Lake. The chapel is open only for services, but you can enjoy the view anytime. ✉*0.5 mi north of Signal Mountain Lodge, off Teton Park Rd., about 3 mi south of Jackson Lake Junction, Oxbow Bend* ☉*Services June–Sept., Sat. 5:30 PM and Sun. 10 AM.*

★ **Fodor'sChoice Jackson Lake.** The biggest of Grand Teton's glacier-carved lakes, this body of water in the northern reaches of the park was enlarged by construction of the Jackson Lake Dam in 1906. You can fish, sail, and windsurf on the lake, or hike trails near the shoreline. Three marinas (Colter Bay, Leeks, and Signal Mountain) provide access for boaters, and several picnic areas, campgrounds, and lodges overlook the lake. ✉*U.S. 89/191/287 from Lizard Creek to Jackson Lake Junction, and Teton Park Rd. from Jackson Lake Junction to Signal Mountain Lodge, Oxbow Bend.*

★ Fodor'sChoice **Oxbow Bend.** This peaceful and much-admired spot overlooks a quiet backwater left by the Snake River when it cut a new southern channel. White pelicans stop here on their spring migration (many stay on through summer), sandhill cranes and trumpeter swans visit frequently, and great blue herons nest amid the cottonwoods along the river. Use binoculars to search for bald eagles, ospreys, moose, beaver, and otter. The Oxbow is known for the reflection of Mt. Moran that marks its calm waters in early morning. ⊠ *U.S. 89/191/287, 2.5 mi east of Jackson Lake Junction, Oxbow Bend.*

★ **Willow Flats.** You will almost always see moose grazing in the marshy area of Willow Flats, in part because it has a good growth of willow trees, which moose both eat and hide in. This is also a good place to see birds and waterfowl. ⊠ *U.S. 89/191/287, 1 mi north of Jackson Lake Junction. Oxbow Bend.*

Grand Teton Hikes & Other Activities

WORD OF MOUTH

"We did lots of hikes, ranger walks and talks, ate dinners at different locations within the park, and woke up early to see the best wildlife. We could see moose outside our room and bears from the [Jackson Lake] Lodge lounge, as well as coyote, trumpeter swans, otter, elk, bison, and lots more on our hikes. Late June is wildflower peak time in the park, but also many mosquitoes (depending on where you hike) so be prepared."

—sms73

By Gil
Brady
IN THE SPIRIT OF ITS FREE-THINKING FOUNDERS AND BENEFACTORS—who include Maud Noble, Horace Albright, and John D. Rockefeller—Grand Teton National Park is ideal for rugged, thrill-seeking individuals, groups with athletic ambitions, and those who prefer solitary recreation, contemplation, and like-minded pursuits. Painters, photographers, scientists, and meditative souls coexist here quite comfortably with hikers, bikers, swimmers, anglers, mountain climbers, boaters, floaters, sailors, paddle sports enthusiasts, cross-country skiers, and snowshoers. Upon arrival, few will question why Smithsonian dubbed this lesser-known national treasure "The Jewel of the Tetons."

With all there is to do, this is not a park where travelers come to stand around waiting for something to happen. And though the fresh, piney air is ideal for kicking back and tailgating upon arrival, many will find irresistible the urge to first knock themselves out exploring this Eden-like wonderland. Here, you'll encounter a landscape inviting self-expression and easily accessed solitude, though without faithful geysers to cue you when it's time to leave or join the crowd. Unlike Yellowstone, Grand Teton is much smaller, compact, and easily navigated. Attractions are closer together, and you can cover the park in some depth in just a few days. Also, most geological wonders here lie above rather than below the active Teton Fault, which runs along the eastern side of the range.

As in Yellowstone, activities are still dependent on the weather and seasons. In the winter months, snowmobiling, cross-country skiing, ice fishing, and snowshoeing are the activities of choice. In the summer, hiking, biking, picnicking, and fishing are the best ways to get out and enjoy the park. Seasons here range from brutal cold and snowy winters—with sub-zero temperatures for weeks at a time—to dry, hot summers. July and August can see temperatures soar above 90°F without a drop of rain for weeks, so don't be surprised if your lips crack or, worse, if sudden forest fires alter your plans. Even still, you can see snow any day of the year in northwestern Wyoming, though summers seem to be getting warmer. If you plan on spending the night camping—or even a long day exploring the backcountry—pack accordingly and prepare for anything. Spring and fall are the most temperate and beautiful. These are the months when the colors of the abundant wildflowers and forest's timbers are richest. This is the perfect time of year to explore a park in transition and witness migrating animals, such as swans, geese, and elk, with less of the noisy distractions that come with summer's seasonal-driven tourism.

Foremost, however, this is bear country. Black and grizzly bears are common, as are mothers with cubs whom they will defend with hair-raising ferocity. However, moose can also be dangerous and have been known to charge and chase people, even bikers (who are also prohibited on the trails). Moose kicks are powerful and deadly; moose are surprisingly fleet of foot, so admire them from afar and avoid the temptation to pet or feed any of the park's wildlife. Bears can become habituated to human food and unexpectedly aggressive in obtaining it. As in Yellowstone, pack your foodstuffs in bear-proof containers, and buy and learn how to use bear spray. Common sense would spare more lives and animals if only people would use it. In 2007 alone, at least nine bears in the area were destroyed by officials because they had come into too close of contact with humans.

5

DAY HIKES

Most of Grand Teton's trails are unpaved, though you will find a few short paved sections in the vicinity of developed areas. You can get trail maps and information about hiking conditions from rangers at any of the park's visitor centers, where you will also find bathrooms or outhouses; there are no facilities along any of the trails themselves.

Of the more than 250 mi of maintained trails, the most popular are around some of the lakes, including Jenny Lake, the Leigh and String lakes area, and Taggart and Bradley lakes (particularly the Taggart Lake Trail with its views of Avalanche Canyon and the Grand Teton). Must-do trails that will whip your legs into mountain shape without too much strain include Taggart Lake via Beaver Creek and Phelps Lake. Frontcountry or backcountry, you may see moose, bears, or mountain lions; keep your distance and don't run from mountain lions. Instead, make lots of noise. Pets are not permitted on trails or in the backcountry, but you can take them on paved frontcountry trails so long as they're on a short leash. Always sign in at trailheads, let someone know where you are going and when you expect to return, and carry plenty of water, snacks, and a cell phone.

Grand Teton Hiking Precautions

Knowing how to pack a backpack well is an asset for long and overnight hikes, but even on shorter trips, make sure to carry plenty of snacks, food, water, a change of socks, and rain gear in case of foul weather.

While plastic bottles work on small trails, a Camelback or something that you can wear is better. It frees your hands, keeps your water colder longer, and is less likely to get dropped or forgotten and litter the park.

Though there's still plenty of solitude to be found with some planning, trails are designed for multiple uses, and hikers should yield to backcountry horse riders, climbers, and passing animals.

Rapidly changing weather is common throughout Jackson Hole. Before arriving and during your stay, be sure to check the Grand Teton public information numbers and Web sites. You can also tune in to the local radio stations for updates on changing weather conditions in the area.

Bring mosquito repellent, sunblock, and bear spray on any long hike, and leave no trace of your passage and the landscape as you found it.

Hiking, especially for city slickers in the mountains, can be a strenuous activity that becomes more pleasurable with experience, overall fitness, and acclimation to high altitudes. For starters, make sure you have good hiking boots or sturdy sneakers that have been broken in and trail tested on rocky terrain with steep drops and inclines. Go up a big hill and down its steep backside with old sneakers, and you may end up with blister-scored heels, busted-out shoes, and squished toes. The lack of proper gear can quickly spoil an otherwise easy and enjoyable trek. You'll quickly learn to pace yourself at these altitudes; breathing can be different until you are acclimated.

SPOTLIGHT HIKE: TAGGART LAKE–BEAVER CREEK TRAIL

★ **Fodors**Choice Named after William B. Taggart, a geologist with the famous 1872 Hayden expedition, this popular loop between Bradley and Phelps lakes, to the north and south, rises 400 feet until leveling off at about 7,080 feet. It circles the base of Static and Grand Teton peaks with views of Avalanche Canyon and has sagebrush meadows where you might spot a moose. Before entering Taggart Lake's southeastern shore, on this path you'll ascend "moraines," cross flower sprinkled foot bridges, and pass a hillside still scarred and recovering from a 1985 lightning fire. The entire round-trip of 4 mi, including short breaks, should take three to four hours at most. ⊠ *The Taggart Lake Trail head is approximately 6 mi south of Jenny Lake on Teton Park Rd.* ☞ *Moderate.*

0.0 MI: TAGGART LAKE TRAILHEAD

The first quarter-mile leg of this hike is flat and lined with sagebrush until you come to the bridge at Taggart Creek and must climb a small moraine (an earthen mound formed by ancient glaciers pushing through the mountains and carving up the valley floor, leaving a lip of dirt and rock in their wake).

0.25 MI: TAGGART CREEK

Footbridges lined with such wildflowers as blue lupine and reddish Indian paintbrush lead to a narrow, somewhat rocky slope up the moraine that levels off in a sagebrush meadow where fires in 1985 scarred the landscape. This stretch will take you another half-mile.

1.1 MI: BRADLEY LAKE JUNCTION

Just a hair past the 1-mi point of the hike, in the middle of an open meadow, a sign marks a fork in the trail. During the approach, you'll encounter progressively seductive views of the Teton Range and Grand Teton peak. Bear left (southwest) at the crossroad for Valley Trail and Taggart Lake. (If you choose to go right (northwest) on Bradley Lake Cutoff Trail, you will travel through a forested grove and end up at a good overlook for Taggart Lake after 1 mi.) This is another area where you may spot a moose.

1.6 MI: TAGGART LAKE

Hiking southwest after the fork will take you to a dirt path (the Valley Trail) that hugs Taggart Lake's southeastern shoreline and outlet into Beaver Creek. Here you can sit on rocks or lay a blanket and contemplate the view of Avalanche Canyon and "The Grand" across the lake. Though some rangers deny it, small snakes hide among the crevices in the rocks. Their heads and bodies can also sometimes be seen breaking the surface of the water here and at other lakes in the park, though to date, no poisonous reptiles have been reported in the area. Geologists theorize Tag-

TAGGART LAKE TRAIL TIPS

■ Because of its descent through lush scenery and accessibility to Taggart Lake's handsome shoreline of lush scenery and glassy waters in the heart of Avalanche Canyon, this trail will appeal to the adventurous as well as the easily winded.

■ On many fair-weather days this trail is crowded, so solitude will be harder to find.

■ During July and August, the trailhead parking lots often fill up fairly early in the day,

so arriving early is preferable if you want to find a parking spot. Rangers urge drivers to park only in designated parking lots and spaces; parking off the road will damage the vegetation.

■ You need to be on the lookout for moose, particularly in the meadows, and follow all warnings about their danger when provoked. Bears can sometimes be encountered on this trail, so do make noise to alert them to your attention.

gart and other lakes in Grand Teton that were first formed around 9,000 years ago by melting glaciers.

2.1 MI: JUNCTION WITH BEAVER CREEK TRAIL

After leaving the lakeshore via the Valley Trail for 0.75 mi, you'll cross a footbridge, which marks a junction with the Beaver Creek Trail. Stay left (east) and continue on the Beaver Creek Trail until you mount a hill and start descending into the open sagebrush fields. The Beaver Creek Trail rejoins the looping Taggart Lake trail at a junction and returns you to the trailhead.

SPOTLIGHT HIKE: PHELPS LAKE TRAIL,

★ **Fodor'sChoice** This easy to moderate hike starts at the Death Canyon Trailhead, which is 5.6 mi from the Moose–Wilson entrance to the park (the turnoff to the trailhead is 4 mi from Moose Junction). It's ideal for beginners, those scouting for an ideal place to campout in the boondocks and couples seeking a romantic outing. You'll summit at the spectacular 700-foot, forested overlook of Phelps Lake and the lower Jackson Hole valley. The turnoff for Whitegrass Rd. which leads to the Death Canyon Trailhead parking lot, is about 3 mi southwest of the Moose Visitor Center; the last mile or so is dirt and can get rough, so be sure your vehicle is adequate for the task. The trail to the Phelps Lake

Overlook is relatively short (less than a mile), but you'll travel a total of 4 mi if you go down to the lake itself. ⊠*Turn off the Moose–Wilson Rd., at Whitegrass Rd., 4 mi southwest of Moose Junction* ☞*Easy to Moderate.*

MILE 0.0: DEATH CANYON TRAILHEAD

Very soon after you depart the parking area at Death Canyon Trailhead, you'll reach a crossroads with the Valley Trail. Head southwest (left) and continue another 0.75 mi up a long hill until you reach the ridge-top overlook of Phelps Lake, which you'll see 700 feet below.

MILE 0.8: PHELPS LAKE OVERLOOK

When you arrive at this shady, breathtaking overlook, don't be surprised to find a small crowd of admirers or couples stealing kisses. With its panoramic views of the lake below and the lower Jackson Hole valley receding into the horizon, this is one of the more awe-inspiring viewpoints in the park. After drinking it all in, you can either head back or navigate the sharp switchbacks down to lake to claim your own beachfront, by veering south (left) at the intersection with Death Canyon Trail, which is heading up If you go all the way down and up, you'll have traveled a total of 4 mi.

OTHER HIKES

Grand Teton is a hiker's paradise. Below you'll find other trails to explore. And if you're in the Jenny Lake region, you should not pass up the chance to visit Hidden Falls, as it's perhaps the most photographic and peaceful spot you can find and enjoy with your entire family.

EASY HIKES

⟳ **Cascade Canyon Trail.** Take the 20-minute boat ride from the Jenny Lake dock to the start of a gentle, 0.5-mi climb to 200-foot Hidden Falls, the park's most popular and crowded trail destination. With the boat ride, plan on a couple of hours to experience this trail. Listen here for the distinctive bleating of the rabbit-like pikas among the glacial boulders and pines. The trail continues 0.5 mi to Inspiration Point over a rocky path that is moderately steep. There are two points on the climb that afford good views of Jenny Lake and the surrounding area, but keep climbing; after passing a rock wall you'll finally reach the true Inspiration Point, with the best views. To avoid crowds, try to make your way to Inspiration Point in early morning or late afternoon. To reach the Cascade Canyon trailhead, go to the Jenny Lake Visitor Center to catch a ride across Jenny Lake with Jenny Lake Boating (see ⇨Boating & Water Sports Outfitters, below). ✉*Jenny Lake Rd., 2 mi off Teton Park Rd., 12 mi south of Jackson Lake Junction* ☎*307/734–9227* 🎫*$5 (one-way) $9 (round-trip) for the Jenny Lake Shuttle* ⊗*June–early Sept.*

Colter Bay Nature Trail Loop. This very easy, 1.75-mi round-trip excursion treats you to views of Jackson Lake and the Tetons. As you follow the level trail from Colter Bay Visitor Center and along the forest's edge, you may see moose and bald eagles. Allow yourself two hours to complete the walk. ✉*2 mi off U.S. 89/191/287, 5 mi north of Jackson Lake Junction.*

Lunchtree Hill Trail. One of the park's easiest trails begins at Jackson Lake Lodge and leads 0.5 mi to the top of a hill above Willow Flats. The area's willow thickets, beaver ponds, and wet, grassy meadows make it a birder's paradise. Look for sandhill cranes, hummingbirds, and the many types of songbirds described in the free bird guide available at visitor centers. You might also see moose. The round-trip walk takes no more than half an hour. ✉*U.S. 89/191/287, 0.5 mi north of Jackson Lake Junction.*

MODERATE HIKES

🕐 ★ **Jenny Lake Trail.** You can walk to Hidden Falls from Jenny Lake ranger station by following the mostly level trail around the south shore of the lake to Cascade Canyon Trail. Jenny Lake Trail continues around the lake for 6.5 mi. It's an easy trail—classed here as moderate because of its length—that will take you two to three hours. You'll walk through a lodgepole pine forest, have expansive views of the lake and the land to the east, and hug the shoulder of the massive Teton range itself. Along the way you are likely to see elk, pikas, golden mantle ground squirrels, a variety of ducks and water birds, plus you may hear elk bugling, birdsong, and the chatter of squirrels. ✉*S. Jenny Lake Junction, 0.5 mi off Teton Park Rd., 8 mi north of Moose Junction.*

Leigh Lake Trail. The flat trail follows String Lake's northeastern shore to Leigh Lake's south shore, covering 2 mi in a round-trip of about an hour. You can extend your hike into a moderate 7.5-mi, four-hour round-trip by following the forested east shore of Leigh Lake to Bearpaw Lake. Along the way you'll have views of Mt. Moran across the lake, and you may be lucky enough to spot a moose.

✉*String Lake trailhead, 0.5 mi west of Jenny Lake Rd., 14 mi north of Moose Junction.*

String Lake Trail. This moderate 3.5-mi, three-hour loop around String Lake lies in the shadows of 11,144-foot Rockchuck Peak and 11,430-foot Mt. Saint John. This is also a good place to see moose, hear songbirds, and view wildflowers. This trail is a bit more difficult than other mid-length trails in the park, which means it is also less crowded. ✉*0.5 mi west of Jenny Lake Rd., 14 mi north of Moose.*

DIFFICULT HIKES

Death Canyon Trail. This 7.6-mi trail is a strenuous hike with lots of hills to traverse, ending with a climb up into Death Canyon. Plan to spend most of the day on this steep trail. ✉*Off Moose–Wilson Rd., 4 mi south of Moose Junction.*

5

SUMMER SPORTS & ACTIVITIES

BICYCLING

Teton Park Road and Jackson Hole Highway are generally flat with long, gradual inclines, and have well-marked shoulders. Grand Teton has few designated bike paths, so cyclists should be very careful when sharing the road with vehicles, especially RVs and trailers. A bike lane allows for northbound bike traffic along the one-way Jenny Lake Loop Road, a one-hour ride. The River Road, 4 mi north of Moose, is an easy four-hour mountain-bike ride along a ridge above the Snake River on a dirt road. Bicycles are not allowed on trails or in the backcountry.

In Jackson, ride the Snow King trails system that begins at Snow King resort. The Cache Creek to Game Creek loop is a 25-mi ride on dirt roads and trails. The two trails systems also link together. In addition, the surrounding Bridger-Teton National Forest has abundant mountain-biking trails and roads.

Teton Cycle Works. The oldest shop in town offers mountain- and road-bike rentals, sales, accessories, and repairs. ✉*175 N. Glenwood St., Jackson* ☎*307/733–4386* ⊙*Mar.–Oct.*

Teton Mountain Bike Tours. Mountain bikers of all skill levels can take guided half-, full-, or multiday tours with this company into both Grand Teton and Yellowstone national parks, as well as to the Bridger-Teton and Caribou–Targhee national forests. *Box 7027, Jackson 83002 *307/733–0712 or 800/733–0788 *www.wybike.com *$55–$125 for half- to full-day trips; multiday trips $379–$400 per day *May–Sept.

BIRD-WATCHING

With more than 300 species of birds in the park, the Tetons make for excellent bird-watching country. Here you might spot both the calliope hummingbird (the smallest North American hummingbird) and the trumpeter swan (the world's largest waterfowl). The two riparian habitats described below draw lots of attention, but there are many other bird-busy areas as well. Birds of prey circle around Antelope Flats Road, for instance—the surrounding fields are good hunting turf for red-tailed hawks and prairie falcons. At Taggart Lake you'll see woodpeckers, bluebirds, and hummingbirds. Look for songbirds, such as pine and evening grosbeaks and Cassin's finches, in surrounding open pine and aspen forests.

Oxbow Bend. Some seriously impressive birds tend to congregate at this quiet spot. In spring, white pelicans stop by during their northerly migration; in summer, bald eagles, great blue herons, and osprey nest nearby. Year-round, you'll have a good chance of seeing trumpeter swans. Nearby Willow Flats has similar bird life, plus sandhill cranes. *U.S. 89/191/287, 2 mi east of Jackson Lake Junction.*

Phelps Lake. The moderate 1.8-mi round-trip Phelps Lake Overlook Trail takes you up conifer- and aspen-lined glacial moraine to a view that's accessible only by trail. Expect abundant birdlife: Western tanagers, northern flickers, and ruby-crowned kinglets thrive in the bordering woods, and hummingbirds feed on scarlet gilia beneath the overlook. *Moose–Wilson Rd., about 3 mi off Teton Park Rd., 1 mi north of Moose Junction.*

BOATING & WATER SPORTS

Water sports in Grand Teton are diverse. You can float the Snake River, which runs high and fast early in the season (May and June) and more slowly during the latter part of the summer. Canoes and kayaks dominate the smaller lakes and share the water with motorboats on the impressively large Jackson Lake. Motorboats are allowed on

Jenny, Jackson, and Phelps lakes. On Jenny Lake, there's an engine limit of 10 horsepower. You can launch your boat at Colter Bay, Leek's Marina, Signal Mountain, and Spalding Bay.

If you're floating the Snake River on your own, you are required to purchase a permit that costs $10 per raft and is valid for the entire season, or one for $5 per raft for seven days. Permits are available year-round at Moose Visitor Center and at Colter Bay, Signal Mountain, and Buffalo (near Moran entrance) ranger stations in summer. Before you set out, check with park rangers for current conditions.

You may prefer to take one of the many guided float trips through calm-water sections of the Snake; outfitters pick you up at the float-trip parking area near Moose Visitor Center for a 10- to 20-minute drive to upriver launch sites. Ponchos and life preservers are provided. Early morning and evening floats are your best bets for wildlife viewing, but be sure to carry a jacket or sweater. Float season runs mid-April to December.

Colter Bay Marina. All types of services are available to boaters, including free parking for boat trailers and vehicles, free mooring, boat rentals, guided fishing trips, and fuel. ⊠*On Jackson Lake.*

Leek's Marina. Both day and short-term parking for boat trailers and vehicles are available for up to three nights maximum. There are no boat rentals, but you can get fuel, and there's free short-term docking plus a pizza restaurant. This marina is operated by park concessionaire Signal Mountain Lodge. ⊠*U.S. 89/191/287, 6 mi north of Jackson Lake Junction* ☎*307/543–2831* ⊘*Mid-May–mid-Sept.*

Signal Mountain Lodge Marina. The marina rents pontoon boats, deck cruisers, motorboats, kayaks, and canoes by the hour or for full-day cruising; rates range from $12 an hour for a kayak to $62 an hour for a pontoon boat. ⊠*Teton Park Rd., 3 mi south of Jackson Lake Junction* ☎*307/543–2831* ⊘*Mid-May–mid-Sept.*

⇨*Outfitters & Expeditions box for boating outfitters.*
Spalding Bay. You can launch your boat here and park your trailer and vehicle for the day. There's no docking or mooring available. ⊠*2 mi off Teton Park Rd., 7 mi south of Jackson Lake Junction.*

BOATING & WATER SPORTS OUTFITTERS

Barker-Ewing Scenic Float Trips. Travel the peaceful parts of the Snake River looking for wildlife as knowledgeable guides talk about area history, plants, and animals. ✆*Box 100–J, Moose 83012* ☎*307/733–1800 or 800/365–1800* ⊕*www.barkerewingscenic.com* ☞*$50* ⊙*May–Sept.*

Grand Teton Lodge Company. You can rent motorboats, rowboats, and canoes at Colter Bay Marina. ✉*2 mi off U.S. 89/191/287, 5 mi north of Jackson Lake Junction* ☎*307/543–3100, 307/543–2811, or 800/628–9988* ⊕*www.gtlc.com* ☞*Motor boats $25 per hour, row boats and canoes $11 per hour* ⊙*Early June–late Sept.*

Grand Teton Lodge Company Snake River Float Trips. Choose from a scenic float trip with lunch, or an evening trip with a steak-fry dinner. Make reservations at the activities desk at Colter Bay Village or Jackson Lake Lodge. ☎*307/543–3100 or 800/628–9988* ⊕*www.gtlc.com* ☞*Scenic float $45, lunch float $53, steak-fry float $60* ⊙*June–Aug.*

Jenny Lake Boating. This company operates a shuttle to ferry hikers across Jenny Lake every 15 minutes to the Cascade Canyon Trailhead, saving time and steps. The company also offers guided boat trips around the lake as well as kayak and canoe rentals. The actual hours vary seasonally. ☎*307/734–9227* ⊕*www.jennylakeboating.com* ☞*Jenny Lake Shuttle $5 (one-way) or $9 (round-trip), scenic cruises $14, canoe and kayak rentals $12 per hour* ⊙*Mid-May–Sept.*

Lewis and Clark River Expeditions. Get in touch with these folks for an exhilarating wet-and-wild ride or a more leisurely scenic float. ✉*335 N. Cache St., Box 720, Jackson 83001* ☎*307/733–4022 or 800/824–5375* ⊕*www.lewisandclarkexpeds.com* ☞*$43–$79* ⊙*Mid-May–mid-Sept.*

Mad River Boat Trips. This company leads a variety of white-water and scenic float trips, some combined with breakfast, lunch, or dinner. ✉*1255 S. U.S. 89, Jackson* ☎*307/733–6203 or 800/458–7238* ⊕*www.mad-river.com* ☞*$44–$83* ⊙*Mid-May–Sept.*

Snake River Kayak and Canoe. Get some instruction in the fine art of paddling here, then test yourself on the river. ✆*Box 4311, Jackson 83001* ☎*307/733–9999 or 800/529–2501* ⊕*www.snakeriverkayak.com* ☞*Raft trips $63–$95, one-day clinics $175–$280, multiday instruction $275–$900* ⊙*Apr.–Oct.*

Triangle X Float Trips. This company offers subdued river trips in Grand Teton National Park, including a sunset supper float. ✉ *2 Triangle X Ranch Rd., Moose* ☎ *307/733–5500 or 888/860–0005* ⊕ *www.trianglex.com* 💲 *$48–$58* ⊙ *Mid-May–late Sept.*

CLIMBING

The Teton Range offers the nation's most diverse general mountaineering. Excellent rock, snow, and ice routes abound for climbers of all experience levels. Unless you're already a pro, it's recommended that you take a course from one of the area's climbing schools before tackling the tough terrain.

Exum Mountain Guides. You'll find a variety of climbing experiences here, ranging from one-day mountain climbs to ice climbing to backcountry adventures on skis and snowboards. ✍ *Box 56, Moose 83012* ☎ *307/733–2297* ⊕ *www.exumguides.com* 💲 *One-day climbs $200–$340, climbing schools $105–$170* ⊙ *Year-round.*

Jackson Hole Mountain Guides. Mountain climbers get a leg up in the Tetons from this outfit, which offers instruction for beginning to advanced climbers in both rock and ice climbing. ✉ *165 N. Glenwood St., Jackson* ☎ *307/733–4979 or 800/239–7642* ⊕ *www.jhmg.com* 💲 *One-day guided climbs $195–$225, climbing classes $125–$275* ⊙ *Year-round.*

FISHING

Rainbow, brook, lake, and native cutthroat trout inhabit the park's waters. The Snake's 75 mi of river and tributary are world-renowned for their fishing. To fish in Grand Teton National Park, you need a Wyoming fishing license. A day permit for nonresidents is $10, and an annual permit is $65 plus a $10 conservation stamp; for state residents a license costs $15 per season plus $10 for a conservation stamp. Children under age 14 can fish free with an adult who has a license. You can buy a fishing license at Colter Bay Marina, Moose Village Store, Signal Mountain Lodge, and at area sporting-goods stores, where you will also be able to get solid information on good fishing spots and the best flies or lures to use. Or you can get one direct from **Wyoming Game and Fish Department.** ✉ *420 N. Cache St., Box 67, Jackson 83001* ☎ *307/733–2321* ⊕ *gf.state.wy.us.*

Grand Teton Lodge Company. The park's major concessionaire operates guided Jackson Lake fishing trips that include boat and tackle, and guided fly-fishing trips on the Snake River. Make reservations at the activities desks at Colter Bay Village or Jackson Lake Lodge, where trips originate. ✉*Colter Bay Marina or Jackson Lake Lodge* ☎*307/543–3100 or 800/628–9988* ⊕*www.gtlc.com* 💲*$130–$375 and up* ☉*June–Sept.*

Signal Mountain Lodge. A variety of guided Lake Jackson fishing trips leave from the marina here. ✉*Teton Park Rd., 3 mi south of Jackson Lake Junction* ☎*307/543–2831* ⊕*www.signalmountainlodge.com* 💲*$65 per hour* ☉*Mid-May–mid-Sept.*

HORSEBACK RIDING

You can arrange a guided horseback tour at Colter Bay Village and Jackson Lake Lodge corrals or with a number of private outfitters. Most offer rides of an hour or two up to all-day excursions. If you want to spend even more time riding in Grand Teton and the surrounding mountains, consider a stay at a dude ranch. Shorter rides are almost all appropriate for novice riders, while more experienced cowboys and cowgirls will enjoy the longer journeys where the terrain gets steeper and you may wind through deep forests. For any ride be sure to wear long pants and boots (cowboy boots or hiking boots). Because you may ride through trees, a long-sleeve shirt is also a good idea and a hat is always appropriate, but it should have a stampede string to make sure it stays on your head if the wind comes up.

Colter Bay Village Corral. One- and two-hour rides leave Colter Bay Village for a variety of destinations, while half-day trips—for advanced riders only—go to Hermitage Point; some rides include a trailside breakfast or dinner. ✉*2 mi off U.S. 89/191/287, 5 mi north of Jackson Lake Junction* ☎*307/543–3100 or 800/628–9988* ⊕*www.gtlc.com* 💲*Short rides $30–$42, breakfast rides $50, dinner rides $56; wagon rides $30 for breakfast and $40 for dinner* ☉*June–Aug.*

Jackson Lake Lodge Corral. One-hour trail rides give an overview of the Jackson Lake Lodge area; two-hour rides go to Emma Matilda Lake, Oxbow Bend, and Christian Pond. Experienced riders can take a half-day ride to Two Ocean

Lake. Some rides include breakfast or dinner eaten along the trail. ⊠*U.S. 89/191/287, 0.5 mi north of Jackson Lake Junction* ☎*307/543–3100 or 800/628–9988* 🖷*307/543– 3143* ⊕*www.gtlc.com* ⊠*Short rides $30–$42, breakfast rides $50 ($30 by wagon), dinner rides $56 ($40 by wagon)* ⊗*June–Aug.*

WINTER SPORTS OUTFITTERS

Jack Dennis Outdoor Shop. This place stocks skis and snowboards for sale and rent, and outdoor gear for any season. ⊠*50 E. Broadway Ave., Jackson* ☎*307/733–3270 Jackson, 307/733–6838 Teton Village* ⊕*www.jackdennis.com* ⊠*Ski rental $25–$44, snowboard and boot rental $25– $35* ⊗*Year-round.*

Pepi Stegler Sports Shop. You can buy or rent skis or snowboards at this Teton Village shop, conveniently located at the base of the Jackson Hole ski mountain. ⊠*Teton Village* ☎*307/733–4505* ⊕*www.jackdennis.com* ⊠*Ski rental $25– $44, snowboard and boot rental $25–$35* ⊗*Nov.–Apr.*

Togwotee Mountain Lodge. You can rent a snowmobile here and then ride it on an extensive trail network along the Continental Divide. ⊠*U.S. 26/287, Box 91, Moran* ☎*307/543–2847 or 800/543–2847* ⊕*www.togwotee lodge.com* ⊠*Snowmobile rentals $139–$205 per day* ⊗*Nov.–Apr.*

EDUCATIONAL PROGRAMS

CLASSES & SEMINARS

Teton Science School. Adults can join one of the school's single- or multiday wildlife expeditions in Grand Teton, Yellowstone, and surrounding forests to see and learn about wolves, bears, mountain sheep, and other animals. Junior high and high school students can take multiweek field ecology courses while living at the school, backpacking, and camping out. Weekdays, kids in grades 1–6 can join Young Naturalists programs that don't involve sleepovers. 🖂*Box 68, Kelly 83011* ☎*1888/945–3567* ⊕*www.teton science.org* ⊠*Adult programs $150–$1,695; youth programs $95–$2,950* ⊗*Year-round.*

RANGER PROGRAMS

Campfire Programs. Park rangers lead free nightly slide shows from June through September at the Colter Bay, Flagg Ranch Resort, Gros Ventre, and Signal Mountain amphitheaters. For schedules of topics check the park newspaper, *Teewinot,* or at visitor centers. ✉*Colter Bay: 2 mi off U.S. 89/191/287, 5 mi north of Jackson Lake Junction* ✉*Flagg Ranch Resort: John D. Rockefeller Jr. Memorial Pkwy., 4 mi north of the national park boundary* ✉*Gros Ventre: 4 mi off U.S. 26/89/191 and 1.5 mi west of Kelly on Gros Ventre River Rd., 7 mi south of Moose Junction* ✉*Signal Mountain: Teton Park Rd., 4 mi south of Jackson Lake Junction* ☎*307/739–3399 or 307/739–3594* ⊙*June and July, nightly at 9:30; Aug. and Sept., nightly at 9.*

Flagg Ranch Resort Campfire Program. Park rangers give talks about park history, wildlife, and geology at this campground north of the park. ✉*John D. Rockefeller Jr. Memorial Pkwy., 4 mi north of Grand Teton National Park boundary* ☎*307/543–2861* ✉*Free* ⊙*June and July, nightly at 8; Aug. and Sept., nightly at 7:30.*

Jackson Lake Lodge Ranger Talks. Visit the Wapiti Room to hear a slide-illustrated ranger presentation on topics such as area plants and animals, geology, and natural history. Also, you can chat with the ranger on the back deck of the lodge 6:30–8 PM daily, early June through early September. ✉*U.S. 89/191/287, 0.5 mi north of Jackson Lake Junction* ☎*307/739–3300* ⊙*Late June–mid-Aug., nightly at 8:30.*

☾ **Ranger Walks.** Rangers lead free walks throughout the park in summer, from a one-hour lakeside stroll at Colter Bay to a three-hour hike from Jenny Lake. The talks focus on a variety of subjects from wildlife to birds and flower species to geology. Call for itineraries, times, and reservations. ☎*307/739–3300, 307/739–3400 TTY* ⊙*Early June–early Sept.*

☾ **Young Naturalist Program.** Children ages 8–12 learn about the natural world of the park as they take an easy 2-mi hike with a ranger. Kids should wear old clothes and bring water, rain gear, and insect repellent. The hike, which takes place at Jenny Lake or Colter Bay, is 1.5 hours long and is limited to 12 children. ✉*Jenny Lake: meet at the flagpole at the visitor center; Colter Bay: meet at the visitor center* ☎*307/739–3399 or 307/739–3594* ⊙*Mid-June–mid-Aug., daily 1:30.*

GUIDED TOURS

Grand Teton Lodge Company Bus Tours. Half-day tours depart from Colter Bay Village or Jackson Lake Lodge and include visits to scenic viewpoints, visitor centers, and other park sites. Interpretive guides provide information about the park geology, history, wildlife, and ecosystems. Buy tickets in advance at Colter Bay Marina or Jackson Lake Lodge activities desks. Tours include Grand Teton, Yellowstone or a combination of the two parks. ⊠*Colter Bay Village or Jackson Lake Lodge* ☎*307/543–2811 or 800/628–9988* ⊠*$40–$80* ☉*Mid-May–early Oct., daily.*

Gray Line Bus Tours. Full-day bus tours provide an overview of Grand Teton National Park. They depart from Jackson and you will learn about the park's geology, history, birds, plants, and wildlife. ⊠*16 W. Martin La., Jackson* ☎*307/733–4325 or 800/443–6133* ⊠*$80 plus $12 park entrance fee* ☉*Memorial Day–Sept.*

Jackson Lake Cruises. Grand Teton Lodge Company runs 1.5-hour Jackson Lake scenic cruises from Colter Bay Marina throughout the day as well as breakfast cruises, and sunset steak-fry cruises. One cruise, known as Fire and Ice, shows how forest fires and glaciers have shaped the Grand Teton landscape. ⊠*2 mi off U.S. 89/191/287, 5 mi north of Jackson Lake Junction* ☎*307/543–3100, 307/543–2811, or 800/628–9988* ⊕*www.gtlc.com* ⊠*Scenic cruise $21; breakfast cruise $33; steak-fry cruise $55* ☉*Late May–mid-Sept.*

Teton Wagon Train and Horse Adventures. Multiday covered wagon rides and horseback trips follow Grassy Lake Road on the "back side" of the Tetons. You can combine the trip with a river trip and a tour of Yellowstone and Grand Teton. ✍*Box 10307, Jackson 83001* ☎*307/734–6101 or 888/734–6101* ⊕*www.tetonwagontrain.com* ⊠*Wagon trip $895; combination trip $1,859* ☉*June–Aug.*

ARTS & ENTERTAINMENT

At Teton Village during the summer you can enjoy performances at the **Grand Teton Music Festival.** *See Festivals & Events on planner.*

Dec. Skiers celebrate Christmas and New Year's Eve with **torchlight parades** at Snow King Mountain in Jackson and at Jackson Hole Mountain Resort. ☎*307/739–2770 or 307/733–5200.*

Throughout the year. **Grand Teton Music Festival** presents monthly concerts featuring solo performers as well as duos and groups at Walk Festival Hall in Teton Village. ☎*307/733–1128 ⊕www.gtmf.org.*

Apr. The **Pole-Pedal-Paddle** is a ski-cycle-canoe relay race starting at Jackson Hole Ski Resort and finishing down the Snake River. ☎*307/733–6433.*

May Jackson's **Old West Days** include a rodeo, Native American dancers, a Western swing-dance contest, and cowboy poetry readings. ☎*307/733–3316.*

May–Aug. Each spring and summer the **Teton County Historical Society** sponsors monthly field trips to regional sites such as pioneer ranches. ☎*307/733–9605.*

May–Sept. Between Memorial Day and Labor Day, gunslingers stage **The Shootout** daily except Sunday in Jackson's Town Square. Don't worry, the bullets aren't real. ☎*307/733–3316.*

July–Aug. During the **Grand Teton Music Festival** a schedule of symphony orchestra performances is presented at Walk Festival Hall in Teton Village and outdoors near Jackson Hole Resort. There's also a winter concert schedule. ☎*307/733–1128.*

July–Aug. Each year, artists in various media show and sell their work in Jackson at the **Jackson Hole Fall Arts Festival.** Special events include poetry readings and dance performances. Jackson's many art galleries have special exhibits and programs. ☎*307/733–3316.*

Each summer, locals and tourists gather day and night in Jackson for the **Teton County Fair** for a full week of rodeo, rides, food, and the usually thrilling and sometimes rowdy demo derby, where cars and streakers clash with over 3,000 hooting spectators. In 2008, festivities commence July 19–27 at the Rodeo Grounds on Snow King Ave. ☎*307/733–5289 ⊕www.tetoncountyfair.com.*

SHOPPING

Inside the park you can buy a wide range of basic items, from food to souvenirs at the stores in Signal Mountain Lodge and Jackson Lake Lodge.

For real grocery shopping, Signal Mountain Lodge and Dornan's in Moose have general stores that also sell ice, but the best prices and selection for groceries, liquor, and other necessities are to be found in Jackson, where other shopping options also are greater. The Jackson Town Square is surrounded by storefronts that house a mixture of galleries and specialty shops with moderate to expensive prices.

Albertson's (✉105 *Buffalo Way* ☎307/ 732–0194) is a large grocery store with the works. **Kmart** (✉510 S. U.S. 89 ☎307/739–0865) is a good store for general purchases, but the grocery offerings are limited, and you won't find fresh produce or meat. **Smith's Grocers** (✉U.S. 89 ☎307/733–8908) is a real grocer that has a wide range of organic foods as well as wine and beer. **Jackson Whole Grocer** (✉974 W. *Broadway* ☎307/733–0450) is a full-service grocer that also sells wine and beer, as well as organic and health food products.

Valley Books (✉125 N. *Cache* ☎307/733–4533) in the Gaslight Shopping Center offers the Valley's widest selection of books.

Lodging & Dining in the Parks

WORD OF MOUTH

"We . . . stayed 2 nights each at Old Faithful, Mammoth [Hot Springs], and Canyon and it was perfect. You will also have opportunities for wildlife viewing at dawn and dusk that are much easier when staying in the park. Yes, the gateway towns are just outside the park entrances, but it still takes awhile to reach the gates—lots of driving."

—Sharondi

By Gil
Brady
and Steve
Pastorino

FOR MORE THAN A CENTURY, visitors to Yellowstone and Grand Teton national parks have had three fairly straightforward choices for lodging within park boundaries—sleep in a tent, wilderness cabin, or hotel room. Xanterra Resorts has a monopoly for lodging in Yellowstone, so you are at their mercy for a hotel room in the park. In smaller Grand Teton National Park, there are, ironically, a greater breadth in lodging choices. Grand Teton Lodge Company operates only three of Grand Teton's hotels, including the Jenny Lake Lodge, the system's most expensive full-service hotel; three other lodging properties are privately owned. The summer season is very short for both parks, the number of rooms limited, and the demand off-the-charts. If you plan ahead (as much as a year in some cases), have realistic expectations, and remember that the attractions at Yellowstone and Grand Teton are outside (not in your room), you will not be disappointed.

Xanterra lodgings tend to be basic, but serviceable. Lake Yellowstone Hotel and Old Faithful Inn are two of the most unique properties in the National Park Service system and worth every penny, and a little inconvenience (the best rooms at Old Faithful Inn don't have private bathrooms!). Grand Teton in-park lodging is similar, though generally more expensive, than equivalent options in Yellowstone, and the Jenny Lake Lodge, offering a more refined and formal atmosphere, is the most expensive of all. A note about service: One of the biggest challenges is finding and housing service staff for national park properties, especially once U.S. universities are back in session in September. Of late, many of the concessionaires have been importing staff from Europe for the busy summer season, so as at many ski resorts, you will find the park has many international employees. The service may be a little erratic at times, but all park properties seem to do an above-average job.

6

WHERE TO EAT IN YELLOWSTONE

Xanterra has competition from Yellowstone General Stores when it comes to dining, but you'll be hard-pressed to ascertain the difference. For the record, Xanterra operates restaurants and cafés inside its hotels (ranging from fast-food style grills to the elegant Lake Hotel). Xanterra restaurants offer "fine dining" at Old Faithful Inn, Lake Hotel, or Mammoth Hotel in the evening, and full-service restaurants at Grant Village and Canyon. ■TIP→**Reserva-**

tions at all the sit-down, full-service restaurants are a must for
dinner during the height of the summer season.

The stand-alone grills, ice cream parlors, and cafeterias at
most villages are operated by Yellowstone General Stores.
You can get a serviceable sandwich or minimalist hot food
(soups, grilled sandwiches, burgers) for lunch or dinner. If
you're planning to picnic or cook at your campsite, Yellowstone General Stores has staples including some vegetables, meats, breads, dairy products, beverages (including
alcohol), and packaged dinners—but the selection is narrow, and you'll pay more than you would outside the park.
West Yellowstone and Jackson have grocery stores with
wider selections and better prices.

When traveling in Yellowstone it's always a good idea to
bring along a cooler—that way you can carry some snacks
and lunch items for a picnic or break and not have to worry
about making it to one of the more developed areas of the
park, where there are restaurants and cafeterias. Generally you'll find burgers and sandwiches at cafeterias and
full meals at restaurants. You will not find any chain restaurants or fast-food establishments in the park, but you
will find a good selection of entrées such as free-range beef
and chicken; game meats such as elk, venison, and trout;
plus organic vegetables. At the several delis and general
stores in the park you can purchase picnic items, snacks,
and sandwiches.

WHAT IT COSTS

RESTAURANTS

¢	$	$$	$$$	$$$$
under $8	$8–$12	$12–$20	$21–$30	over $30

Restaurant prices are per person for a main course at dinner and do not
include tax.

★ Fodor'sChoice ✕**Lake Yellowstone Hotel Dining Room.** Opened in
$$$–$$$$ 1893 and renovated by Robert Reamer beginning in 1903,
this double-colonnaded dining room off the hotel lobby is
the most elegant dining experience in the park. This dining
room is an upgrade from Old Faithful Inn in every way—
service, china, view, menu sophistication, and even the
quality of the crisp salads. Arrive early and enjoy a bever-
age in the airy sunroom. The menu includes elk medallions,
buffalo prime rib, and fettuccine with wild smoked salmon.

The wine list focuses on wines from California, Oregon, and Washington—with prices as high as $120 for a bottle of Mondavi Reserve Cabernet. ⊠*Lake Village Rd., Lake Village* ☎*307/344–7311* ⌾*Reservations essential* ⊟*AE, D, DC, MC, V* ⊘*Closed early Oct.–mid-May.*

$$-$$$$ ✕**Obsidian Dining Room.** From the wood-and-leather chairs
★ etched with figures of park animals to the intricate lighting fixtures that resemble snowcapped trees, there's lots of atmosphere at Old Faithful Snow Lodge. The huge windows give you a view of the Old Faithful area, and you can sometimes see the famous geyser as it erupts. Aside from Mammoth Hot Springs Dining Room, this is the only place in the park where you can enjoy a full lunch or dinner in winter. The French onion soup will warm you up on a chilly afternoon; among the main courses, look for elk, beef, or salmon. ⊠*Old Faithful Village, far end of Old Faithful Bypass Rd., Old Faithful* ☎*307/344–7311* ⊟*AE, D, DC, MC, V* ⊘*Closed mid-Oct.–mid-Dec. and mid-Mar.–mid-May.*

$$-$$$ ✕**Old Faithful Inn Dining Room.** Just behind the lobby, the original dining room designed by Robert Reamer in 1903—and expanded by him in 1927—has lodgepole-pine walls and ceiling beams and a giant volcanic rock fireplace graced with a contemporary painting of Old Faithful by the late Paco Young. Note the etched glass panels featuring partying cartoon animals that separates the dining room from the Bear Pit Lounge. These are reproductions of oak panels commissioned by Reamer in 1933 to celebrate the end of Prohibition. A buffet offers quantity over quality: bison, chicken, shrimp, two salads, two soups, and a dessert. You're better off choosing from nearly a dozen entrees on the à la carte menu, including grilled salmon, baked chicken, prime rib, and bison rib eye. Expect at least one vegetarian entree (pasta and/or tofu) in addition to a choice of salads and soups (roasted red pepper and Gouda, for example). Save room for a signature dessert such as The Caldera, a chocolate truffle torte with a molten middle. The most extensive wine list in the park offers more than 50 (all American) choices, including sparkling and nonalcoholic varieties (from $20 to $70 per bottle). ⊠*Old Faithful Village, Old Faithful* ☎*307/344–7311* ⌾*Reservations essential* ⊟*AE, D, DC, MC, V* ⊘*Closed late Oct.–early May.*

$$-$$$ ✕**Roosevelt Lodge Dining Room.** At this rustic log cabin in
☾ a pine forest, the menu ranges from barbecued ribs and

6

Roosevelt beans to hamburgers and french fries. For a real Western adventure, call ahead to join the popular chuck-wagon cookout that includes an hour-long trail ride or a stagecoach ride. ✉*Tower-Roosevelt* ☎*307/344–7311* ⚓*Reservations essential for cookout* ▤*AE, D, DC, MC, V* ⊘*Closed early Sept.–early June.*

$–$$$ ✕**Grant Village Dining Room.** The floor-to-ceiling windows of this lakeshore restaurant provide views of Yellowstone Lake through the thick stand of pines. The most contemporary of the park's restaurants, it makes you feel at home with pine-beam ceilings and cedar-shake walls. You'll find dishes ranging from pork and duck to prime rib; in late season you'll find a sandwich buffet on Sundays. ✉*Grant Village* ☎*307/344–7311* ⚓*Reservations essential* ▤*AE, D, DC, MC, V* ⊘*Closed late Sept.–late May.*

$–$$$ ✕**Mammoth Hot Springs Dining Room.** A wall of windows overlooks an expanse of green that was once a military parade and drill field at Mammoth Hot Springs. The Art Deco–style restaurant, decorated in shades of gray, green, and burgundy, has an airy feel with its bentwood chairs. Beef, pork, and chicken are on the menu as well as a selection of pasta and vegetarian dishes. ✉*Mammoth Hot Springs* ☎*307/344–7311* ⚓*Reservations essential* ▤*AE, D, DC, MC, V* ⊘*Closed mid-Oct.–mid-Dec. and mid-Mar.–mid-May.*

$$ ✕**Canyon Lodge Dining Room.** An ambitious but well-priced dinner menu features main courses such as pine nut–crusted trout and chili-rubbed chicken with Manchego and green chili salsa. You can also choose from assorted appetizers, burgers, soups, and salads—plus three dozen American wines (California, Oregon, and Washington). The building, which was built as part of the "Mission 66" upgrade of park facilities in the 1950s, lacks any appreciable character other than some attractive photos of park flora, fauna, and landscapes. For breakfast, there's both a full menu and a buffet. ✉ ☎*307/344–7311* ▤*AE, D, DC, MC, V* ⊘*Closed mid-Sept.–early June.*

¢–$$ ✕**Canyon Lodge Cafeteria.** This busy lunch spot serves such traditional and simple American fare as country-fried steak and hot turkey sandwiches. It stays open for light dinners as well, and for early risers, it also has a full breakfast menu. ✉*Canyon Village* ☎*307/344–7311* ▤*AE, D, DC, MC, V* ⊘*Closed mid-Sept.–early June.*

¢–$$ ✕**Lake Lodge Cafeteria.** This casual eatery, popular with fam-
ⓒ ilies, serves hearty lunches and dinners such as spaghetti,
pot roast, and fried chicken. It also has a full breakfast
menu. ✉*Lake Village Rd., Lake Village* ☎*307/344–7311*
▤*AE, D, DC, MC, V* ☉*Closed mid-Sept.–early June.*

¢–$$ ✕**Old Faithful Lodge Cafeteria.** Serving kid-friendly fare such
ⓒ as pizza, this noisy, family-oriented eatery also has some of
the best views of Old Faithful. ✉*South end of Old Faithful Bypass Rd.* ☎*307/344–7311* ▤*AE, D, DC, MC, V*
☉*Closed mid-Sept.–mid-May.*

¢–$ ✕**Bear Paw Deli.** You can grab a quick bite and not miss a
geyser eruption at this snack shop located off the lobby
in the Old Faithful Inn. Burgers, chicken sandwiches, and
chili typify your choices for hot meals. ✉*Old Faithful Village, Old Faithful* ☎*307/344–7311* ▤*AE, D, DC, MC, V*
☉*Closed early Oct.–late May.*

¢–$ ✕**Geyser Grill.** When the kids are hungry, stop by this spot
ⓒ in the Old Faithful Snow Lodge for burgers, sandwiches,
and french fries. ✉*Old Faithful Village, Old Faithful*
☎*307/344–7311* ▤*AE, D, DC, MC, V* ☉*Closed early
Oct.–late May.*

¢–$ ✕**Mammoth Terrace Grill.** Although the exterior looks rather
elegant, this restaurant in Mammoth Hot Springs serves
only fast food, ranging from biscuits and gravy for breakfast to hamburgers and veggie burgers for lunch and dinner. ✉*Mammoth Hot Springs* ☎*307/344–7311* ▤*AE, D,
DC, MC, V* ☉*Closed late Sept.–mid-May.*

PICNIC AREAS IN YELLOWSTONE

There are 49 picnic areas in the park, ranging from secluded
spots with a couple of tables to more popular stops with
a dozen or more tables and more amenities. Only nine
areas—Snake River, Grant Village, Spring Creek, Nez
Perce, Old Faithful East, Bridge Bay, Cascade Lake Trail,
Norris Meadows, and Yellowstone River—have fire grates.
Only gas stoves may be used in the other areas. None have
running water; all but a few have pit toilets.

You can stock up your cooler at any of the general stores
in the park; there is one in each major developed area. It is
also possible to purchase box lunches that include drinks,
snacks, sandwiches, and fruit, or vegetarian or cheese-and-
crackers selections from restaurants within Yellowstone.

When you choose a picnic area, keep an eye out for wild-life; you never know when a herd of bison might decide to march through. In that case, it's best to leave your food and move a safe distance away from the big animals.

✕**Firehole River.** The Firehole River rolls past and you might see elk grazing along its banks. This picnic area has 12 tables and one pit toilet. ✉*Grand Loop Rd., 3 mi (5 km) south of Madison.*

✕**Fishing Bridge.** This picnic area has 11 tables within the busy Fishing Bridge area. It's walking distance to the amphitheater, store, and visitor center. ✉*East Entrance Road, 1 mi (2 km) from Grand Loop Rd., Fishing Bridge.*

✕**Gibbon Meadows.** You are likely to see elk or buffalo along the Gibbon River from one of nine tables at this area, which has a wheelchair-accessible pit toilet. ✉*Grand Loop Rd., 3 mi (5 km) south of Norris.*

✕ **Sedge Bay.** On the northern end of this volcanic beach, look carefully for the large rock slabs pushed out of the lake bottom. Nearby trees offer shade and a table, or hop onto the level rocks for an ideal lakeside picnic. You may see bubbles rising from the clear water around the rocks—these indicate an active underwater thermal feature. Kids can have a field day throwing rocks in the water here, and the only company you may have all day could be crickets, birds, and bison. (✉*East Entrance Rd., 8 mi (13 km) east of Fishing Bridge Junction*)

WHERE TO STAY IN YELLOWSTONE

Park lodgings range from two of the national park system's magnificent old hotels to simple cabins to bland, modern motels. Old Faithful Snow Lodge and Mammoth Hot Springs Hotel are the only accommodations open in winter; rates are the same as in summer.

Ask about the size of beds, bathrooms, thickness of walls, and room location when you book a hotel, especially in the older hotels, where accommodations vary and upgrades are ongoing. Historic hotels may be grand, but the rooms are still very basic. The same applies to newer, motel-like facilities at Canyon and Grant villages. Telephones have been installed in some rooms, but there is no Internet service—and no TVs—anywhere in the park, except for two very expensive suites in Mammoth Hotel. All park lodging is no-smoking.

In general, cabins are rustic—spartan even. All have beds and locking doors (phew!), but in-room baths, showers, and electric or gas heat are not a given. Prices in Yellowstone are generally comparable to costs outside the park, though some of the budget options, such as simple cabins, are often less expensive in the park. In general, accommodations in the park will have fewer amenities. For example, park lodgings have no televisions, most have no telephones, and there is no air-conditioning (though it's not needed at these elevations).

All Yellowstone hotels are operated by **Xanterra Parks & Resorts** (⌂ *Yellowstone National Park, Box 165, Mammoth Hot Springs 82190* ☎ *307/344–7901 general information, 307/344–7311 reservations* ⊕ *www.travelyellowstone. com*), and all accept major credit cards. Make reservations at least two months in advance for July and August for all park lodgings.

6

WHAT IT COSTS				
HOTELS				
¢	$	$$	$$$	$$$$
under $50	$51–$100	$101–$150	$151–$200	over $200

Hotel prices are per night for two people in a standard double room in high season, excluding taxes and service charges.

CANYON VILLAGE

$$$ ⊞ **Cascade Lodge.** Pine wainscoting and brown carpets set the tone in this lodge built in 1992 in the trees above the Grand Canyon of the Yellowstone. The location is at the farthest edge of the Canyon Village, which means it's quite a hike to the nearest dining facilities—and you have to pass through rows upon rows of cabins, parking lots, and roads to get anywhere; the payoff is a much quieter environment because it's away from the major traffic. **Pros:** Canyon location is central to the entire park. **Cons:** far from dining and other service, with children you'll need to drive to restaurants. ⊠ *North Rim Dr. at Grand Loop Rd., Canyon Village* ☎ *307/344–7901* ⊕ *www.travelyellowstone.com* ⇲ *40 rooms* ⅋ *In-Room: no a/c, no TV. In-hotel: bar, no*

How to Get the Room You Want

All Yellowstone campgrounds and lodging fills to capacity well in advance during the season. Plan early, and make your reservations one year ahead of your trip for rooms in premier venues like Lake Yellowstone Hotel and Old Faithful Inn.

Start at Xanterra's Web site. It is not as user-friendly as the best travel Web sites, but with patience and persistence you will find the information you want.

If you can't find all of your preferred dates and properties on-line, call Xanterra's reservations line directly. Yellowstone lodging reservations are handled by a call center in Mammoth Hot Springs, with operators who tend to be quite knowledgeable about the park. Also, check the Web site frequently as cancellations occur—even right up to your trip departure (for that matter, even after you depart if you have access to the Web while in transit). **Xanterra Parks & Resorts** (☎866/439–7375 ⊕www. travelyellowstone.com).

---

elevator, no-smoking rooms. |○|*EP* ⊟*AE, D, DC, MC, V* ☉*Closed mid-Sept.–late May.*

$$$ 🏠**Dunraven Lodge.** This motel-style lodge with pine wainscoting and brown carpets is in the pine trees at the edge of the Grand Canyon of the Yellowstone, adjacent to the essentially identical Cascade Lodge. It's at the farthest edge of the Canyon Village, so it's a distance to the nearest dining facilities. **Pros:** Canyon location is central to the entire park. **Cons:** far from dining and other services, with children you'll need to drive to restaurants. ⊠*North Rim Dr., at Grand Loop Rd., Canyon Village* ☎*307/344–7901* ⊕*www.travelyellowstone.com* ➪*41 rooms* ♨*In-room: no a/c; no TV. In-hotel: bar, no-smoking rooms* |○|*EP* ⊟*AE, D, DC, MC, V* ☉*Closed mid-Sept.–late May.*

$–$$ 🏠**Canyon Cabins.** Unattractive and unassuming, these pine-frame cabins are mostly in clusters of four, six, and eight units. Their popularity is a testament to their location. They have been upgraded recently, so all now have private bathrooms (some with baths, others with showers only), and higher-end cabins also have knotty pine bed frames, hand sinks, and coffeemakers. Even the lowest-priced cabins are worth the price for the location—you're less than 30 minutes away from Lamar Valley, Hayden Valley, and Lake Yellowstone; Old Faithful is less than 45 minutes away—but the cabins are on several loops and cul-de-sacs that it's possible to forget you're in a national park. **Pros:** affordability, location. **Cons:** too much asphalt, too many neighbors. ⊠*North Rim Dr. at Grand Loop Rd., Canyon Village* ☎*307/344–7901* ⊕*www.travelyellowstone.com* ⊅*428 cabins* &*In-room: no a/c, no phone, no TV. In-hotel: 3 restaurants, bar, no-smoking rooms.* ⦿*EP* ⊟*AE, D, DC, MC, V* ⊘*Closed mid-Sept.–late May.*

GRANT VILLAGE

$$ ⊞**Grant Village Lodge.** The six humble lodge buildings that make up this facility have rough pine exteriors painted gray and rust. Grant Village is a great location to visit the southern half of the park, but the lodge itself is reminiscent of a big-city motel, the complex offering basic rooms with few features beyond a bed and nightstand. **Pros:** excellent location to explore southern half of park, many nearby facilities. **Cons:** merely the basics, with absolutely no extras. ⊠*Grant Village* ☎*307/344–7901* ⊕*www.travel yellowstone.com* ⊅*300 rooms* &*In-room: no a/c, no TV. In-hotel: 2 restaurants, bar, no-smoking rooms* ⊟*AE, D, DC, MC, V* ⊘*Closed mid-Sept.–late May* ⦿*EP.*

MAMMOTH HOT SPRINGS

$–$$ ⊞**Mammoth Hot Springs Hotel and Cabins.** Built in 1937, this hotel has a spacious Art Deco lobby, where you'll find an espresso cart after 4 PM. The rooms are smaller and less elegant than those at the park's other two historic hotels, but the Mammoth Hot Springs Hotel is less expensive and usually less crowded. In summer, the rooms can get hot, but you can open the windows, and there are fans. More than half the rooms do not have their own bathrooms; shared baths are down the hall. The cabins, set amid lush lawns, are the nicest inside the park, but most do not have private bathrooms; only two very expensive suites have TVs. This is one of only two lodging facilities open in winter. Some cabins have hot tubs, a nice amenity after a day of cross-country skiing or snowshoeing. **Pros:** great rates for a historic property, beautiful setting near picturesque Fort Yellowstone, no better place to watch elk in the fall. **Cons:** those elk grazing on the lawn can create traffic jams, many hotel rooms and cabins without private bathrooms, rooms can get hot during the day. ⊠*Mammoth Hot Springs* ☎*307/344–7901* ⊕*www.travelyellowstone.*

com ➾*97 rooms, 67 with bath; 2 suites; 115 cabins, 76 with bath* ⌂*In-room: no a/c, no phones (some), no TV. In-hotel: restaurant, bar, no-smoking rooms.* ⦿*EP* ▭*AE, D, DC, MC, V* ⊘*Closed early Oct.–late-Dec. and mid-Mar.–early May.*

OLD FAITHFUL AREA

$$$ Old Faithful Snow Lodge. Built in 1998, this massive structure brings back the grand tradition of park lodges by making good use of heavy timber beams and wrought-iron accents in a distinctive facade. Inside you'll find soaring ceilings, natural lighting, and a spacious lobby with a stone fireplace. Nearby is a long sitting room, where writing desks and overstuffed chairs invite you to linger. Guest rooms combine traditional style with modern amenities. This is one of only two lodging facilities in the park that are open in winter, when the only way to get here is on over-snow vehicles. **Pros:** the most modern hotel in the park, lobby and adjacent hallway are great for relaxing, the only property on the interior of the park open in winter. **Cons:** pricey, but you're paying for location. ✉*Far end of Old Faithful Bypass Rd., Old Faithful* ☎*307/344–7901* ⊕*www.travel yellowstone.com* ➾*100 rooms* ⌂*In-room: no a/c, no TV. In-hotel: restaurant, bicycles, no-smoking rooms* ⦿*EP* ▭*AE, D, DC, MC, V* ⊘*Closed mid-Oct.–mid-Dec. and mid-Mar.–early May.*

★ **Fodor's**Choice ⚅**Old Faithful Inn.** It's no accident that this Rob-
$$–$$$ ert Reamer signature building has been declared a National
☿ Historic Landmark—and has been a favorite of five generations of park visitors. The so-called Old House was originally built in 1904 and is worth a visit regardless of whether you are staying the night. The lobby has a 76-foot-high, eight-sided fireplace; bright red iron-clad doors, and two balconies (both open to the public) as well as a fantasy-like "treehouse" of platforms, ladders, and dormer windows high above the foyer. Believe it or not, you can stay in 1904-era rooms with thick wood timber walls and ceilings for under $100 if you are willing to forsake a private bathroom. Rooms with bathrooms in either the Old House or the "modern" wings (built in 1913 and 1927) can rent for as high as $200+, especially if they have geyser views. Renovations in the hotel will continue throughout 2008 but shouldn't compromise one of America's most distinctive buildings. **Pros:** a truly historic property, Old House

rooms are truly atmospheric with lodgepole pine walls and ceilings. **Cons:** waves of tourists in the lobby, some rooms lack private bathrooms. ⊠*Old Faithful Village, Old Faithful* ☎*307/344–7901* ⊕*www.travelyellowstone. com* ⚲*324 rooms (246 with bath), 6 suites* ♿*In-room: no a/c, no phone (some), no TV. In-hotel: Restaurant, bar, no-smoking rooms* ⊙*EP* ⊟*AE, D, DC, MC, V* ⊘*Closed late Oct.–early May.*

$–$$ ⊞**Old Faithful Snow Lodge Cabins.** A few cabins, designated "frontier" by Xanterra, predate and survived the fire of 1988; the others burned down. These frontier cabins are older, and not as nice as their replacements; thus, these are the cheaper options. Western cabins built the year after the fire are spacious and have full bathrooms. Either is an affordable option—and cozy for families—in the summer only. **Pros:** location and price; easy access to Snow Lodge's grand lobby and sitting room, in addition to its restaurants, gift shop, and bike rentals. **Cons:** it's easy to confuse these cabins with ones several hundred yards away by Old Faithful Lodge. ⊠*Far end of Old Faithful Bypass Rd.* ☎*307/344–7901* ⊕*www.travelyellowstone.com* ⚲*34 cabins (24 with bath)* ♿*In-room: no a/c, no phone, no TV. In-hotel: restaurant, bar, bicycles, no-smoking rooms* ⊙*EP* ⊟*AE, D, DC, MC, V* ⊘*Closed mid-Oct.–mid-Dec. and mid-Mar.–early May.*

$ ⊞**Old Faithful Lodge Cabins.** There are no rooms inside the Old Faithful Lodge, though there are 97 cabins sitting at the northeast end of the village. Typical of cabins throughout the park, these are very basic—lacking most amenities (including bathrooms about one third of the cabins), views, or character. However, the location can't be beat—cabins are almost as close to the geyser as Old Faithful Inn. If you plan to spend a day or three exploring the geyser basins or the central area of the park, this is a great budget-conscious option to lay down your head since you'll be out and about most of the time anyway. **Pros:** a stone's throw from Old Faithful Geyser, all area services are within walking distance. **Cons:** some cabins lack private bathrooms, they're pretty basic. ⊠*South end of Old Faithful Bypass Rd.* ☎*307/344–7901* ⊕*www.travelyellowstone.com* ⚲*96 cabins (60 with bath)* ♿*In-room: no a/c, no phone, no TV. In-hotel: restaurant, no-smoking rooms* ⊙*EP* ⊟*AE, D, DC, MC, V* ⊘*Closed mid-Sept.–mid-May.*

6

TOWER-ROOSEVELT

$ 🏠**Roosevelt Lodge Cabins.** Near the beautiful Lamar Valley in the park's northeast corner, this simple lodge dating from the 1920s surpasses some of the more expensive options. All lodging is in rustic cabins set around a pine forest. Some cabins have bathrooms, but most do not, though there is a bathhouse nearby. Roughrider cabins may have woodstoves as the only heating system. You can make arrangements here for horseback and stagecoach rides. **Pros:** closest cabins to Lamar Valley and its world-famous wildlife, authentic western ranch feel, Roughrider cabins are the most inexpensive in the park. **Cons:** cabins are very close together and many lack private bathrooms, you may have to draw straws to stoke the fire at 3 AM if your Roughrider cabin has only a woodstove. ✉*Tower-Roosevelt Junction on Grand Loop Rd., Tower-Roosevelt* ☎*307/344–7901* ⊕*www.travelyellowstone.com* ⇄*80 cabins, 14 with bath* &*In room: no a/c, no TV. In hotel: restaurant, no-smoking rooms* ⏀*EP* ⊟*AE, D, DC, MC, V* ⊘*Closed early Sept.–early June.*

YELLOWSTONE LAKE AREA

$$-$$$$ 🏠**Lake Yellowstone Hotel.** More Kennebunkport than Western, this distinguished hotel is the park's oldest. Dating from ★   1891, the white-and-pastel colored hotel has maintained an air of refinement that Old Faithful Inn can't—due to its constant tour buses full of visitors. Just off the lobby, a spacious sunroom offers priceless views of Lake Yellowstone at sunrise or sunset. It's also a great place to play cards, catch up on a newspaper from the gift shop or just soak in the grandeur of a 117-year-old National Historic Landmark. Note the tile-mantel fireplace, the etched windows of the gift shop, and the beautiful bay windows. Rooms have white wicker furnishings, giving them a light, airy feeling; some have lake views. There is one two-room suite with lake views that has been used as accommodations for more than one U.S. president. The least expensive rooms are in an annex, not the original building. **Pros:** an oasis of elegance in the park, with the best views of any park lodging. **Cons:** the most expensive property in the park (even Old Faithful Inn has some shared-bath rooms under $100), restaurant expensive and not particularly kid-friendly. ✉*Lake Village Rd., Lake Village* ☎*307/344–7901* ⊕*www.travelyellowstone.com* ⇄*194 rooms* &*In-room: no a/c, no TV.*

In-hotel: restaurant, bar, no-smoking rooms ⊚EP ⊟AE, *D, DC, MC, V* ⊘*Closed early Oct.–mid-May.*

$$ ▣**Lake Yellowstone Hotel Cabins.** Located behind the Yellowstone Lake Hotel, these cabins were renovated and brightened up with yellow paint in 2003–04. The simple duplexes provide basic, no-frills accommodations, but unlike some cabins in the park, all of these have private bathrooms. **Pros:** active area for bison and other wildlife. **Cons:** the cabins feel like they were plunked adjacent to the unattractive rear parking lot without much thought; nearby Lake Lodge cabins are a better deal in a nicer setting. ✉*Lake Village Rd., Lake Village* ☎*307/344–7901* ⊕*www.travelyellowstone.com* ⌕*110 cabins* ⌂*In-room: no a/c, no TV. In-hotel: restaurant, no-smoking rooms* ⊟*AE, D, DC, MC, V* ⊘*Closed mid-Oct.–mid-May.*

$–$$ ▣**Lake Lodge Cabins.** Just beyond the Lake Yellowstone ♺ Hotel lies one of the park's hidden treasures: Lake Lodge, built in 1920. The 140-foot lobby and porch offer one of the best sunrise views in the park. The lodge itself no longer offers rooms. Rather, check in at the lobby (make a note to return to enjoy the two fireplaces, a visiting speaker, or a meal), and then head for your cabin, which is just north of the lodge. The accommodations are basic Yellowstone no-frills style—clean, with one to three beds, and a sink (some also have a shower/tub). There are views of the lake from the lodge but not from the cabins. **Pros:** the best front porch at a Yellowstone lodge and a great lobby, affordability, good for families. **Cons:** absolutely no frills of any kind. ✉*Lake Village Rd., Lake Village* ☎*307/344–7901* ⊕*www.travelyellowstone.com* ⌕*186 rooms (100 with bath)* ⌂*In-room: no a/c, no phone, no TV. In-hotel: restaurant, bar, no-smoking rooms* ⊚EP ⊟*AE, D, DC, MC, V* ⊘*Closed mid-Sept.–mid-June.*

WHERE TO CAMP IN YELLOWSTONE

There are a variety of campgrounds both inside Yellowstone National Park and in the surrounding national forests and gateway communities. Yellowstone has a dozen campgrounds scattered around the park.

ABOUT CONCESSIONAIRE-MANAGED SITES

Some 80% of the developed campsites in the park are operated by **Xanterra Parks & Resorts** (☎*307/344–7311 for reservations* ⊕*www.travelyellowstone.com*). Xanterra operates five large campgrounds—Canyon, Fishing Bridge RV Park, Grant Village, Bridge Bay, and Madison. You can reserve Xanterra sites in advance, although you'll pay about a $5 premium over the National Park Service campsites. These campgrounds are in great settings, but they are large—more than 250 sites each—and can feel very crowded. Tents and RVs coexist, although Xanterra designates certain areas as "tent only." Larger groups can reserve space in Bridge Bay, Grant, and Madison from late May through September.

ABOUT NATIONAL PARK SERVICE SITES

The National Park Service operates seven small campgrounds: Norris, Lewis Lake, Mammoth, Indian Creek, Tower Fall, Slough Creek, and Pebble Creek. These are first-come, first-served—with smaller, choice sites like Slough Creek filling up by 10 AM each day in the summer. To get a site in an NPS campground, arrive in the morning, pick out your site, pay (cash only, no change available) at a drop box near the campground host (look for a sign near the entrance to the campground), and leave your receipt and an inexpensive item (empty cooler, water jug, etc.) at the campsite. NPS limits campers to 14 days maximum at any one location in the summer.

ABOUT BACKCOUNTRY SITES

If you're prepared to carry your own water and other necessities, you could also consider a backcountry campsite. Located as little as 2 mi from parking lots and trailheads, there are more than 300 backcountry sites in the park. Check availability and obtain the required (though free) permit at any ranger station, visitor center, or backcountry office; you may also pay $20 to reserve one of these sites in advance (the reservations open on April 1 each year). Talk to the park's Accessibility Coordinator about ADA-accessible backcountry sites. All backcountry campsites have restrictions on group size and length of stay. Boating is prohibited throughout the backcountry, and pit fires are prohibited at certain campsites. *For more information about backcountry exploration, see* ⇨*Exploring the Backcountry, in Chapter 3.*

WHAT IT COSTS				
CAMPING				
¢	$	$$	$$$	$$$$
under $8	$9–$14	$15–$20	$21–$25	over $25

Camping prices are for a campsite including a tent area, fire pit, bear-proof food storage box, picnic table; potable water and pit toilets or restrooms will be nearby.

CAMPGROUNDS IN YELLOWSTONE

$$$$ ⚠**Fishing Bridge RV Park.** Xanterra emphasizes "Park" not "Campground" in this area. There are no picnic tables or fire pits at individual RV sites here. However, full hookups are available for RVers to empty septic tanks, refill their potable water tank, and plug-in to electricity, but plan on parking your RV and spending the majority of your time away from the park. Boat access is via nearby Bridge Bay Marina. This is the only facility in the park that caters exclusively to recreational vehicles. Because of bear activity in the area, only hard-sided campers are allowed. Liquid propane, as well as basic RV supplies, are available upon check-in. Generators are allowed from 8 AM to 8 PM. ♿*Flush toilets, full hookups, dump station, drinking water, guest laundry, showers, bear boxes, public telephone, ranger station ⇌344 sites ✉East Entrance Rd. at Grand Loop Rd., Fishing Bridge ☎307/344–7311 ⊕www.travelyellowstone. com ⊟AE, D, DC, MC, V ⊙Mid-May–late Sept.*

$$ ⚠**Bridge Bay.** The park's largest campground, Bridge Bay rests in a wooded grove above Lake Yellowstone and adjacent to the park's major marina. Ask for one of the few sites with a lake view. Xanterra tries to keep tent and RV campers separate—make sure you ask if you have a preference. If you end up on one of the inner loops, you may find yourself surrounded. You can rent boats at the nearby marina, take guided walks, or listen to rangers lecture about the history of the park. Don't expect solitude, as there are more than 400 campsites. Generators are allowed from 8 AM to 8 PM. Hot showers and laundry are 4 mi (6 km) north at Fishing Bridge. ♿*Flush toilets, dump station, drinking water, showers, bear boxes, fire pits, picnic tables, public telephone, ranger station ⇌432 sites ✉3 mi (5 km) southwest of Lake Village on Grand Loop Rd., Bridge Bay*

6

CAMPING IN YELLOWSTONE

CAMPGROUND NAME	Total # of Sites	# of RV sites	# of hook-ups	Drive-to sites	Hike-to sites	Flush toilets	Pit toilets	Drinking water	Showers	Fire grates/pits	Swimming	Boat access	Playground	Dump station	Ranger station	Public telephone	Reservations Possible	Daily fee per site	Dates open
Bridge Bay	432	432		Y		Y		Y		Y		Y		Y	Y	Y	Y**		May-Sept.
Canyon	272	272		Y		Y		Y	Y	Y					Y	Y	Y		Jun-Sept.
Fishing Bridge RV Park	344	344	344	Y		Y		Y	Y					Y	Y	Y	Y		May-Sept.
Grant Village	425	425		Y		Y		Y	Y	Y		Y		Y	Y	Y	Y		Jun-Sept.
Indian Creek	75	75		Y			Y	Y		Y									Jun-Sept.
Lewis Lake	85	85		Y			Y	Y		Y		Y			Y				Jun-Oct.
Madison	280	280		Y		Y		Y		Y				Y	Y	Y	Y		May-Sept.
Mammoth Hot Springs	85	85		Y		Y		Y							Y	Y			Y/R
Norris	116	116		Y		Y		Y							Y	Y			May-Sept.
Pebble Creek	32	32		Y			Y			Y									Jun-Sept.
Slough Creek	29	29	200	Y			Y			Y									May-Oct.
Tower Fall	32	32	0	Y			Y			Y									May-Sept.

Y/R = year-round / ** = Summer Only

☎307/344–7311 ⊕*www.travelyellowstone.com* ☰*AE, D, DC, MC, V* ⊙*Late May–mid-Sept.*

$$ ▲**Canyon.** A massive campground with 400+ sites, the ⟳ Canyon campground accommodates everyone from hiker/ biker tent campers to large RVs. The campground is accessible to Canyon's many short trails. Nearby Canyon Village offers every service—stores, laundry, ranger station, ice, etc.—which makes this campground a hit with families. The location is near laundry facilities and the visitor center. Generators are allowed from 8 AM to 8 PM. ♿*Flush toilets, drinking water, guest laundry, showers, bear boxes, fire pits, picnic tables, public telephone, ranger station* ⇌*272 sites* ✉*North Rim Dr., ¼ mi east of Grand Loop Rd., Canyon Village* ☎*307/344–7311* ⊕*www.travelyellowstone. com* ☰*AE, D, DC, MC, V* ⊙*Mid-June–early Sept.*

$$ ▲**Grant Village.** Sprawling over dozens of acres, this campground has a mixed bag of tent, RV, and group campsites. Some sites have views of Yellowstone Lake while others back up to lodgepole pine forest. Some sites are wheelchair-accessible. Generators are allowed from 8 AM to 8 PM. ♿*Flush toilets, dump station, drinking water, guest laundry, showers, bear boxes, picnic tables, public telephone, ranger station* ⇌*425 sites* ✉*South Entrance Rd., 2 mi south of West Thumb, Grand Village* ☎*307/344– 7311* ⊕*www.travelyellowstone.com* ☰*AE, D, DC, MC, V* ⊙*Late June–late Sept.*

$$ ▲**Madison.** The largest NPS-operated campground (meaning no advance reservations are accepted), Madison has eight loops and nearly 300 sites. The outermost loop backs up to the Madison River, but other sites feel a bit claustrophobic. You can't beat the location, though; you're minutes from Old Faithful, five different geyser basins, and three picturesque rivers (the Firehole, Madison, and Gibbon). Visit the adjacent ranger station (a National Historic Landmark) and view National Park Mountain. This campground can accommodate trailers up to 45 feet. Generators are allowed from 8 AM to 8 PM. ♿*Flush toilets, dump station, drinking water, bear boxes, fire pits, picnic tables, public telephone, ranger station* ⇌*277 sites* ✉*Grand Loop Rd., Madison* ☎*307/344–7311* ⊕*www.travelyellowstone. com* ☰*AE, D, DC, MC, V* ⊙*Early May–Oct.*

$ ▲**Indian Creek.** In a picturesque setting next to a creek, this campground is in the middle of a prime wildlife-viewing area. There are some combination sites that can accommodate trailers of up to 45 feet. ♿*Pit toilets, bear boxes, fire pits, picnic tables* ⇝*75 sites* ✉*8 mi south of Mammoth Hot Springs on Grand Loop Rd.* ☎*307/344–2017* ⊟*No credit cards* ☉*Early June–mid-Sept.*

$ ⚠**Lewis Lake.** Set among lodgepole pine trees that didn't burn in 1988, this hilly campground above Lewis Lake has comfort and character. Used primarily by visitors from Grand Teton, fishermen, and backcountry hikers, it's fairly quiet. Launch your boat into Lewis Lake, hike several popular trails, and otherwise avoid the crowds of the Grand Loop campgrounds—if you can get a spot here. It's a bit off the beaten track, which means this campground south of Grant Village is quieter than most. This is the only campground besides Bridge Bay and Grant Village that has a boat launch. ♿*Pit toilets, drinking water, bear boxes, fire pits, picnic tables* ⇝*85 sites* ✉*6 mi south of Grant Village on South Entrance Rd.* ☎*307/344–2017* ⊟*No credit cards* ☉*Mid-June–early Nov.*

$ ⚠**Mammoth Hot Springs.** At the base of a sagebrush-covered hillside, this campground can be crowded and noisy in the summer. It's surrounded on three sides by the North Entrance Road, so expect to hear a lot of auto traffic encircling you and climbing the hill to Mammoth Hot Springs. The campground lacks shade, so it's one of the few places in the park that can get pretty hot in the summer. Located just 4 mi (6 km) from the North entrance and adjacent to the busy Mammoth village, it fills up early in busy season. Be extremely aware of bison, mule deer, and, in particular, elk, which are especially active in autumn due to their annual mating patterns. There are wheelchair-accessible sites at this campground. Generators are allowed from 8 AM to 8 PM. ♿*Flush toilets, drinking water, bear boxes, fire pits, picnic tables, public telephone, ranger station* ⇝*85 sites* ✉*North Entrance Rd., Mammoth Hot Springs* ☎*307/344–2017* ⊟*No credit cards* ☉*Open year-round.*

$ ⚠**Norris.** Astride the Gibbon River, this is a quiet, popular campground. A few of its "walk-in" sites are amongst the best in the park (if you don't mind carrying your tent, food, and other belongings a few yards). Anglers love catching brook trout and grayling here. The campground can accommodate trailers up to 45 feet. Generators are allowed from 8 AM to 8 PM. ♿*Flush toilets, drinking water, bear boxes, fire pits, picnic tables, ranger station* ⇝*116 sites*

⊠*Grand Loop Rd., Norris* ☎*307/344–2177* ▬*No credit cards* ⊘*Mid-May–late Sept.*

$ ⛰**Pebble Creek.** For nine of the past 10 years, Darlene and
★ Ray Rathmell have served as campground hosts here. It's no wonder. Beneath multiple 10,000-foot peaks (Thunderer, Barronnette Peak, and Mt. Norris) this easternmost campground in the park is set creek-side in a forested canopy. Pebble Creek is a babbling stream here, but hike a few yards north of the canyon to see the small canyon the river has carved. Great fishing, hikes, and wildlife abound in the vicinity. Along with nearby Slough Creek, this is the best campground in the park. Due to its small size, it fills up by 10 AM on busy days. It's also smaller than most, which means it tends to be a little quieter. Sites can accommodate trailers up to 45 feet. ⛴*Pit toilets, bear boxes, fire pits, picnic tables* ⛺*32 sites* ⊠*Northeast Entrance Rd., 22 mi east of Tower-Roosevelt Junction* ☎*307/344–2017* ▬*No credit cards* ⊘*June–late Sept.*

$ ⛰**Slough Creek.** Down the most rewarding 2 mi of dirt
★ road in the park, Slough Creek is a gem. Nearly every site is adjacent to the creek, which is prized by anglers. The campground sits at the edge of the wildlife-rich Lamar Valley, and one of the famous wolf packs introduced in 1995 has taken residence several miles up the river and bears the name "Slough Creek Pack." Listen carefully for grunting bison, howling wolves, and bugling elk. If you want to stay here in the summer, make this your first stop in the morning—on many days it will fill up by 10 AM. ⛴*Pit toilets, bear boxes, fire pits, picnic tables* ⛺*29 sites* ⊠*Northeast Entrance Rd., 10 mi east of Tower-Roosevelt Junction* ☎*307/344–2017* ▬*No credit cards* ⊘*Late May–Oct.*

$ ⛰**Tower Fall.** Save for its location in the heart of the northernmost Grand Loop, Tower Fall campground has no appeal. There is no tranquil stream or towering peak. The U-shaped layout of the campground makes everyone feel claustrophobic since there are too many sites on too small a footprint. If you've come this far, ask a ranger at nearby Tower Ranger Station if there is room at Slough Creek or Pebble Creek—the extra miles are more than worth it. It's within hiking distance of the roaring waterfall, so this campground gets a lot of foot traffic. It can accommodate shorter trailers. Hot water and flush toilets are available at the Tower Store, which also has restrooms. ⛴*Pit toilets, bear boxes, fire pits, picnic tables* ⛺*32 sites* ⊠*3 mi south-*

6

east of Tower-Roosevelt on Grand Loop Rd. ☎307/344–2017 ▭*No credit cards* ⊙*Mid-May–late Sept.*

WHERE TO EAT IN GRAND TETON

Dining in Grand Teton National Park offers more upscale alternatives than neighboring Yellowstone. Simply put, there's more menu variety, greater price ranges, and more ambience to choose from. Grand Teton National Park's restaurants bridge the gap between Yellowstone's mass-market allure and nearby Jackson's sophisticated epicurean scene quite nicely. No one should presume you can't eat well in Yellowstone. You can, just not as easily as in Grand Teton, which once was—and to some degree still is—the playground of aristocrats. But there's a measurable difference between the quality of restaurants in the two parks.

For the unassuming, going out for a fine meal in Grand Teton National Park can leave you wondering whether you've wandered into a very gracious country club. Excluding the snack bars and Signal Mountain Lodge, which offer similar fare at similar prices to much of what is served in Yellowstone, many of the restaurants in Grand Teton tend to appeal more to discriminating foodies or hip locals from Jackson who like to think they know better. This is particularly true since Grand Teton is closer to Jackson and must compete with that ritzy town's finicky tastes. On all levels there are more choices in Grand Teton since the monolithic presence of Xanterra does not dominate the park's restaurants, as it does in Yellowstone.

And though the park has some excellent restaurants, don't miss dining in Jackson and neighboring Wilson, where restaurants combine game, fowl, and fish with the enticing spices and sauces of European cuisine and the lean ingredients, vegetarian choices, and meat cuts that reflect the desires of health-consciousness diners. Steaks are usually cut from grass-fed Wyoming beef, but you'll also find buffalo and elk on the menu; poultry and pasta are offered by most restaurants, and you'll find fresh salads and fish (trout, tilapia, and salmon are most common). Just about everywhere you can order a burger or a bowl of homemade soup. Casual is the word for most dining both within and outside the park. However, ethnic and gourmet dining in Jackson are becoming more popular. An exception is Jenny Lake Lodge, where jackets and ties are recommended for dinner. Breakfast is big: steak and eggs, pancakes, biscuits and gravy; lunches are lighter, often taken in a sack to enjoy on the trail.

For Dining price category information, see Where to Eat in Yellowstone, above.

$$$$ ✕**Jenny Lake Lodge Dining Room.** Elegant yet rustic, this is
★ one of Grand Teton National Park's finest dining establishment, with jackets suggested for men. The menu is ever-changing and offers fish, pasta, chicken, and beef; the wine list is extensive. Gourmet five-course dinners are prix-fixe; lunch is à la carte. Unless children are particularly well-behaved, families with youngsters should probably find a babysitter or go elsewhere. ⊠*Jenny Lake Rd., 2 mi off Teton Park Rd., 12 mi north of Moose Junction, Jenny Lake* ☎*307/733–4647 or 800/628–9988* ⚐*Reservations essential* ☰*AE, MC, V* ☉*Closed early Oct.–late May. No lunch.*

★ Fodor'sChoice ✕**Jackson Lake Lodge Mural Room.** If you're look-
$$–$$$$ ing for upscale, this fine-dining restaurant might be the ultimate in Wyoming's national parks' culinary experiences. This large room houses a 700-square-foot mural painted by late 20th-century Western artist Carl Roters that details an 1837 Wyoming mountain man rendezvous. Select from a menu that includes trout, elk, lamb, beef, and pasta. The cedar plank salmon is a great choice, or try a buffalo steak. One cannot exaggerate the scene beyond the windows of this establishment. The riparian area below and Willow Flats, where moose love to feast, compete with Jackson Lake and the Teton's Cathedral Group. If you can, book a window table at sunset and drink in the luscious panorama. Other delicious sights include Roters's mural, which covers two walls of the dining room. This elegant restaurant might not work as a first choice for casual or budget-conscious diners. ⊠*U.S. 89, 5 mi north of Moran Junction* ☎*307/543–2811 Ext. 3463 or 800/628–9988* ☰*AE, MC, V* ☉*Closed mid-Oct.–late May.*

$$–$$$$ ✕**The Peaks.** Part of Signal Mountain Lodge, this casual room has exposed ceiling beams and big square windows creating a rustic atmosphere overlooking southern Jackson Lake and the Tetons. The emphasis here is on fish: Rocky Mountain trout is marinated, lightly floured, and grilled, or simply grilled and topped with lemon-parsley butter. But there's also filet mignon and elk stew, not to mention free-range chicken and vegetable lasagna for the health-

conscious or vegetarian diner. Families should call about menu selections in advance. ⊠ *Teton Park Rd., 4 mi south of Jackson Lake Junction, Oxbow Bend* ☎ *307/543–2831* ⊟ *AE, D, MC, V* ⊗ *Closed mid-Oct.–mid-May.*

$$–$$$ ✕ **Dornan's Chuck Wagon.** This legendary chuck wagon oper-
☼ ates only during the summer and has been feeding hun-
★ gry wranglers, cowboys, travelers, and dudes since 1948. It is owned and operated by the same family as Dornan's restaurant and operates on the same grounds. Locals know that here they can catch a hearty meal of beef stew, short ribs, steak, prime rib, trout, chicken, cowboy beans, mashed potatoes, with lemonade or hot coffee, and cobbler for dessert in the spring and summers. At breakfast, count on old-fashioned staples such as sourdough pancakes, eggs, bacon, sausage, or biscuits and gravy. You can eat your chuck wagon meal inside one of Dornan's tepees (which kids are sure to enjoy) if it happens to be raining or windy. Otherwise, sit at outdoor picnic tables with pristine views of the Snake River and the Tetons. In recent years, the food at Dornan's chuck wagon has not been as consistently good as that of the Bar J in Wilson; however, the quick service and inexpensive prices make this a good choice for fami-lies or travelers on a budget. ⊠ *200 Moose Street., at the Moose Entrance to Grand Teton National Park, off Teton Park Rd. at Moose Junction, Moose* ☎ *307/733–2415* ⊟ *AE, MC, V* ⊗ *Oct.–May.*

$$ ✕ **Dornan's Restaurant.** Tasty pizzas and pastas are the main standbys at Dornan's, but you'll also find generous mar-garitas, a surprisingly diverse wine list, and occasional live music. Located in Moose inside Grand Teton National Park, this family-style restaurant operates year-round on a longtime family inholding. Place your order at the front counter, and your food is brought out to you—either at a picnic table facing the Tetons, inside one of the huge teepees (perfect in rainy weather, or for those traveling with kids), or upstairs on the roof with stunning mountain views, the perfect hangout to unwind with a margarita after a strenu-ous day's hike. The extremely popular eatery serves both steak and pasta and has an extensive salad bar. There's also a long inside bar with stellar views and friendly bar-keeps. Check Dornan's schedule for live music and be sure to explore the wine shop next door: one of the most varied and well-stocked in the valley. It's where local resident and movie star Harrison Ford has been seen buying his vino. ⊠ *200 Moose St., 2 mi off U.S. 89/191/287, 5 mi north*

Legendary Signal Mountain

Even if you're just passing through the area, try the winding drive to the top of Signal Mountain for one of the best 360-degree panoramas in the park. Going south on Teton Park Road, Signal Mountain Road cuts east 4.1 mi south of Jackson Lake Junction, 1.1 mi beyond the turnoff for Signal Mountain Lodge (Signal Mountain *Resort* Road); it's a left turn onto the road. It's a steep 4-mi ascent to the top of Signal Mountain, but at the top, you can park and follow the well-marked dirt path for a view of the Jackson Hole valley that's particularly dramatic at sunset. There are also some hiking trails on Signal Mountain worth exploring. In 1877, William H. Jackson first made Signal Mountain famous when he ascended to the summit and took the earliest photograph of Jackson Lake. This idyllic respite is now accessible to nearly anyone.

of Jackson Lake Junction, Moose ☎307/733–2415 ▭*AE, MC, V* ⊗*Closed early Sept.–May.*

¢–$ ✕**Jackson Lake Lodge Pioneer Grill.** With its old-fashioned soda fountain, frontier antiques, friendly service, and seats along a winding counter, this eatery recalls a 1950s-era luncheonette. Serves breakfast, lunch, and dinner. Good spot for hikers starting out to grab a bagel, eggs, or flapjacks before hitting the trails. The grill also offers buffalo burgers, turkey diners, and fried trout. Diners looking for something more substantial or sophisticated should look elsewhere. ✉*U.S. 89, 5 mi north of Moran Junction, Oxbow Bend* ☎307/543–2811 Ext. 1911 ▭*AE, MC, V* ⊗*Closed early Oct.–late May.*

¢–$ ✕**John Colter Café Court.** This Colter Bay Village resting spot serves Mexican-America fare such as tacos, burritos, and quesadillas as well as ice cream. You can also buy a boxed lunch and take it to the beach. It's just right for what it is, but don't expect the moon. ✉*Just under 5 mi north of Jackson Lake Lodge, Colter Bay* ☎307/543–2811 ▭*AE, MC, V* ⊗*Closed Oct.–mid-May.*

PICNIC AREAS

The park has 11 designated picnic areas, each with tables and grills, and most with pit toilets and water pumps or faucets. In addition to those listed here you can find picnic areas at Colter Bay Village Campground, Cottonwood

Creek, Moose Visitor Center, the east shore of Jackson Lake, and South Jenny Lake, and String Lake trailhead.

✕**Chapel of the Sacred Heart.** From this intimate lakeside picnic area you can look across southern Jackson Lake to Mt. Moran. For wedding information contact "Our Lady of the Mountains" Catholic Church in Jackson. ⊠ *0.25 mi east of Signal Mountain Lodge, off Teton Park Rd., 4 mi south of Jackson Lake Junction, Oxbow Bend.*

✕**Chapel of The Transfiguration & Maud Noble Cabin.** Near Menor's Ferry, the tiny chapel built in 1925 is still an active Episcopal church. The nearby homesteader's cabin of Maud Noble is the original 1917 meeting site where the plan to set aside a portion of Jackson Hole as a national recreation area for the people of the United States was hatched. In summer, you can have ice cream and soda, or eat a packed lunch, at the old General Store by Menor's Ferry. Just walk northeast down the footpath along the Snake River. ⊠ *0.5 mi off Grand Teton Park Road, 2 mi (3 km) north of Moose Junction in Grand Teton National Park.* ⊙ *Late Sept.–late May.*

✕**Colter Bay Visitor Center.** This big picnic area, spectacularly located right on the beach at Jackson Lake, gets crowded in July and August. It's near the visitor center and museum, which has an impressive collection of Native American artifacts including clothing, tools, pottery, and beadwork. It's also conveniently close to flush toilets and stores. ⊠ *25 mi (40 km) north of Moose, 2 mi (3 km) off U.S. 89/191/287, 5 mi (8 km) north of Jackson Lake Junction, Colter Bay* ⊙ *Early Sept.–mid-May.*

✕**East shore of Jackson Lake.** North of Colter Bay, four scenic roadside picnic spots dot this area. ⊠ *U.S. 89/191/287, 6 mi (10 km), 8 mi (13 km), 9 mi (14 km), and 12 mi (19 km) north of Jackson Lake Junction, Colter Bay.*

★ Fodor's Choice ✕**Hidden Falls.** Adjacent to the Jenny Lake shuttle boat dock is a shaded, pine-scented scenic trail. An easy 0.5-mi hike takes you to the falls. Because of problems with bears, park rangers advise that hikers to the falls refrain from eating there. You might also want to pack "bear spray" to repel any sudden unwanted visitors. At the least, hikers should take extra precautions to carefully wrap food in bear proof containers and not leave behind scraps or crumbs. Take the shuttle boat across Jenny Lake to reach the Cascade Canyon trailhead. ⊠*At the Cascade Canyon trailhead, Jenny Lake.*

✕**Signal Mountain Lodge.** Slightly less crowded than the picnic area at Colter Bay Visitor Center, this lakeside picnic area has staggeringly beautiful views of the surrounding landscape, meadows and mountains but contains only a few tables. Flush toilets and stores are nearby. ⊠*Teton Park Rd., 4 mi south of Jackson Lake Junction, Oxbow Bend.*

✕**String Lake trailhead.** Scenic but crowded, the picnic area lies in pine forest at the base of the Teton Range. A one-way drive south at entrance of String Lake connects to Jenny Lake. ⊠*Jenny Lake Rd., 2 mi off Teton Park Rd., 12 mi north of Moose Junction, Jenny Lake.*

✕**Two Ocean Lake.** One of the park's most isolated and uncrowded picnic sites is about 6 mi (10 km) northwest of the Moran entrance station at the east end of Two Ocean Lake. About 1 mi (2 km) north of the entrance station, turn east onto Pacific Creek Road, and about 2 mi (3 km) in from U.S. 191/287 take a left (turning north) on the first dirt road. Two Ocean Lake is about 2.5 mi (4 km) down Two Ocean Lake Rd. ⊠*Off Pacific Creek Rd., 2 mi east of U.S. 26/89/191, Oxbow Bend.*

6

WHERE TO STAY IN GRAND TETON

The choice of lodging properties within the park is as diverse as the landscape itself. Here you'll find simple campgrounds, cabins, and basic motel rooms. You can also settle into a homey B&B, or a luxurious suite in a full-service resort. Between June and August, room rates go up and are harder to get without advanced reservations. Nonetheless, if you're looking to stay in a national park that's tailored to individual pursuits, this is it. Although this park is becoming more popular and crowded each year, it's still closer to the original vision of a haven for man to interact with nature (while contemplating it), as its idealistic founders first imagined back in 1929 and again in 1950.

For Lodging price category information, see "Where to Stay in Yellowstone," above.

For information on lodging and dining (as well as tours) in the park, contact the park's largest concessionaire, **Grand Teton Lodge Company.** ⌂*Box 250, Moran, WY83013* ☎*307/543–3100 or 800/628–9988* ⊕*www.gtlc.com.*

You can reserve rooms near the park through two agencies. **Jackson Hole Central Reservations** (☎*307/733–4005 or 800/443–6931 ⊕www.jacksonholewy.com*) handles hotels as well as B&Bs. **Resort Reservations** (☎*307/733–6331 or 800/329–9205 ⊕www.jacksonhole.net*) is the place to call for reservations for most motels in Jackson.

$$$$ ▣**Jenny Lake Lodge.** This lodge (the most expensive lodging in any U.S. national park) has been serving tourists, sportsmen and travelers since the 1920s. Nestled off the scenic one-way Jenny Lake Loop Road, bordering a wildflower meadow, its guest cabins are well spaced in lodgepole-pine groves. Cabin interiors, with sturdy pine beds and handmade quilts and electric blankets, live up to the elegant rustic theme, and cabin suites have fireplaces. Breakfast, bicycle use, and horseback riding, and dinner are always included the price. Room telephones are provided only on request. **Pros:** maximum comfort in a pristine setting, perhaps the best hotel in the national park system. **Cons:** very expensive, not suitable for families with kids under 17, pretty formal for a national park property. ⊠*Jenny Lake Rd., 2 mi off Teton Park Rd., 12 mi north of Moose Junction, Jenny Lake* ☎*307/733–4647 or 800/628–9988 ⊕www.gtlc.com* ⇆*37 cabins* ⌂*In-room: no a/c, no TV. In-hotel: restaurant, bicycles, public Internet, no elevator* ⊟*AE, DC, MC, V* ⊘*Closed early Oct.–late May* ⦿*MAP.*

$$$–$$$$ ▣**Dornan's Spur Ranch Cabins.** Near Moose Visitor Center in Dornan's all-in-one shopping–dining–recreation development. These one and two-bedroom cabins have queen-sized beds, as well as great views of the Tetons and the Snake River. Each of the cabins has a full kitchen, with electric stove, toaster, pots, pans, dishes, coffeemaker, and utensils as well as a generously sized living-dining room and a furnished porch with a Weber grill in summer. However, at this writing, there's only one microwave on site, so you'll want to request it early. **Pros:** cabins are simple but clean; full kitchens allow you to make your own meals to save money. **Cons:** proximity of cabins means not much privacy, cabins have little atmosphere and no fireplaces. ⊠*10 Moose Rd., off Teton Park Rd. at Moose Junction, Moose* ☎*307/733–2522* ⊕*www.dornans.com* ⇆*8 1-bedroom cabins, 4 2-bedroom cabins* ⌂*In-room: no a/c, kitchen, no TV. In-hotel: 2 restaurants, bar, no elevator* ⊟*D, MC, V* ⦿*EP.*

$$$–$$$$ ⚅Jackson Lake Lodge. This large, full-service resort stands on a bluff with spectacular views across Jackson Lake to the Tetons. (And we do mean full service: there's everything from live music in the bar to in-house religious services.) The upper lobby has 60-foot picture windows and a collection of Native American artifacts and Western art. Many of the guest rooms have lake and mountain views, while others have little or no view, so ask when you book. **Pros:** central location for visiting both Grand Teton and Yellowstone, heated outdoor pool, on-site medical clinic. **Cons:** rooms without views are pricey for what you get, the hotel hosts a lot of large meetings. ⌧*U.S. 89/191/287, 0.5 mi north of Jackson Lake Junction, Oxbow Bend* ☎*307/543–3100 or 800/628–9988* ⊕*www.gtlc.com* ⌁*385 rooms* ⌂*In-room: no a/c, refrigerator (some), no TV, dial-up. In-hotel: 2 restaurants, bar, pool, public Wi-Fi, airport shuttle, some pets allowed* ⊟*MC, V* ⊙*Closed early Oct.–mid-May.*

$$–$$$ ⚅Signal Mountain Lodge. These relaxed, pine-shaded cabins sit on Jackson Lake's southern shoreline. The main building has a cozy lounge and a grand pine deck overlooking the epic lake. Some cabins are equipped with sleek kitchens and pine tables. The smaller log cabins are in shaded areas, and eight of them have a fireplace. Rooms 151–178 have lake views. **Pros:** restaurants and bar are popular hot spots, on-site gas station, general store sells ice. **Cons:** rooms are pretty motel-basic, fireplaces are gas. ⌧*Teton Park Rd., 3 mi south of Jackson Lake Junction, Oxbow Bend* ☎*307/543–2831* ⊕*www.signalmountainlodge.com* ⌁*79 rooms, 32 log cabins* ⌂*In-room: no a/c, kitchen (some), refrigerator (some), no TV. In-hotel: 2 restaurants, bar, no elevator* ⊟*AE, D, MC, V* ⊙*Closed mid-Oct.–mid-May.*

★ Fodor'sChoice⚅Moulton Ranch Cabins. Along Mormon Row,
$–$$$ these cabins stand a few dozen yards south of the famous Moulton Barn, which you see on brochures, jigsaw puzzles, and photographs of the park. The land was once part of the T. A. Moulton homestead, and the cabins are still owned by the Moulton family. The quiet property has views of the Teton and the Gros Ventre ranges, and the owners can regale you with stories about early homesteaders. There's a dance hall in the barn, making this an ideal place for family and small group reunions. No smoking on the premises. **Pros:** quiet and secluded. **Cons:** fairly basic accommodations, little nightlife nearby. ⌧*Off Antelope Flats Rd., U.S. 26/89/191, 2 mi (3 km) north of Moose Junction, Antelope Flats* ☎*307/733–3749 or 208/529–2354* ⊕*www.moult*

onranchcabins.com ⮕*5 units* ⟨⟩*In-room: no a/c, kitchen (some), no TV. In-hotel: no elevator, no-smoking rooms* ⊟*MC, V* ⊘*Closed Oct.–May. No Sun. check-in.*

¢–$$ 	▭**Colter Bay Village.** Near Jackson Lake, this complex of Western-style cabins—some with one room, others with two or more rooms—are within walking distance of the lake. The property has splendid views and an excellent marina and beach for the windsurfing crowd (you'll need a wet suit because of the cold). There are also tent cabins, which aren't fancy (*see* ⇨ *"Where to Camp in Grand Teton," below*) and share communal baths, but they do keep the wind and rain off. There's also a 116-space RV park. **Pros:** prices are good for what you get, many nearby facilities. **Cons:** little sense of privacy, not all cabins have bathrooms. ✉*2 mi off U.S. 89/191/287, 10 mi north of Jackson Lake Junction, Colter Bay* ☎*307/733–3100 or 800/628–9988* ⊕*www.gtlc.com* ⮕*166 cabins, 66 tent cabins* ⟨⟩*In-room: no a/c, no phone, no TV. In-hotel: 2 restaurants, bar, no elevator, laundry facilities, some pets allowed* ⊟*AE, MC, V* ⊘*Closed late Sept.–late May.*

WHERE TO CAMP IN GRAND TETON

You'll find a variety of campgrounds ranging from small areas where only tents are allowed, to full RV parks with all services. If you don't have a tent but want to bring your sleeping bags, you can take advantage of the tent cabins at Colter Bay, where you have a hard floor, cots, and canvas walls to keep the weather at bay. Standard campsites include a place to pitch your tent or park your trailer/camper, a fire pit for cooking, and a picnic table. All developed campgrounds have toilets and potable drinking water, but plan to bring your own firewood. Check-in at campsites as early as possible as many are assigned on a first-come, first-served basis and are run by park concessionaires.

For Camping price category information, see "Where to Camp in Yellowstone," above.

ABOUT BACKCOUNTRY SITES

You can camp in the park's backcountry year-round, provided you have the requisite permit and are able to gain access to your site. Between June 1 and September 15, backcountry campers in the park are limited to one stay of up to 10 days. Campfires are prohibited in the backcountry except at designated lakeshore campsites. *For more information about backcountry exploration, see ⇨Exploring the Backcountry, in Chapter 5, "Grand Teton Hikes & Activities."* You can reserve a backcountry campsite between January 1 and May 15 for a $25 nonrefundable fee (Social Security numbers must be included on all checks) by faxing a request or writing to the **GTNP-Backcountry Permits** (✆Box 170, Moose, WY83012 ⊜307/739–3443). You can also take a chance that the site you want will be open when you show up, in which case you pay no fee at all, but park officials seem less inclined recently to accommodate walk-ins.

At this writing, the Jackson Hole Mountain Resort tram will not be running during the entire summer season of 2008. Consequently, there is no access to the park's backcountry except on foot, so backcountry campers should plan accordingly. Updates are posted on the park's Web site.

$$$$ ⚠ **Colter Bay Tent Village & RV Park.** Adjacent to the National Park Service–this concessionaire-operated campground is the only RV park in Grand Teton Park. And you'll find showers here, too. ⊠*2 mi (3 km) off U.S. 89/191/287, 10 mi (16 km) north of Moran Junction, Colter Bay* ⊜*307/543–2811 or 800/628–9988* ⟿*66 tent cabins, 112 RV sites with full hookups* ⚹*Flush toilets, full hookups, drinking water, guest laundry, showers, bear boxes, fire grates, picnic tables* ⚶*Campground is first come, first served. RV park takes reservations* ⊟*AE, D, MC, V* ☉*Open June–Sept.*

$$ ⚠ **Colter Bay Campground.** Busy, noisy, and filled by noon,
★ this campground has both tent and trailer/RV sites. One of its great advantages: it's centrally located. Try to get a site as far from the nearby cabin road as possible. This campground also has hot showers at Colter Bay Village. The maximum stay is 14 days. ⊠*2 mi (3 km) off U.S. 89/191/287, 5 mi (8 km) north of Jackson Lake Junction, Colter Bay* ⊜*307/543–2100 or 800/628–9988* ⟿*350 tent or RV sites* ⚹*Flush toilets, dump station, drinking water, guest laundry, showers, bear boxes, fire grates, picnic tables* ⚶*Reservations not accepted* ⊟*AE, MC, V* ☉*Late-May–late Sept.*

$$ ⚠ **Gros Ventre.** The park's biggest campground is in an open, grassy area on the bank of the Gros Ventre River, away from the mountains and 2 mi (3 km) southwest of Kelly. Try to get a site close to the river. The campground usually doesn't fill until nightfall, if at all. There's a maximum stay of 14 days. ⊠*4 mi (6 km) off U.S. 26/89/191,*

CAMPING IN GRAND TETON

CAMPGROUND NAME	Total # of Sites	# of RV sites	# of hook-ups	Drive-to sites	Hike-to sites	Flush toilets	Pit toilets	Drinking water	Showers	Fire grates/pits	Swimming	Boat access	Playground	Dump station	Ranger station	Public telephone	Reservations Possible	Daily fee per site	Dates open
Colter Bay	350	238	0	Y		Y		Y	Y	Y		Y		Y	Y	Y		$14	May-Sept
Colter Bay Trailer Village	116	116	116	Y		Y		Y	Y			Y		Y	Y	Y	Y	$44	May-Sept.
Gros Ventre	360	360	0	Y		Y		Y		Y				Y	Y	Y		$12	May-Oct.
Jenny Lake	50	0	0	Y		Y		Y		Y		Y			Y	Y		$12	May-Sept.
Lizard Creek	60	60	0	Y		Y		Y		Y								$15	Jun-Sept.
Signal Mountain	86	86	0	Y		Y		Y		Y		Y		Y	Y	Y		$15	May-Oct.

Y/R = year-round
** = Summer Only

1½ mi (2 km) west of Kelly on Gros Ventre River Rd., 6 mi (10 km) south of Moose Junction, Moose ☎*307/739–3603 or 800/628–9988* ⌕*360 tent or RV sites, 5 group sites* ♿*Flush toilets, dump station, drinking water, bear boxes, fire grates, picnic tables* ♿*Reservations not accepted* ⊟*AE, MC, V* ⊗*May–mid-Oct.*

$$ ⛺ **Jenny Lake.** Wooded sites and Teton views make this the
★ most desirable campground in the park, and it fills early. The small, quiet facility allows tents only, and limits stays to a maximum of seven days. Maximum one vehicle per campsite, no longer than 14 feet. ✉*Jenny Lake Rd., ½ mi off Teton Park Rd., 8 mi north of Moose Junction, Jenny Lake* ☎*800/628–9988* ⌕*50 tent sites (10 walk-in)* ♿*Flush toilets, drinking water, bear boxes, fire grates, picnic tables* ♿*Reservations not accepted* ⊟*No credit cards* ⊗*Mid-May–late Sept.*

$$ ⛺ **Lizard Creek.** Views of Jackson Lake, wooded sites, and the relative isolation of this campground make it a relaxing choice. You can stay here no more than 14 days. No vehicles over 30 feet are allowed. ✉*U.S. 89/191/287, 13 mi north of Jackson Lake Junction* ☎*307/543–2831 or 800/672–6012* ⌕*61 tent/trailer sites* ♿*Flush toilets, drinking water, bear boxes, fire grates, picnic tables* ♿*Reservations not accepted* ⊟*No credit cards* ⊗*Early June–early Sept.*

$$ ⛺ **Signal Mountain Campground.** This campground in a hilly setting on Jackson Lake has boat access to the lake. Campsites offer spectacular views of the Tetons across Jackson Lake. No vehicles or trailers over 30 feet are allowed. There's a maximum stay of 14 days. ✉*Teton Park Rd., 3 mi south of Jackson Lake Junction, Oxbow Bend* ☎*No phone* ⌕*81 sites (tent or RV)* ♿*Flush toilets, dump station, drinking water, fire grates, picnic tables* ♿*Reservations not accepted* ⊟*AE, D, MC, V* ⊗*Early May–mid-Oct.*

What's Nearby

WORD OF MOUTH

"Jackson is a good place to stay if you are visiting Grand Teton [National Park], [but it's a] long and possibly a slow drive to Yellowstone from there. If no lodging [is] available inside the park, try one of the other gateway towns of West Yellowstone, Cooke City/Silver Gate, or Gardiner."

—RedRock

By Gil
Brady
and Steve
Pastorino

LOCATED IN THE NORTHWEST CORNER OF WYO-MING, bordered to the north by Montana and to the west by Idaho, Yellowstone and Grand Teton national parks, while isolated, are still easily accessible through several gateways. Nearby gateways for Yellowstone include Bozeman and Livingston to the north, Cody to the east, and West Yellowstone to the west. To the south is Jackson, the primary gateway for Grand Teton National Park, but there are some small towns in Idaho and Wyoming that could also be classified as gateways, though they are relatively isolated. All are within a couple of hours from the parks (West Yellowstone being the closest to Yellowstone and Jackson being the closest to Grand Teton), but be sure and check for road closures as sometimes winter can make roads impassable.

Remember that these parks are destinations, not something to see as you pass through. There are several upscale resorts for those who appreciate sleeping on beds, but there are literally thousands of possible campsites for those looking to rough it. Plan on spending several days in one or both of the parks if you want to see all that they have to offer.

GATEWAYS TO YELLOWSTONE NATIONAL PARK

The town of **West Yellowstone** abuts the park's West Entrance, where the open plains of southwestern Montana and northeastern Idaho come together along the Madison River Valley. Affectionately known among winter recreationists as the "snowmobile capital of the world," this town of 1,000 is also a good place to go for fishing, horseback riding, and downhill skiing. There's also plenty of culture, as this is where you'll find the Museum of the Yellowstone.

As the only entrance to Yellowstone that's open by car the entire year, **Gardiner** is always bustling. The town's Roosevelt Arch has marked the park's North Entrance since 1903, when President Theodore Roosevelt dedicated it. The Yellowstone River slices through town, beckoning fishermen and rafters. The town of 800 has quaint shops and good restaurants.

Named for William F. "Buffalo Bill" Cody, the town of **Cody** sits near the park's East Entrance. Situated at the mouth of the Shoshone Canyon (where the north and south forks of the Shoshone River join), Cody is a good base for hiking trips, horseback riding excursions, and white-water rafting on the North Fork of the Shoshone or the Clarks Fork of the Yellowstone. Cody is also home to one of the

7

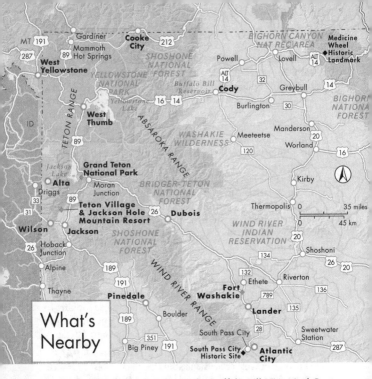

nation's finest museums—the Buffalo Bill Historical Center, sometimes called the "Smithsonian of the West."

With both Yellowstone and the Absaroka-Beartooth Wilderness at its back door, the village of **Cooke City** is a good place for hiking, horseback riding, mountain climbing, and other outdoor activities. Some 50 mi to the east, **Red Lodge** provides a lot more options for dining and lodging. At the base of the Beartooth Mountains, the town is one of Montana's premier ski destinations. These communities guard the Northeast Entrance, least used of all entry points to the park. But it's by far the most spectacular entrance. Driving along the Beartooth Scenic Byway between Red Lodge and Cooke City you'll cross the southern tip of the Beartooth range, literally in the ramparts of the Rockies.

GATEWAYS TO GRAND TETON NATIONAL PARK

A major gateway to both Grand Teton and Yellowstone, **Jackson** is the busiest town in the region—but don't confuse this with Jackson Hole. Jackson Hole is the mountain-ringed valley that houses Jackson and much of Grand Teton National Park. The town of Jackson, located south of the park, is a small community (roughly 7,000 residents) that gets flooded with more than 3 million visitors annually due to its excellent restaurants, upscale resorts, and airport. Expensive homes and fashionable shops have sprung up all over, but Jackson manages to maintain at least part of its true Western character. With its raised wooden sidewalks and old-fashioned storefronts, the town center still looks a bit like a Western movie set. There's a lot to do here, both downtown and in the surrounding countryside.

If it's skiing you're after, **Teton Village,** located on the south-western side of the park, is the place for you. This cluster of businesses centers around the facilities of the Jackson Hole Mountain Resort—a ski and snowboard area with gondola and various other lifts. There are plenty of places to eat, stay, and shop here.

WEST YELLOWSTONE

The West entrance for Yellowstone National Park is at the eastern edge of West Yellowstone.

In the summer of 2008, the gateway community of **West Yellowstone,** Montana, celebrated the 100th anniversary of passengers arriving on the Union Pacific railroad. Trains no longer come, but visitors do, in droves. The town of about 1,000 people has four times as many hotel rooms as it has people, and dozens of dining options. Known as the "snow-mobile capital of the world" by some, it's also a hub for fly-fishing, with six world-class rivers close by. The town is becoming a year-round home for outdoor enthusiasts and residents alike. Snowmobile riders are joined by cross-country skiers throughout the winter, but especially for two crowded festival weekends: the Thanksgiving weekend ski-season kickoff and the Yellowstone Rendezvous Race that takes place in late February or early March. In the summer, cyclists, runners, horseback riders, and bird-watchers descend as well.

If you look beyond the myriad souvenir shops, you'll find a live theater, the renowned Grizzly & Wolf Discovery Center, the Museum of Yellowstone, and several other worth-while attractions to keep you occupied when you're not in the park itself.

Many businesses close from mid-November through Christmas and again mid-March through April, to coincide

West Yellowstone

KEY

① Exploring

① Restaurants & Hotels

Exploring

Grizzly & Wolf Discovery Center, **4**

Playmill Theatre, **1**

Yellowstone Historic Center, **2**

Yellowstone IMAX Theatre, **3**

Restaurants

Bar N Ranch, **3**

Beartooth BBQ, **13**

Bullwinkle's, **15**

Ernie's Deli & Bakery, **2**

Morning Glory Coffee & Tea, **11**

Oregon Shortline Restaurant, **9**

Pete's Rocky Mountain Pizza & Pasta, **12**

Running Bear Pancake House, **7**

TJ's Bettola, **6**

Wild West Pizzeria, **14**

Hotels

Bar N Ranch, **4**

Clubhouse Inn, **17**

Greywolf Inn & Suites, **20**

Grizzly RV Park, **22**

Hibernation Station, **21**

Holiday Inn Sunspree Resort, **8**

Kelly Inn, **19**

Madison Hotel, **16**

Stage Coach Inn, **10**

Wagon Wheel Campground & Cabins, **1**

West Yellowstone Bed & Breakfast, **5**

Yellowstone Park Hotel, **18**

with the seasonal closing of Yellowstone's West Entrance, so be sure to plan ahead during the shoulder season.

Numbers in the margins correspond to bullets on the West Yellowstone map.

TOWN INFORMATION

West Yellowstone Chamber of Commerce ⊠ *30 Yellowstone Ave., West Yellowstone, MT 59758* ☎ *406/646–7701* ⊕ *www. westyellowstonechamber.com.*

WHAT TO SEE & DO

If you need something to do other than experiencing the beautiful scenery in the park, West Yellowstone also has a movie theater, fun center, old-time photo studios, and rodeos, among other events and activities, to keep you and yours busy.

❹ **Grizzly & Wolf Discovery Center.** Home to eight grizzlies and a pack of four wolves (although a second pack is scheduled to be introduced in 2008), the center gives visitors a fun, hands-on, up-close experience with two of America's most fierce predators. Accredited by the Associations of Zoos & Aquariums, the extensive programming provides educational opportunities for kids and parents alike, but the center is also home to important scientific research. In case you're wondering, the animals were saved from death in the U.S. and Canada and given a "second chance" at the Center. ✉ *201 South Canyon St., West Yellowstone, MT* ☎ *406/646–7001* ⊕ *www.grizzlydiscoveryctr.com* 💲 *$9.75* ⊙ *Open 365 days a year, 8 AM–dusk.*

❸ **Yellowstone IMAX Theatre.** This theater shows multiple titles on its 60-foot-high screen, but skip it if you'd rather see Lower Yellowstone Falls' 300-foot drop in person less than one hour away. Kids may enjoy it, however. ✉ *101 South Canyon St., West Yellowstone, MT* ☎ *406/646–4100* ⊕ *www.yellowstoneimax.com* 💲 *$9* ⊙ *Open 7 days a week, year-round, but film schedules vary.*

❷ **Yellowstone Historic Center.** Your time will be spent at ⟳ the 10-acre outdoor museum. The **Union Pacific Depot,** which was built in 1909, has been transformed into a museum dedicated to modes of travel to Yellowstone in the years before World War II. The collection includes trains, stagecoaches, and examples of many other conveyances. You can also watch films about the 1988 Yellowstone fire, earthquakes, and more. ✉ *104 Yellowstone Ave., West Yellowstone, MT* ☎ *406/646–1100* ⊕ *www.yellowstonehistoriccenter.org* 💲 *TK* ⊙ *Mid-May–mid-June and mid-Sept.–Oct., 9–6; mid-June–mid-Sept. 9–9; mid-Nov.–mid-Apr., weekdays 10–3.*

❶ **Playmill Theatre.** West Yellowstone's local community theater presents its 45th summer season in 2008. With a company drawn primarily from Montana, Idaho, Wyoming, and Utah, you can expect family favorites almost every night but Sunday from Memorial Day through Labor Day. ✉ *29 Madison Ave., West Yellowstone, MT* ☎ *406/646–7757* ⊕ *www.playmill.com* 💲 *$15* ⊙ *May–Aug., Mon.–Sat., but showtimes vary.*

WHERE TO EAT

West Yellowstone has a surprising number of restaurants to choose from, the majority of which offer a casual and kid-friendly atmosphere. Fine dining is a little harder to come by, but flourishes at Bar N Ranch and TJ's Bettola. If you're hungry for American food after a day of exploring Yellowstone National Park, you will find a broader selection of burgers, steaks, and the like outside the park, at comparable prices to the cookie-cutter menus inside the park. Throughout the year, ice cream and other sweets seem ubiquitous.

WHAT IT COSTS				
RESTAURANTS				
¢	$	$$	$$$	$$$$
under $8	$8–$12	$12–$20	$21–$30	over $30

Restaurant prices are per person for a main course at dinner and do not include tax.

$$$–$$$$ ✕**Bar N Ranch Restaurant.** Executive Chef Jack Cole oversees a restaurant with full bar and wide-ranging wine list. Starters mostly feature fish and seafood. Broiled halibut with sweet red Thai chili sauce is the "must try" main course, but cilantro scallops, buffalo rib eye, rainbow trout, and steaks will tempt you as well. Save room for exquisite desserts such as huckleberry cornbread cake, crème brûlée, and fresh berry cobbler. High-back chairs and tables made from reclaimed barn wood are both formal and rustic. ⊠*890 Buttermilk Creek Rd., 5 mi west of town via U.S. 20* ☎*406/646–0300* ⚇*Reservations essential* ▤*AE, D, MC, V* ⊘*No lunch.*

$$–$$$ ✕**Bullwinkle's Saloon & Eatery.** A Green Bay Packers' bar in Montana? Even if you and the owners don't root for the same team, this is a carnivore's dream. Buffalo, elk, and steak are all featured, but extensive seafood, soups, and salads warrant a look. You can also order dozens of beers and mixed drinks in addition to more than 20 wines. It's a saloon, so the place can get noisy. Expect to wait 30 minutes or more on busy summer nights. ⊠*19 Madison Ave.,* ☎*406/646–7974* ⚇*Reservations not accepted* ▤*AE, D, DC, MC, V.*

$$–$$$ ✕**TJ's Bettola.** Unable to secure a liquor license in town, this Italian fine-dining establishment was known for candlelit tables, Italian music, and artwork on the walls—at the airport! At this writing, the owner was in the process of shuttering the airport location and reopening in town in the old Protestant Church. Call ahead to find out if the move has been completed—it's worth it if you have a taste for pasta, gnocchi, or chicken marsala. ⊠*316 Canyon St.,* ☎*406/646–4700* ▤*MC, V.*

$$ ✕**Beartooth BBQ.** "St. Louis style" ribs (a meatier cut than baby back ribs), not to mention barbecued chicken and pork, are highlights on the menu in this meat-eater's paradise. The tiny joint seats maybe 40 diners—including a few at the cramped corner bar. The tasty homemade tabbouleh and huckleberry vinaigrette dressing indicate that the chef has put some thought and effort into something other than his smoker. Select from a dozen local beers to accompany your meal. If you like sweet and spicy barbeque, it's well worth the stop. ✉*111 Canyon St.* ☎*406/646–0227* ⊟*MC, V* ⊙*Closed mid-Nov. to late Dec. and mid-March to mid- April.*

$–$$ ✕**Oregon Short Line Restaurant.** Connected to the Holiday
☺ Inn Sunspree Resort, this family eatery offers typical fare with a nod to some local favorites like salmon and bison. Kids will love wandering through the restored 1903 Union Pacific railroad car (it's museum-quality) in the lobby. You'll love the fact that kids under 12 eat free if you're staying at the Holiday Inn. ✉*315 Yellowstone Ave.* ☎*406/646–7365* ⊟*AE, D, MC, V.*

$–$$ ✕**Pete's Rocky Mountain Pizza & Pasta.** Although it might lose out to Wild West Pizzeria for the best pizza in town, Pete's wins hands down for its homemade pasta, elk sausage, and Italian favorites like chicken parmesan. Ideal for families, Pete's features both indoor and outdoor seating. ✉*104 Canyon St.* ☎*406/646–7820* ⊟*D, MC, V* ⊙*Closed Nov.–late Dec. and Mar.–Apr.*

¢–$$ ✕**Running Bear Pancake House.** You can get buttermilk or
☺ buckwheat pancakes topped with blueberries, coconut, strawberries, peaches, walnuts, or chocolate chips, not to mention omelets, skillet breakfasts, and eggs to order. For lunch, there are sandwiches and burgers. Pies are housemade here, as are muffins and cinnamon rolls. But trust the name and go for the best pancakes in West Yellowstone, and enjoy the extremely friendly service. Open only from 7 AM to 2 PM. ✉*Corner of Madison & Hayden Sts.,* ☎*406/646–7703* ⊟*D, MC, V* ⊙*No dinner. Closed Nov.– late Dec. and mid-Mar. to May 1.*

$ ✕**Wild West Pizzeria.** Good pizza seems to taste better in
☺ mountain resort towns, and Wild West is no exception.
★ Owner Aaron Hecht set out to make the best pizza in West Yellowstone a decade ago. The crisp crust, flavorful sauce, and "celebrity" frontier combinations work. Sitting Bull features Italian pepperoni, sausage, and salami—plus

Canadian Bacon. Calamity Jane offers white sauce, mush-rooms, artichoke hearts, minced garlic, and fresh tomatoes. You can also get pasta and sandwiches, but everyone seems to relish the pizza. Beer is poured in the adjacent Strozzi's Bar, but you can bring it into the pizzeria—it's just a minor inconvenience. ⊠*14 Madison Ave.,* ☎*406/646–4400* ▭*MC, V.*

¢ ✕**Ernie's Deli & Bakery.** Add to one of five types of fresh-baked bread every day a bevy of tasty meats, cheeses, and fixings, and you can create your own special sandwich. There are literally thousands of possibilities. You can also pick from such favorites as The Yellowstone, which features four kinds of salami; or The Firehole, with its spicy turkey breast on garlic bread. Box lunches are also available with a sandwich, apple, drink, candy, cookie, chips, and a mint for under $8. Beer, wine, coffee, soups, and fresh bagels are also available. Dawn and her team at Ernie's are super friendly, too. ⊠*406 U.S. 20,* ☎*406/646–9467* ▭*No credit cards.*

¢ ✕**Morning Glory Coffee & Tea.** You don't expect to find a store that imports, roasts, and grinds its own coffee beans in this hamlet, but Morning Glory does just that—and it hits the spot for a perfect cup of coffee. One of only two manufacturers "of anything" in West Yellowstone, says one local businesswoman, Morning Glory's storefront may not inspire, but the coffee does. They also ship coffee anywhere. Fresh-baked scones and pastries are available daily, but otherwise your food choices are slim. ⊠*129 Dunraven St.* ☎*406/646–7061* ▭*No credit cards.*

WHERE TO STAY

West Yellowstone has become a busy bedroom community for the adjacent national park, with four times more rooms than residents. Properties range from decades-old motels to cookie-cutter chain hotels built since the mid-1990s. Prices at the nicer properties, which are reviewed here, tend to be higher than the lodging in the park, but you do have more access to modern suburban amenities such as grocery stores and a variety of restaurants and shopping.

WHAT IT COSTS

HOTELS

¢	$	$$	$$$	$$$$
under $50	$51–$100	$101–$150	$151–$200	over $200

Hotel prices are per night for two people in a standard double room in high season, excluding taxes and service charges.

★ Fodor'sChoice ☷ **Bar N Ranch.** A deluxe option for the increas-
$$$$ ing number of affluent anglers, hunters, and visitors to
West Yellowstone, this supersized B&B combines Midwest-
ern hospitality of its Chicago-born owners with big-timber
architecture and a frontier feel. Seven rooms in the main
lodge (above a spacious living room and the community's
finest restaurant), plus seven stand-alone cabins sleep from
two to eight. The 200-acre ranch, which first welcomed
visitors in 2006, is 6 mi (10 km) from the entrance to Yellowstone National park. **Pros:** all rooms have a fireplace,
Jacuzzi, and antique furniture, in addition to modern con-
veniences such as Wi-Fi and a DVD player. **Cons:** there
are no room phones and cellular service is spotty, nothing
within walking distance, dirt/gravel driveway can be dusty.
⊠*890 Buttermilk Creek Rd., 59758* ☎*406/646–0300*
⊕*www.bar-n-ranch.com* ⇆*14 rooms* △*In-room: no a/c,
no phone, refrigerator, DVD, Wi-Fi. In-hotel: restaurant,
bar, pool, no elevator, public Internet, public Wi-Fi, some
pets allowed, no-smoking rooms.* ⓘ*BP* ⊟*AE, D, MC, V.*

$$$–$$$$ ☷ **Holiday Inn Sunspree Resort.** Definitely a notch above most
ⓒ West Yellowstone hotels, this so-called resort is merely
average by big-city standards. Rooms are spacious and
have been renovated in the recent past, and each has a sofa
seating area. An indoor pool and waterslide will occupy
the kids. It's also one of the few properties in town with
substantial meeting space. There's an attached restaurant
and snowmobiling packages in the winter. **Pros:** full-ser-
vice hotel, the adjoining Oregon Short Line restaurant has
a restored 1903 deluxe railroad car. **Cons:** breakfast not
included. ⊠*315 Yellowstone Ave., 59758* ☎*406/646–7365
or 800/646–7365* ⊕*www.doyellowstone.com* ⇆*123 rooms*
△*In-hotel: refrigerator, Wi-Fi. In-hotel: restaurant, room
service, bar, pool, gym, laundry facilities, airport shuttle,
no-smoking rooms.* ⓘ*EP* ⊟*AE, D, DC, MC, V.*

$$$–$$$$ ☷ **Yellowstone Park Hotel.** The newest hotel in West Yellow-
stone was built in 2007. Under the same ownership as the

7

Stage Coach Inn and Gray Wolf Inn, it's a cookie-cutter property. Still, it's clean, has friendly service, and is in a good location. Some suites have a fireplace and/or a Jacuzzi. You could do worse. Snowmobiles are available on-site for rental in the winter. **Pros:** clean and new. **Cons:** devoid of personality. ⊠*201 Grizzly Ave., 59758* ☎*406/646–0255 or 866/920–0255* ⊕*www.yellowstoneparkhotel.com* ⇴*66 rooms* ⌂*In-room: refrigerator, Ethernet. In-hotel: pool, gym, laundry facilities, public Wi-Fi, no-smoking rooms* ⌾*CP* ⊟*AE, D, DC, MC, V.*

$$–$$$$ ▫**Hibernation Station.** An impressive bronze statue of two
⟳ elk greets you as you enter this 50-cabin complex on nearly 5 acres of land. It's on the southern edge of town, about four blocks from the Yellowstone National Park entrance and even closer to world-class snowmobile and cross-country skiing trails in Gallatin National Forest. Finely appointed cabins have tapestry-covered walls, frontier decor including bronze sculptures in some rooms, and luxurious down comforters; some cabins are heated by gas fireplaces. Rent from the hotel's own fleet of snowmobiles, and you even get clothing, instructors, and guides if necessary. **Pros:** friendly staff, rooms are large and nicely finished, geared toward snowmobile and ski enthusiasts in the winter. **Cons:** unpaved drives and parking areas detract in summer, no on-site breakfast available. ⊠*212 Gray Wolf Ave., 59758* ☎*406/646–4200 or 800/580–3557* ⊕*www.hibernationstation.com* ⇴*50 cabins* ⌂*In-room: no a/c, kitchen (some), refrigerator (some), DVD (some). In-hotel: public Wi-Fi, some pets allowed, no-smoking rooms.* ⌾*EP* ⊟*AE, D, MC, V.*

$$$ ▫**Gray Wolf Inn & Suites.** Large families are drawn to the suites, which range from 750 square feet to 1,000 square feet, include full-size kitchen appliances, and sleep six comfortably. There's a sufficient kitchen to roast a complete turkey dinner in your room if you visit for the Thanksgiving Ski Rendezvous. Rooms are clean and modern, and the location is fantastic. **Pros:** heated indoor parking, location, large and reasonably priced suites. **Cons:** fast-food chains are your closest choices for meals, rooms are a bit expensive for what you get. ⊠*250 S. Canyon Ave., 59758* ☎*406/646–0000 or 800/852–8602* ⊕*www.graywolf-inn.com* ⇴*84 rooms, 18 suites* ⌂*In-room: kitchen (some), refrigerator, VCR (some), Wi-Fi. In-hotel: pool, laundry facilities, airport shuttle, some pets allowed, no-smoking rooms* ⌾*CP* ⊟*AE, D, MC, V.*

$$$ 🏨**Kelly Inn.** Of the five substantially similar properties south of Yellowstone Avenue, Kelly Inn adds a few personal touches to try to separate it from the pack. Look for the timber accents and wooden bears "climbing" the exterior of the hotel. The pool is a little larger than those at other hotels, and the lobby and service is warm and welcoming. Built in 1996, it maintains a clean, neat appearance. **Pros:** location (turn left at the first light as you exit the park and you will see the Kelly Inn on your right). **Cons:** no gym, the modest upgrades between this and neighboring properties may not justify its higher rates. ⊠*104 S. Canyon St., 59758* ☎*406/646–4544 or 800/635-3559* ⊕*www.yellowstonekellyinn.com* ⇨*78 rooms* ⚴*In-room: refrigerator, Wi-Fi. In-hotel: pool, laundry facilities, public Internet, some pets allowed.* ❆*CP* ═*AE, D, DC, MC, V.*

$$–$$$ 🏨**Clubhouse Inn.** Located directly behind the Yellowstone Historic Center, this clean, modern, and bright chain hotel is one of the closest properties to the park entrance. Service is attentive and friendly. **Pros:** location, cleanliness, friendliness. **Cons:** closes for the winter. ⊠*105 S. Electric Ave., 59758* ☎*406/646–4892 or 800/565–6803* ⊕*www.yellowstoneclubhouseinn.com* ⇨*77 rooms* ⚴*In-room: refrigerator (some), Wi-Fi. In-hotel: pool, gym, airport shuttle, no-smoking rooms.* ❆*CP* ═*AE, D, DC, MC, V* ☉*Closed mid-Oct. to early May.*

$$ 🏨**Stage Coach Inn.** An impressive two-story lobby with piano and fireplace greets guests. Although one of Yellowstone's oldest properties (construction started in 1946), the property has been maintained well and renovated frequently. Most recently renovated rooms are larger and have modern Western decor. The attached Coachman Lounge and Casino is homey and welcoming (especially on a snowy winter night), with pool tables, TVs, and legal poker games with licensed dealers. **Pros:** all rooms are comfortable and clean, the property has character. In the winter, the inn rents snowmobiles. **Cons:** lacks some services such as Wi-Fi, a pool, gym, and in-room microwaves. ⊠*209 Madison Ave., 59758* ☎*406/646–7381 or 800/842–2882* ⊕*www.yellowstoneinn.com* ⇨*83 rooms* ⚴*In-room: refrigerators (some). In-hotel: bar, laundry facilities, no-smoking rooms* ❆*CP* ═*AE, D, DC, MC, V.*

$$ 🏨**West Yellowstone Bed & Breakfast.** Just 4 mi (6 km) west of town on U.S. 20, Debbie and Scott Clark operate a quiet, traditional B&B. Join fellow guests each morning

7

for a full breakfast (with menu options for every palate) in an airy common kitchen/dining area. Retire each night to one of three rooms, each with its own private entrance and bathroom. The lodge, which opened in 2003, is exquisitely clean and well-maintained. Timber beds are handmade by Scott, who also leads fly-fishing expeditions with Blue Ribbon Flies. "Our guests prefer the peace and quiet," says proprietor Debbie Clark. "If they wanted television, they [could] stay at a Comfort Inn." **Pros:** more personality, value, and attentive service than any property in its modest price range; pets and kids are welcome. **Cons:** no restaurants or businesses within walking distance; with just three rooms, getting a reservation can be tricky; no public Internet access at this writing. ⊠ *20 Crane Lane, 59758* ☎ *406/646–7754* ⊕ *www.westyellowstonebandb.com* ⏎ *3 rooms* ⌂ *In-room: no a/c, no phone, refrigerator, no TV. In-hotel: no elevator, some pets allowed, no-smoking rooms* ⏏ *BP* ⊟ *AE, D, MC, V.*

¢–$ 🏚 **Madison Hotel.** The oldest hotel in West Yellowstone opened in 1912 and has earned a place on the National Register of Historic Places. As you might expect from a 96-year-old wooden building, the floors are uneven and creaky—and not all rooms have a private bath. The ceilings are also very low, compounded by the small size of the rooms. Somehow, presidents Harding and Hoover, plus actor Clark Gable, stayed here, or so the story goes. Perhaps it's the folksy and friendly service, which is welcoming. The original building has hostel-style dorm rooms (no bath, no a/c) as well as some private rooms with both a private bath and a/c. If you're traveling solo, the $25 hostel rate is the best bargain in town. There are also motel-style rooms off the rear parking lot; although these have private bathrooms, a/c, and TVs, avoid them— they're dated. **Pros:** the original hotel evokes 1912 (in a good way); rough timber walls, handmade furniture, hand sinks, and quilts are unique; family-owned and operated. **Cons:** the lobby/gift shop/Internet café is either a collector's dream or a cluttered mess depending on your perspective; definitely not for everyone. ⊠ *139 Yellowstone Ave., 59758* ☎ *406/646– 7745 or 800/838–7745* ⊕ *www.madisonhotelmotel.com* ⏎ *8 multi-person rooms without private bath; 6 rooms in original hotel with private bath; 17 motel-style rooms in rear* ⌂ *In-room: no a/c (some), no phone, refrigerator (some), no TV. In-hotel: no elevator, public Internet, airport shuttle, some pets allowed, no-smoking rooms.* ⏏ *EP* ⊟ *AE, D, MC, V* ☾ *Closed for winter from early Oct. through mid-May.*

WHERE TO CAMP

The "urban" campsites of West Yellowstone might be a welcome sight if you arrive late at night and don't want to navigate Yellowstone National Park in darkness—or if every single campsite in the park is full. Otherwise, it's hard to comprehend why anyone would camp here since the campsites and RV parks in West Yellowstone are more expensive than those inside the park, which are much closer to the reason for your trip. Plus, there's a steady flow of traffic through West Yellowstone at all hours, so expect noise.

WHAT IT COSTS				
CAMPING				
¢	$	$$	$$$	$$$$
under $8	$9–$14	$15–$20	$21–$25	over $25

Camping prices are for a campsite including a tent area, fire pit, bear-proof food storage box, picnic table; potable water and pit toilets or restrooms will be nearby.

$$$$ ⚠**Grizzly RV Park.** Adjacent to the Rendezvous Ski Trails at the south end of West Yellowstone, this campground is clean and modern, with cabins as well as tent and RV sites. ✉*210 S. Electric St., 59758* ☎*406/646–4466* ⊕*www.grizzlyrv.com* ⌂*Flush toilets, full hookups, drinking water, guest laundry, showers, public telephone, public Wi-Fi* ⌁*191 RV sites, 16 tent sites; 7 cabins* ▭*AE, D, MC, V* ⊙*May–Oct.*

$$$$ ⚠**Wagon Wheel Campground and Cabins.** Located within West Yellowstone a few blocks west of the park, this campground has tent and RV sites along with cozy one-, two-, and three-bedroom cabins with porches, barbecue grills, and cable TV. No pets are allowed, and there's no smoking in the cabins. Two cabins are open year-round. ✉*408 Gibbon Ave., 59758* ☎*406/646–7872* ⊕*www.wagonwheelrv.com* ⌂*Flush toilets, full hookups, drinking water, guest laundry, showers, public telephone* ⌁*32 RV sites, 6 tent sites; 9 cabins* ▭*No credit cards* ⊙*Memorial Day–Sept. 15.*

SHOPPING

West Yellowstone has dozens of souvenir shops, tiny boutiques, and galleries. There is a certain sameness to all of it, but a few stores have withstood the test of time. Also, with six world-class rivers to fish nearby, it's no wonder that at least four fly-fishing shops are clustered within a block of one another. All the stores also offer guided fishing and lodging packages, equipment rental and sale, and a wealth of expertise about the angling opportunities in and around Yellowstone National Park.

Arrick's (⊠37 Canyon St. ☎406/646–7290 ⊕www.arricks. com) rents pontoon boats as well as fly-fishing and fly tying gear.

Bud Lilly's Trout Shop (⊠39 Madison Ave. ☎406/646–7796 ⊕www.budlillys.com), the oldest fishing shop in West Yellowstone, opened its doors in the 1950s. The basement has fishing-themed artwork and gifts.

Bob Jacklin's Fly Shop (⊠105 Yellowstone Ave. ☎406/646–7336 ⊕www.jacklinsflyshop.com) dates to the 1970s. Jacklin, a member of the fly-fishing hall of fame, still offers regular free clinics.

Bookworm (⊠14 N. Canyon St. ☎406/646–7796) is a cluttered treasure trove for readers and collectors of fine books. You will find hundreds of titles (including first editions and autographed copies) of books and memorabilia related to Yellowstone, the Western United States, and frontier history.

Book Peddler (⊠115 N. Canyon St. ☎406/646–9358) is a neat, modern bookstore featuring regional books as well as best sellers in paperback and hardcover. You can also get a decent cup of coffee at its coffee bar.

Madison River Outfitters (⊠117 Canyon St. ☎406/646–9644 ⊕www.madisonriveroutfitters.com) is the largest outdoor recreation store in West Yellowstone, and it's the only one that also carries a broad selection of outdoor clothing as well as tents, backpacks, and other hiking equipment.

★ **Silver Heels** (⊠115 Yellowstone Ave. ☎406/646–7796) owner Greg Huth has been custom-designing silver and gold jewelry in the heart of West Yellowstone for nearly 40 years. The store is located on Yellowstone Avenue about two blocks from the park entrance. Silver Heels also displays gems found in the region 100 years ago by Huth's family.

RED LODGE

60 mi southwest of Billings via U.S. 212.

Nestled against the foot of the pine-draped Absaroka-Beartooth Wilderness and edged by the Limestone Palisades, this little burg is listed on the National Register of Historic Places and has become a full-blown resort town, complete with a ski area, trout fishing, access to backcountry hiking, horseback riding, and a golf course. Red Lodge was named for a band of Cheyenne who marked their tepee lodges with paintings of red earth. It became a town in the late 1880s, when the Northern Pacific Railroad laid tracks here to take coal back to Billings. One of Red Lodge's most colorful characters from this time was former sheriff "Liver Eatin' " Jeremiah Johnson, the subject of much Western lore and an eponymous movie starring Robert Redford. Red Lodge is a favored stopover for motorcyclists and others heading over the Beartooth Highway to Yellowstone National Park. Maps for self-guided historical walking tours of the town are available at the Chamber and the museum.

EN ROUTE. **Joliet, a neonless ranching community midway between I–90 and Red Lodge on Hwy. 212, claims its own bit of glamour at The Homestead Café (⊠ 606 W. Front Ave. ☎ 406/962–3911). The owners spent years in Las Vegas as Marilyn Monroe and Elvis Presley impersonators, as dozens of photos lining the walls attest. Your chicken-fried steak may taste extra special when served by legends.**

The folks in Red Lodge, all 2,300 of them, relish festivals. For a complete list and exact dates, contact the **Red Lodge Area Chamber of Commerce** ⊠ *601 N. Broadway 59068* ⌂ *P. O. Box 988* ☎ *406/446–1718 or 888/281–0625* ⊕ *www. redlodge.com.*

Each August, the **Festival of Nations** (⊕ *www.festivalofna tions.us*) celebrates the varied heritages of early settlers, many of whom migrated to work in now-defunct coal mines. The weekend festival includes ethnic music, food, and dance.

From kindergartners to seniors, fiddlers of all ages head for Red Lodge each July to compete in the two-day **Montana State Old-Time Fiddlers Contest** ⊕ *www.montanafiddlers.org.*

☽ For 10 days in July, the fur trade/Mountain Man era lives again during **Rendezvous at Red Lodge** (⊕*www.redlodge. com/rendezvous*). Participants from around the country set up tents, don period dress, and trade tools, beads, and other items at this historical reenactment.

☽ When the snow flies in late February, the annual **Winter Carnival** (⊕*www.redlodgemountain.com*) draws skiers, snowboarders, and other fans of the cold to three days of events such as the zany Classic Cardboard Downhill Race with construction materials limited to cardboard, glue, and tape. Other events include kids' activities and live music.

☽ The **Beartooth Nature Center** provides a home for more than 70 injured or orphaned mammals and raptors, including bears, mountain lions, bobcats, wolves, and golden eagles. ⊠*615 Second Ave. E., 59068* ☎*406/446–1133* ⊕*www. beartoothnaturecenter.org* ⊡*$6* ⊙*June–Oct., daily 10–5; Nov.–May, daily 10–2.*

In addition to memorabilia that once belonged to rodeo greats, the Ridin' Greenoughs and Bill Linderman, the **Carbon County Historical Society Museum** houses a historic gun collection, simulated coal and hard rock mines, and Crow Indian and Liver Eatin' Johnson exhibits. ⊠*224 N. Broadway, 59068* ☎*406/446–3667* ⊕*www.carboncountyhistory. com* ⊡*$3* ⊙*Late-May–early-Sept., Mon.–Sat. 10–5; Sept.– May, Tues.–Sat. 11–3.*

OFF THE BEATEN PATH. **A bar and a museum may seem an unlikely pairing, but Shirley Smith, owner of the Little Cowboy Bar & Museum (** ⊠*105 W. River St., Fromberg 59029* ☎*406/668–9502*), **makes it work. A rodeo enthusiast and lover of local lore, she has packed the one-room museum with rodeo memorabilia and objects ranging from projectile points to bottled beetles. Smith loves to spin tales of regional heroes/outlaws and the legendary Little People of the nearby Pryor Mountains.** ⊹*20 mi east on Hwy. 308, then 19 mi north on Hwy. 72* ⊡*Free.*

SPORTS & THE OUTDOORS

DOWNHILL SKIING

☽ There are 84 ski trails on 1,600 acres at **Red Lodge Mountain Resort** (⊠*305 Ski Run Rd., 59068* ☎*406/446–2610 or 800/444–8977* ⊕*www.redlodgemountain.com*). The family-friendly resort has a 2,400-foot vertical drop, a large beginner area, plenty of groomed intermediate terrain, and 30 acres of extreme chute skiing. Slopes are accessed by two high-speed quads, one triple, and four double chairs. Lift tickets are $46. The season runs late-November–early April.

FISHING

Montana Trout Scout (⊠ *213 W. 9th St., 59068* ☎ *406/855–3058* ⊕ *www.montanatroutscout.com*) conducts fly-fishing float trips and wade fishing on local streams and rivers such as the Yellowstone, Clark's Fork, Stillwater, and Rock Creek.

GOLF

The surrounding mountains form a backdrop for the 18-hole, par 72 **Red Lodge Mountain Golf Course** (⊠ *828 Upper Continental Dr., 59068* ☎ *406/446–3344 or 800/444–8977* ⊕ *www.redlodgemountain.com*).

HORSEBACK RIDING

☾ With **Whispering Winds Horse Adventures** (⊠ *55 Ladvala Rd., Roberts 59070* ☎ *406/671–6836*) enjoy riding lessons in the ranch's arena or daytime or sunset trail rides among rolling hills. Lunch or dinner is optional. A half-day Family Fun program customizes the riding experience. The company's owner is certified in equine-assisted learning which uses horses in problem-solving techniques and practical therapy. ≙ *Reservations required.*

NORDIC SKIING

At the **Red Lodge Nordic Ski Center,** escape to the solitude of forests along 14.5 km (9 mi) of groomed trails at the base of the Beartooth Mountains. You also can experience on- and off-trail backcountry skiing and snowboarding. Trails are maintained by volunteers and there is no lodge. ⊹ *1 mi from town on Hwy. 78, then 2 mi west on Fox Trail* ☎ *406/446–1771* ⊕ *www.beartoothtrails.org* ☉ *Dec.–Mar.*

WHITE-WATER RAFTING

The Stillwater River's foaming white water flows from the Absaroka-Beartooth Wilderness, providing exhilarating rafting with **Adventure Whitewater** (⊠ *310 W. 15th St., 59068* ☎ *406/446–3061 or 800/897–3061* ⊕ *www.adventurewhitewater.com*), which also has a combined rafting and horseback-riding trip.

WHERE TO EAT

$$–$$$$ ✕ **Bridge Creek Backcountry Kitchen & Wine Bar.** This restaurant's signature entrée is naturally raised Montana strip

loin, dry-aged for 28 days to enhance flavor. Bridge Creek has an extensive wine list, occasional wine tastings, theme buffets in the off-season, and patio dining in summer. For lunch, try one of the soup and half-sandwich combos. ⊠*116 S. Broadway 59068* ☏*406/446–9900* ⊕*www.eat foodrinkwine.com* ▤*MC, V.*

$-$$ ✕**Bogart's.** Not surprisingly, Bogie's photos, movie ads, and memorabilia cover the walls. But this casual eatery's most notable features are great Mexican food, margaritas, burgers, and specialty pizzas. Expect to wait for seating in summer. ⊠*11 S. Broadway, 59068* ☏*406/446–1784* ▤*MC, V.*

$-$$ ✕**Foster and Logan's Pub & Grill** Multiple TVs, each tuned to a different sport, line the brick walls of this friendly place. The bar claims 20 beers on tap, the better to enjoy what locals call the town's best hamburgers. In winter, opt for buffalo chili topped with diced onions and shredded cheddar. ⊠*17 S. Broadway, 59068* ☏*406/446–9080* ▤*AE, D, MC, V.*

WHERE TO STAY

$$-$$$ ▩**Pollard Hotel.** This 1893 landmark in the heart of Red
★ Lodge's historic district has been restored to the charms of an earlier era, when the likes of Calamity Jane and Liver Eatin' Johnson frequented the hotel. Reproduction Victorian furniture throughout vivifies a fin de siècle feel, and handsome oak paneling adds a rich touch to some public rooms. The Pollard's restaurant ($$$–$$$$) specializes in steaks, chops, duck, and fresh fish. ⊠*2 N. Broadway* ✑*P. O. Box 650 59068* ☏*406/446–0001 or 800/765–5273* ☍*406/446–0002* ⊕*www.pollardhotel.com* ⇌*39 rooms* ♒*In-hotel: restaurant, gym* ▤*AE, D, MC, V* ⊙*BP.*

$$ ▩**Rock Creek Resort.** A wooden bear's raised paw welcomes you to this 35-acre get-away, where a Southwestern motif decorates the wood, log, and stone lodge, cabin, and condos perched beside a babbling, boulder-strewn creek. Some of the rooms have hot tubs and/or fireplaces. A historic old cabin holds the wonderful Old Piney Dell restaurant ($$–$$$), where the steaks, Wiener schnitzel, and Sunday brunch are especially popular. In summer the Kiva restaurant serves breakfast and lunch. ⊠*6380 U.S. 212 S., 5 mi south of Red Lodge, 59068* ☏*406/446–1111 or 800/667–1119* ☍*406/237–9851* ⊕*www.rockcreekresort.com* ⇌*38 rooms, 48 condos, 1 cabin* ♒*In-room: kitchen (some), dial-*

up. In-hotel: 2 restaurants, bar, tennis courts, pool, laundry facilities ☰*AE, D, DC, MC, V* ⊚*CP.*

$–$$ ⊠**Weatherson Inn B&B.** European antiques, collected during the owners' 10 years in Switzerland, fill the interior of this 1910 Victorian home, situated two blocks from the center of town. Rooms have private baths and one, a spa tub. Breakfast is served in the sun-filled breakfast room or on the deck. ✉*314 N. Broadway* ⊡*P.O. Box 2449, 59068* ☎*406/446–0213 or 886/806–2142* ⊕*www.weather soninn.com* ⇆*2 rooms* ☰*MC, V* ⊚*BP.*

WHERE TO CAMP

$ ⚠**Greenough Campground and Lake.** Pine trees, a small trout-stocked lake, and gentle hiking trails provide summer respite in Greenough, one of a dozen U.S. Forest Service campgrounds in the Red Lodge vicinity. ⚐*Vault toilets, drinking water, fire grates, picnic tables, fishing for kids in small shallow lake* ⇆*13 sites* ✉*10.5 mi south of Red Lodge on U.S. 212, then 1 mi west on Hwy. 421, 59068* ☎*406/4462103 Beartooth Ranger District Office, 877/444–6777 for campground reservations* ⊕*www.fs.fed. us/r1/custer or www.recreation.gov (for reservations)* ⚐*Reservations essential* ☰*AE, D, MC, V only if reservations made through National Reservation Service* ⊙*May–Sept.*

$$–$$$$ ⚠**Red Lodge KOA.** With its heated pool, playground, trout-filled brook, and access to Rock Creek for fishing, this tidy campground is ideal for families. Sites are along the banks of small creeks and among shady willows and pine trees. ⚐*Pool, laundry facilities, flush toilets, full hookups, partial hookups (water), drinking water, showers, fire grates, picnic tables, food service, electricity, public telephone, play area, public Wi-Fi* ⇆*13 full hookups, 35 partial hookups, 20 tent sites; 6 cabins* ☎*7464 U.S. 212, 4 mi north of Red Lodge, 59068* ☎*406/446–2364 (disconnected in winter) or 800/562–7540* ⊕*www.koa.com* ⚐*Reservations essential during July* ☰*AE, D, MC, V* ⊙*Mid-May–Sept.*

NIGHTLIFE & THE ARTS

NIGHTLIFE

You can sit back with a beer and watch the Bearcreek Downs' Pig Races at the **Bear Creek Saloon & Steakhouse** (✉*108 W. Main St., 7 mi east of Red Lodge on Hwy. 308, Bearcreek 59007* ☎*406/446–3481*). Oinkers in numbered jerseys streak around an outdoor oval while patrons bet on their favorites; proceeds fund local scholarships. The races take place summer evenings at 7, Thursday through Sunday; December through March the restaurant serves dinner Friday–Sunday, but no racing.

THE ARTS

★ Located in a 1889 train depot, the **Carbon County Arts Guild & Depot Gallery** (⊠*11 W. Eighth St., 59068* ☎*406/446–1370* ⊕*www.carboncountydepotgallery.org*) showcases paintings and sculptures by some 200 Western artists. The **Coleman Gallery and Studio** (⊠*223 S. Broadway, 59068* ☎*406/446–1228 or 800/726–2228* ⊕*www.colemangallery.biz*) features works by award-winning photographer Merv Coleman. Natural scenery and wildlife are his specialties. Internationally recognized painter Kevin Red Star, whose works draw on his Crow Indian heritage, displays his oils, acrylics, lithographs, and etchings at **Kevin Red Star Gallery** (⊠*1 N. Broadway, 59068* ☎*406/446–4646* ⊕*www.kevinredstar.com*). Red Star's works are in the permanent collections of the Smithsonian Institution, the Institute of American Indian Art, and the Pierre Cardin Collection in Paris. The **Red Lodge Clay Center** (⊠*123 S. Broadway, 59068* ☎*406/446–3993* ⊕*www.redlodgeclaycenter.com*) promotes local, regional, and national ceramic artists. Exhibits change monthly.

SHOPPING

You'll find high-end Western-style decor pieces, woven blankets and rugs, art, and jewelry at **Common Ground** (⊠*3 N. Broadway, 59068* ☎*406/446–2800* ⊕*www.comngrndartgallery.com*). Pick up a paper bag and fill it from the bushel baskets overflowing with what once was called "penny candy" at the **Montana Candy Emporium** (⊠*7 S. Broadway, 59068* ☎*406/446–1119*). At **Rocky Fork Juniper** (⊠*1123 S. Adams, 59068* ☎☎*406/446–1832* ⊕*www.rockyforkjuniper.com*), three local fellows handcraft rocking chairs and other furniture from fallen juniper gathered in the nearby foothills. From hiking accessories to cross-country-skiing gear and snowshoes, **Sylvan Peak Enterprises** (⊠*9 S. Broadway, 59068* ☎*406/446–1770 or 800/249–2563*) carries a large selection of top-quality mountain-country dry goods, locally made fleece jackets, hats, and kids' togs. Distinctive clothing, handmade jewelry, china, and gifts are just some of the offerings at **Twin Elk** (⊠*6382 U.S. 212,*

59068 ☎406/446–3121 or 877/894–6355), at the Rock Creek Resort.

EN ROUTE. **Driving south from Red Lodge along the 68-mi Beartooth Highway (U.S. 212) will take you over the precipitous 11,000-foot Beartooth Pass as the road winds its way through lush alpine country to the "back door" of Yellowstone National Park in Wyoming. With multiple steep climbs and switchbacks, this officially designated All American Road was a feat of 1930s engineering. The highway is usually open from mid-May to mid-October, but snow can close it at any time of the year. It's a good idea to fill the gas tank and cooler before you leave Red Lodge, because it's 64 mi to the next gas station at Cooke City, Montana. Several hiking trails lead off the highway; for hiking maps and more information, contact the Beartooth Ranger District (☎406/446–2103) in Red Lodge.**

LIVINGSTON & THE YELLOWSTONE RIVER

7

35 mi west of Big Timber via I–90; 116 mi west of Billings via I–90.

The stunning mountain backdrop to the town of Livingston was once Crow territory, and a chief called Arapooish said about it: "The Crow country is good country. The Great Spirit has put it in exactly the right place. When you are in it, you fare well; when you go out of it, you fare worse."

Livingston, along the banks of the beautiful Yellowstone River, was built to serve the railroad and the white settlers it brought. The railroad still runs through the town of 12,000, but now tourism and outdoor sports dominate the scene, and there are some 14 art galleries. Robert Redford chose the town, with its turn-of-the-20th-century flavor, to film parts of the movie *A River Runs Through It.*

Antique creels, fly rods, flies, and aquarium exhibits are among the displays at the Federation of Fly Fishers' **Fly Fishing Discovery Center,** housed in a former school. The museum–education center hosts year-round classes, such as the free summer casting lesson every Tuesday and Thursday evening from 5 to 7. ✉*215 E. Lewis St., 59047* ☎406/222–9369

⊕*www.fedflyfishers.org* ⊠*$3* ☉*June–Sept., Mon.–Sat. 10–6, Sun. noon–5; Oct.–May, weekdays 10–4.*

The old **Livingston Depot Center in the Northern Pacific Depot** served as the gateway to Yellowstone for the park's first 25 years. It is now a museum with displays on Western and railroad history. The 1902 depot, an Italian villa-style structure, has mosaic trim, a terrazzo floor, and wrought-iron ticket windows. ⊠*200 W. Park St., 59047* ☎*406/222–2300* ⊕*www.livingstonmuseums.org* ⊠*$3* ☉*Late-May–mid-Sept., Mon.–Sat. 9–5, Sun. 1–5.*

The **Yellowstone Gateway Museum,** on the north side of town in a turn-of-the-20th-century schoolhouse, holds an eclectic collection, including finds from a 10,000-year-old Native American dig site and a flag fragment associated with the Battle of the Little Bighorn. Outdoor displays include an old caboose, a sheep wagon, a stagecoach, and other pioneer memorabilia. ⊠*118 W. Chinook St., 59047* ☎*406/222–4184* ⊠*$4* ☉*Late May–early Sept., daily 8–5; rest of Sept., Tues.–Sat. noon–4.*

Just south of Livingston and north of Yellowstone National Park, the **Yellowstone River** comes roaring down the Yellowstone Plateau and flows through Paradise Valley. Primitive public campsites (available on a first-come, first-served basis; for information contact Montana Fish, Wildlife and Parks Department at ☎*406/247–2940*) and fishing access sites can be found at various places along the river, which is especially popular for trout fishing, rafting, and canoeing. With snowcapped peaks, soaring eagles, and an abundance of wildlife, a float on this section of the Yellowstone is a lifetime experience. U.S. 89 follows the west bank of the river, and East River Road runs along the east side.

Since the 1920s, cowboys and cowgirls have ridden and roped at the annual **Livingston Roundup Rodeo,** held at the Park County Fairgrounds. All members of the Professional Rodeo Cowboy Association (PRCA), participants descend on Livingston from around the U.S. A June 30 hoedown, a 3 PM July 2 parade, and a queen-selecting contest kick off the three-day rodeo. ⊠*46 View Vista Dr., 59047* ☎*406/222–0850 (Livingston Chamber)* ⊕*www.livingston-chamber.com* ⊠*$12* ☉*July 2–4, 8 PM nightly.*

Since the 1950s, the **Wilsall Rodeo** (⊠*U.S. 89 N, east on Clark St. past grain elevator to rodeo grounds, Wilsall, 59086* ☎*406/578–2371*) has been showcasing cowboy and cowgirl events in mid-June at this ranching community at the base of the Crazy Mountains 35 mi east of Livingston.

OFF THE BEATEN PATH. Paradise Valley Loop. A drive on this loop takes you along the spectacular Yellowstone River for a short way and then past historic churches, schoolhouses, hot springs, and expansive ranches, all backed by the peaks of the Absaroka-Beartooth Wilderness. From Livingston head 3 mi south on U.S. 89, turn east onto East River Road, and follow it over the Yellowstone River and for 32 mi through the tiny towns of Pine Creek, Pray, Chico, and Emigrant. You'll eventually hit U.S. 89 again, where roadside historic markers detail early inhabitants' lives; follow it north to Livingston. ☎*406/222–0850* ⊕*www. livingston-chamber.com.*

SPORTS & THE OUTDOORS

From the spring hatch of "Mother's Day" caddis flies through late-fall streamer fishing, the Yellowstone River and its tributary streams draw fly fishers from around the globe to the blue-ribbon streams for Yellowstone cutthroat, brown, and rainbow trout. Hiking trails lead into remote accesses of surrounding peaks, often snowcapped through June.

BOATING
With **River Source Outfitters** (⊠*5237 Hwy. 89, 59047* ☎*406/223–5134* ⊕*www.riversourcerafting.com*) you can take multiday canoe trips on the Yellowstone or Marias rivers, half- or full-day whitewater (class II and III rapids) rafting trips, or kayak lessons and tours. Canoe rentals and dogsledding are also offered. Boaters eager to explore the Yellowstone River will find a one-stop shop at **Rubber Ducky River Rentals** (⊠*15 Mt. Baldy Dr., 59047* ☎*406/222–3746* ⊕*www.riverservices.com*). Aside from guide and drop-off services, the store rents and sells boats and equipment, including its own line of rafts and kayaks. Guided rafting and kayaking trips down the Yellowstone, Gallatin, and Madison rivers are available from the **Yellowstone Raft Company** (⊠*406 Hwy. 89, Gardiner 59030* ☎*800/858–7781* ⊕*www.yellowstoneraft.com*). Be sure to make reservations for your trip in advance.

FISHING
George Anderson's Yellowstone Angler (⊠*5256 U.S. 89 S, 59047* ☎*406/222–7130* ⊕*www.yellowstoneangler.com*)

specializes in catch-and-release fly-fishing float trips on the Yellowstone River, wade trips on spring creeks, access to private lakes and streams, and fly-casting instruction.

The fishing experts at **Dan Bailey's Fly Shop** (⊠*209 W. Park St., 59047* ☏*406/2221673 or 800/356–4052* ⊕*www. dan-bailey.com*) can help you find the right fly, tackle, and outdoor clothing. Rental equipment, fly-fishing clinics, and float and wade trips are also available at this world-renowned shop.

HORSEBACK RIDING

Bear Paw Outfitters (⊠*136 Deep Creek Rd., 59047* ☏*406/222–6642 or 406/222–5800*) runs day rides and pack trips in Paradise Valley, the Absaroka-Beartooth Wilderness, and Yellowstone National Park; prices start at $30 per hour aboard horses or mules.

WHERE TO EAT

$–$$$ ✕**Montana's Rib & Chop House.** Here, in the middle of cattle country, you can expect the juiciest, tenderest steaks—such as the flavorful hand-cut rib eye—all made from certified Angus beef. Jambalaya, baby back ribs, and catfish are also on the menu. ⊠*305 E. Park St., 59047* ☏*406/222–9200* ▬*AE, D, MC, V.*

¢–$ ✕**Paradise Valley Pop Stand & Grill.** You can dine in or order takeout from this 1950s-style burger and ice-cream joint. The ice cream is made locally. ⊠*5060 U.S. 89, 2 mi south of Livingston, 59047* ☏*406/222–2006* ▬*MC, V* ☉*Daily.*

WHERE TO STAY

$$$$ ▦**63 Ranch.** Owned by the same family since 1929, this 2,000-acre working cattle ranch is one of Montana's oldest dude ranches. Only weeklong packages are available, and they include a full range of activities, from horseback riding to fishing to helping check or move cattle. The rustic cabins are commodious yet comfortable, with log furniture and private baths. ⊠*Off Bruffey La., 12 mi southeast of Livingston;* ⌂*Box 979, 59047* ☏*406/222–0570* ☒*406/222–6363* ⊕*www.sixtythree.com* ⇜*12 cabins* ⚷*In-room: no a/c, no phone, no TV. In-hotel: no elevator, laundry facilities* ▬*No credit cards* ☉*Closed mid-Sept.– mid-June* †⊙*FAP.*

$$$$ ⚑B Bar Ranch. In winter, this 9,000-acre working cattle
★ ranch invites guests for spectacular winter adventures in
cross-country skiing and wildlife tracking. The ranch shares
a 6-mi boundary with Yellowstone National Park, in Tom
Miner Basin, 36 mi south of Livingston. Some of the 18.6
mi of impeccably groomed trails are created by rare Suf-
folk Punch draft horses from the country's largest herd,
which lives here on the B Bar. Sleigh rides and naturalist-
led trips into Yellowstone are some of the activities. Rates
include meals and activities, and there's a two-night minimum stay. ✉*818 Tom Miner Creek Rd., Emigrant 59027*
📞*406/848–7729* 📠*406/848–7793* 🌐*www.bbar.com* 🛏*6*
cabins, 3 lodge rooms ⚬*In-room: no a/c, no phone, no TV.*
In-hotel: no elevator ═*MC, V* ⊘*mid-Dec.–Feb.* ❍*FAP.*

$$$$ ⚑Mountain Sky Guest Ranch. This full-service guest-ranch
resort in the middle of scenic Paradise Valley and 30 mi
north of Yellowstone National Park is a family favorite.
The cabins feel luxurious after a day in the saddle. The
children's programs offer age-appropriate activities such as
hiking, swimming, crafts, hayrides, campfires, and a talent
show. Dinners range from Western barbecue to gourmet
treats such as grilled lamb loin topped with fig-and-port-
wine glaze. Everyone learns to dance the two-step to a
local band. There's a seven-night minimum stay in summer only. ✉*Big Creek Rd.; U.S. 89 S, then west 4.5 mi on*
Big Creek Rd., Emigrant 59027 ✉*Box 1219, Bozeman*
59715 📞*406/333–4911 or 800/548–3392* 📠*406/333–*
4537 🌐*www.mtnsky.com* 🛏*30 cabins* ⚬*In-room: no a/c,*
no phone, refrigerator, no TV. In-hotel: bar, tennis court,
pool, no elevator, children's programs (ages 1–18), laundry
facilities, airport shuttle, public Internet ═*MC, V* ❍*FAP.*

¢–$$ ⚑Chico Hot Springs Resort & Day Spa. During the gold rush
★ of the 1860s, a miner noted that he "washed [his] dirty
duds" in the hot-springs water near the Yellowstone River.
Soon, a series of bathhouses sprang up, attracting people
to the medicinal waters. The Chico Warm Springs Hotel
opened in 1900, drawing famous folks such as painter
Charlie Russell (1864–1926) to the 96°F–103°F pools. The
hotel is surrounded by two large outdoor soak pools, a
convention center, and upscale cottages that open to views
of 10,920-foot Emigrant Peak and the Absaroka-Beartooth
Wilderness beyond. The dining room ($$$) is considered
among the region's best for quality of food, presentation,
and service. Pine nut–encrusted halibut with fruit salsa and
Gorgonzola filet mignon are among the biggest draws. ✉*1*

7

Old Chico Rd., Pray 59065 ☎*406/333–4933 or 800/468–9232* 🖨*406/333–4694* ⊕*www.chicohotsprings.com* ⤶*82 rooms, 4 suites, 16 cottages* ♿*In-room: no a/c (some), kitchen (some), refrigerator (some), no TV, dial-up. In-hotel: restaurant, room service, bar, pool, spa, no elevator, some pets allowed* ☰*AE, D, MC, V.*

$ 🏨 **The Murray Hotel.** Even cowboys love soft pillows, which is why they come to this 1904 town centerpiece, whose floors have seen silver-tipped cowboy boots, fly-fishing waders, and the sparkling heels of Hollywood celebrities. Antiques reflect a different theme in each guest room. Ask to see the third-floor suite that film director Sam Peckinpah once called home. Historic photos, a player piano, and stuffed game animals decorate the lobby and surround the antique elevator, which is still in use. ⊠*201 W. Park St., 59047* ☎*406/222–1350* 🖨*406/222–2752* ⊕*www.murray-hotel.com* ⤶*30 rooms* ♿*In-room: dial-up. In-hotel: bar* ☰*AE, D, MC, V.*

WHERE TO CAMP

$$–$$$$ ⛺ **Paradise Valley/Livingston KOA.** Set among willows, cottonwoods, and small evergreens, this full-service campground is well situated along the banks of the Yellowstone River, 40 mi north of Yellowstone National Park. It's popular with families, who enjoy the heated pool. To reach the campground, go 10 mi south of Livingston on U.S. 89, then 0.5 mi east on Pine Creek Rd. It's a good idea to reserve ahead. ♿*Laundry facilities, flush toilets, full hookups, dump station, drinking water, showers, fire grates, picnic tables, electricity, public telephone, general store, swimming (indoor pool)* ⤶*82 RV sites, 27 tent sites, 22 cabins, 2 cottages* ⊠*163 Pine Creek Rd., 59047* ☎*406/222–0992 or 800/562–2805* ⊕*www.livingstonkoa.com* ☰*D, MC, V* ☉*May–mid-Oct.*

$ ⛺ **Pine Creek Campground.** A thick growth of pine trees surrounds this Paradise Valley campground at the base of the mountains. It's near the trailhead for challenging hikes to Pine Creek Waterfalls and the Absaroka-Beartooth Wilderness. ♿*Toilets, drinking water, fire pits, picnic tables, playground, live music on weekends* ⤶*26 sites* ⊠*9 mi south of Livingston on U.S. 89, then 2.5 mi east on Pine Creek Rd., 59047* ☎*406/222–1892 or 877/444–6777 (latter is National Reservation Service)* ⊕*www.fs.fed.us/r1/gallatin* ☰*AE, MC, V (cards through National Reservation Service only)* ☉*Late May–early Sept.*

NIGHTLIFE & THE ARTS

NIGHTLIFE

With dancing and country music, microbrews, video poker, and keno, the **Buffalo Jump Steakhouse & Saloon** (⊠*5237 U.S. 89 S, 59047* ☎*406/222–2987*) has livened up many a Saturday night in Livingston. Locals voted the jukebox at the **Murray Bar** the best in town and its staff the friendliest. There's live music most weekends. (⊠*201 W. Park St., 59047* ☎*406/222–6433* ⊕*www.themurraybar.com*). Friday and Saturday evenings June through August, the **Pine Creek Cafe** (⊠*2496 East River Rd., 59047* ☎*406/222–3628*) serves up live bluegrass music, barbecue burgers, and beer under the stars. The fun starts at 7.

THE ARTS

★ Livingston's beauty has inspired artists, as evidenced by the many fine art galleries in town. The **Danforth Gallery** (⊠*106 N. Main St., 59047* ☎*406/222–6510*) is a community art center that displays and sells paintings, sculptures, and jewelry by local and regional artists. Subtle, moody images by renowned artist Russell Chatham line the walls of **Chatham Fine Art** (⊠*120 N. Main St., 59047* ☎*406/222–1566* ⊕*www.russellchatham.com*). Works on display include oils, lithographs, drawings, and posters.

Visions West Gallery (⊠*108 S. Main St., 59047* ☎*406/222–0337* ⊕*www.visionswestgallery.com*) specializes in contemporary Western and wildlife art, including numerous works on the fly-fishing theme, from paintings and bronzes to hand-carved flies.

The historic district's **Blue Slipper Theatre** (⊠*113 E. Callender St., 59047* ☎*406/222–7720*) presents various full-length productions, including one-act plays, popular melodramas, and an annual Christmas variety show. The **Firehouse 5 Playhouse** (⊠*Sleeping Giant Trade Center, 5237 U.S. 89 S59047* ☎*406/222–1420*) stages comedies, dramas, and musicals year-round.

SHOPPING

★ At **The Cowboy Connection** (⊠*110 S. Main St., 59047* ☎*406/222–0272*), you'll find two rooms filled with pre-1940 Western boots, art, photos, spurs, holsters, even the occasional bullet-riddled hat. For contemporary Western and Native American items, such as fringed jackets and skirts, and rattlesnake earrings, visit **Gil's Indian Trading Post**

(✉207 W. Park St., 59047 ☎406/222–0112). The floorboards creak as you walk through **Sax and Fryer** (✉109 W. Callender St., 59047 ☎406/222–1421), an old-time bookstore specializing in Western literature, especially books by Montana authors. It's the oldest store in Livingston.

In addition to selling outdoor clothing, boots, and bicycles, **Timber Trails** (✉309 W. Park St., 59047 ☎406/222–9550) helps mountain bikers, hikers, and cross-country skiers with trail maps, directions, and friendly advice.

CODY

84 mi northwest of Thermopolis via Hwy. 120; 52 mi east of Yellowstone via U.S. 14/16/20.

Cody, founded in 1896 and named for Pony Express rider, army scout, Freemason, and entertainer William F. "Buffalo Bill" Cody, is the eastern gateway community for Yellowstone National Park. The North Fork Highway—as the route leading east to Yellowstone is locally known—follows the North Fork of the Shoshone River past barren rock formations strewn with tumbleweeds, then enters lush forests and green meadows as the elevation increases roughly 3,000 feet in 70 mi. Cody is within easy reach of Shoshone National Forest, the Absaroka Range, the Washakie Wilderness, and the Buffalo Bill Reservoir.

But Cody is much more than a base for exploring the surrounding area. Several excellent museums make up the outstanding Buffalo Bill Historical Center, and the Western lifestyle is alive and well on dude ranches and in both trendy and classic shops. Part of the fun in Cody is sauntering down Main Street, stopping by the Irma Hotel (built by Buffalo Bill and named for his daughter) for some refreshment, and attending the nightly rodeo.

Pick up a brochure ($1 donation) with a self-guided walking tour of the town's historic sites at the Chamber of Commerce on Sheridan Avenue.

The **Wyoming Vietnam Veterans Memorial** is a small-scale version of the Vietnam Veterans Memorial wall in Washington, D.C. The Cody memorial recognizes the Wyoming residents who died during the conflict. ✉U.S. 14/16/20, east of Cody.

The **Cody Mural,** at the Church of Jesus Christ of Latter-day Saints, is an artistic interpretation of Mormon settlement in the West. Edward Grigware painted the scene on the domed ceiling in the 1950s. ✉ *1010 Angler Ave.* ☎ *307/587–3290 or 307/587–9258* ⚑ *Free* ☉ *June–mid-Sept., Mon.–Sat. 8–8, Sun. 3–8.*

☼ On the west side of Cody are some of the finest museums anywhere and true jewels of the West: the **Buffalo Bill Historical Center,** which houses five museums in one. The **Buffalo Bill Cody Museum** is dedicated to the incredible life of William F. "Buffalo Bill" Cody. Shortly after Cody's death, some of his friends took mementos of the famous scout and Wild West showman and opened the Buffalo Bill Museum in a small log building. The museum has since been moved to the historical center and includes films, huge posters from the original Wild West shows, illustrated books as well as personal effects such as clothing, guns, saddles, and furniture. The **Cody Firearms Museum** traces the history of firearms through thousands of models on display, from European blunderbusses to Gatling guns and modern firearms. Included are examples of Winchester and Browning arms, as well as a model of an arms-manufacturing plant. There are also the 1881 Navy revolvers belonging to Cody's friend James "Wild Bill" Hickok. Legend has it that Hickok's revolvers had to be sold after his death, following a lethal card game in Deadwood, to bury him. At the time of his death, Hickok was holding a pair of black aces and a pair of eights–since known as a "Dead Man's Hand." Through exhibits, outdoor activities, tours, and seminars, the **Draper Museum of Natural History** explores the Yellowstone ecosystem. There are children's discovery areas in addition to life-size animal mounts. Recordings play the sounds of wolves, grizzly bears, birds, and other animals that make their home in the Yellowstone area. At the **Plains Indian Museum,** interactive exhibits and life-size dioramas explore the history and culture of the Lakota, Blackfeet, Cheyenne, Shoshone, and Nez Perce tribes. Among the exhibits are rare medicine pipes, clothing, and an earth-house interpretive area. The **Whitney Gallery of Western Art** is devoted to the West's greatest artists. On display are works by such masters as Frederic Remington, Charles M. Russell, Albert Bierstadt, George Catlin, and Thomas Moran, plus contemporary artists such as Harry Jackson, James Bama, and Peter Fillerup. ✉ *720 Sheridan Ave.* ☎ *307/587–4771* ⊕ *www.bbhc.org* ⚑ *$15 (2 days)* ☉ *Apr.,*

7

daily 10–5; May, daily 8–8; June–mid-Sept., daily 8 AM*–8* PM*; mid-Sept.–Oct., daily 8–5; Nov.–Dec. 10–3, Jan.–Mar., daily 10–3, closed Mon.*

Cody Nite Rodeo, more dusty and intimate than big rodeos such as Cheyenne Frontier Days, offers children's events, such as goat roping, in addition to the regular adult events. Contact the Cody Chamber of Commerce for more information. ⊠ *West Cody Strip* ☎ *800/207–0744* ⊕ *www.codyniterodeo.com* ⤳ *$20–$8; seat prices vary with location* ☉ *June–Aug., daily at 8:30* PM.

Summer evenings, the **Cody Gunslingers Shootout** takes place on the porch at the Irma Hotel. ⊠ *1192 Sheridan Ave.* ☎ *307/587–4221* ⤳ *Free* ☉ *June–late Sept., daily at 6* PM.

If you give the folks at **Cody Trolley Tours** an hour of your time, they'll take you on a journey through 100 years of Cody history. The tour takes in historic sites, scenery, geology, and wildlife attractions. A combination ticket also grants you admission to the Buffalo Bill Historical Center. ⊠ *Ticket booth in front of Irma Hotel, 1192 Sheridan Ave.* ☎ *307/527–7043* ⊕ *www.codytrolleytours.com* ⤳ *Tour ticket $20, combination ticket with Buffalo Bill Historical Center $30* ☉ *Early June–Sept., Mon.–Sat. at 9, 11, 1, 3, and 6:30; Sun. at 9, 11, 1, and 3.*

Dioramas at **Tecumseh's Wyoming Territory Old West Miniature Village and Museum** depict early-Wyoming and Native American history and Western events. The gift shop sells deerskin clothing handmade on the premises. ⊠ *142 W. Yellowstone Hwy.* ☎ *307/587–5362* ⤳ *$3 adults; $1 children; $10 max per family* ☉ *mid-May–mid-Sept., daily 8–8; rest of yr by appointment.*

On Cody's western outskirts, off the West Yellowstone Highway, is **Old Trail Town,** a collection of historic buildings from Wyoming's frontier days. Also here are a cemetery for famous local mountain men and Native American and pioneer artifacts. The buildings aren't fancy and the displays are rustic, so you really get a feel for an Old West town. Sometimes in summer Bobby Bridger, great-grandnephew of mountain man Jim Bridger, performs his "Ballad of the West" ($12) in the barn here. The three-night program describes the settlement of the West and includes stories of mountain men, Buffalo Bill Cody, and the Lakota. ⊠ *1831 Demaris Dr.* ☎ *307/587–5302* ⤳ *$6 adults; $2 children* ☉ *mid-May–mid-Sept., daily 8–8.*

Fishing and boating on the Buffalo Bill Reservoir are popular activities at **Buffalo Bill State Park,** west of Cody. A visitor center here focuses on the history of the reservoir, which was completed in 1910. ✉*47 Lakeside Rd., west of Cody on U.S. 24/26/20; then State Route 291* ☎*307/587–9227* ⊕*wyoparks.state.wy.us* ✑*Park $4, camping $12* ⊙*Park daily 24 hrs, visitor center May–Sept., daily 8–8.*

The **Shoshone National Forest** was the country's first national forest, established in 1891. You can hike, fish, mountain bike, and ride horses in warmer weather, and snowmobile and cross-country ski in winter. There are picnic areas and campgrounds. ✉*U.S. 14/16/20, west of Cody* ☎*307/527–6241* ⊕*www.fs.fed.us/r2/shoshone* ✑*Free* ⊙*Daily 24 hrs.*

OFF THE BEATEN PATH. **Chief Joseph Scenic Byway.** In 1877, a few members of the Nez Perce tribe killed some white settlers in Idaho as retribution for earlier killings by whites. Fearing that the U.S. Army would punish the guilty and innocent alike, hundreds of Nez Perce fled on a five-month journey toward Canada that came to be known as the Nez Perce Trail. Along the way they passed through what is now Yellowstone National Park, across the Sunlight Basin area north of Cody, and along the Clarks Fork of the Shoshone River before turning north into Montana. To see the rugged mountain area they traveled through, follow Highway 120 north 17 mi to Highway 296, the Chief Joseph Scenic Byway. The byway eventually leads to Cooke City and Red Lodge, Montana. Along the way you'll see open meadows, pine forests, and a sweeping vista of the region from the top of Dead Indian Pass.

SPORTS & THE OUTDOORS

CANOEING, KAYAKING & RAFTING

To get out on the Shoshone River, charter a guided trip. In Cody it's not possible to rent equipment for unguided trips.

Family river trips on the Shoshone River are offered by **River Runners** (✉*1491 Sheridan Ave.* ☎*307/527–7238*). **Wyoming River Trips** (✉*Buffalo Bill Village, 1701 Sheridan Ave.* ☎*307/587–6661 or 800/586–6661*) arranges Shoshone River trips.

FISHING

The fish are big at the private **Monster Lake** (☎800/840–5137), filled with rainbow, brook, and brown trout weighing up to 10 pounds. For a fee you can fish all or part of the day at this lake on the east side of town; accommodations are available as well.

You can buy fishing tackle, get information on fishing in the area, or take a guided half- or full-day trip with **Tim Wade's North Fork Anglers** (✉1107 *Sheridan Ave.* ☎307/527–7274 ⊕*northforkanglers.com*)

GOLF

Olive Glenn Golf and Country Club (✉*802 Meadow La.* ☎*307/587–5551 or 307/587–5308*) is a highly rated 18-hole course open to the public; a Jacuzzi, pool, and two tennis courts are also here.

HORSEBACK RIDING

Ride for one to four hours or all day with **Cedar Mountain Trail Rides** (✉*U.S. 14/16/20, 1 mi west of rodeo grounds* ☎307/527–4966). You can ride horses into Shoshone National Forest with **Goff Creek Lodge** (✉*995 E. Yellowstone Hwy.* ☎*307/587–3753 or 800/859–3985* ⊕*goffcreek.com*); lunch rides are also available.

SKIING

In the Wood River valley near Meeteetse, 32 mi south of Cody, **Wood River Ski Touring Park** (✉*1010 Park Ave.* ☎307/868–2603) has 32 km (20 mi) of cross-country trails.

WHERE TO EAT

$–$$$ ✕**Maxwell's.** A turn-of-the-20th-century Victorian structure with huge windows and a porch houses this upscale contemporary restaurant that serves free-range beef entrées, homemade soups, pastas, and sandwiches. The baby back pork ribs are always a good bet, and the Mediterranean pizza with Greek olives, feta cheese, and fresh tomatoes is also a good, very filling choice. In summer there's outdoor dining on the deck. ✉*937 Sheridan Ave.* ☎307/527–7749 🖃AE, D, MC, V.

$–$$ ✕**Proud Cut Saloon.** At this popular downtown eatery and watering hole, owner Del Nose serves what locals call "kick-ass cowboy cuisine": butterfly steaks, prime rib, shrimp, fish, and chicken. Western paintings, vintage photographs of Cody country, and large game mounts decorate the place. ⊠*1227 Sheridan Ave.* ☎*307/527–6905* ▬*D, MC, V.*

¢–$$ ✕**Granny's.** This family-style diner has a kids and senior ☺ menu and is popular with locals and old-timers, serving good coffee, omelets, biscuits with gravy, patty melts, hot sandwiches, fried chicken, soups and salads. ⊠*1550 Sheridan Ave.* ☎*307/587–4829* ▬*MC, V.*

¢–$$ ✕**La Comida.** Making no claim to authentic Mexican cooking, this restaurant nevertheless receives praise for its "Cody-Mex" cuisine. You may order enchiladas, burritos, tacos, and chiles rellenos, but they won't be as spicy as similar foods would be in the Southwest. Mexican wall hangings contribute to the festive atmosphere. ⊠*1385 Sheridan Ave.* ☎*307/587–9556* ▬*AE, D, DC, MC, V.*

WHERE TO STAY

$$$$ ☷**Rimrock Dude Ranch.** Dating to 1956, this is one of the oldest guest ranches on the North Fork of the Shoshone River. Rimrock offers both summer and winter accommodations and activities, from horseback riding in the surrounding mountain country to snowmobile trips in Yellowstone National Park. Lodging is in one- and two-bedroom cabins. There's a one-week minimum stay. ⊠*2728 North Fork Rte., 82414* ☎*307/587–3970 or 800/208–7468* ⬚*307/527–5014* ⊕*www.rimrockranch.com* ↵*9 cabins* ☉*May–Sept.* ⚫*In-room: no a/c, refrigerator, no TV. In-hotel: pool, airport shuttle, no-smoking rooms* ▬*MC, V* ⦿*FAP.*

$$$$ ☷**UXU Ranch.** One of the cabins at the UXU guest ranch ☺ is a historic late-19th-century stage stop moved to the site and decorated with Molesworth-style furnishings made by New West of Cody; other cabins here date to the 1960s or 1920s. The ranch, along the North Fork of the Shoshone River, offers outstanding horseback riding, pack trips into the nearby mountains, and the opportunity to really get away from it all. There's a minimum one-week stay. Open year round, inquire about winter rates. No pets. ⊠*1710 North Fork Hwy., Wapiti 82450* ☎*800/373–9027* ⬚*307/587–8307* ⊕*www.uxuranch.com* ↵*11 cabins* ⚫*In-room: no a/c, no phone. In-hotel: bar, children's programs (ages 6 and up), no-smoking rooms* ▬*MC, V* ⦿*FAP.*

$–$$$$ ☷**Cody Guest Houses.** You have several house-rental options ★ here, from a Victorian guest house with lace curtains and antique furnishings to a four-bedroom lodge with a fire-place. The 10 different guest houses have one to four bed-rooms, and all of them have been lovingly restored and elegantly decorated. These houses are meant to make you feel truly at home, so you'll find refrigerators, full kitchens, outdoor barbecue grills, and children's play areas at most of them. ⊠*1525 Beck Ave., 82414* ☎*307/587–6000 or 800/587–6560* 🖷*307/587–8048* ⊕*www.codyguesthouses. com* ➾*10 houses* ⌂*In-room: no a/c (some), kitchen, no TV (some). In-hotel: laundry facilities, no-smoking rooms* ☰*AE, D, MC, V.*

$–$$$ 🖭**Best Western Sunset Motor Inn.** This inn sits on a large grassy property with shade trees and has an enclosed play area for children. Numerous amenities, clean rooms, and a quiet and relaxed atmosphere make this a favorite with families. It's a block from the Buffalo Bill Historical Center. ⊠*1601 8th St., 82414* ☎*307/587–4265 or 800/624–2727* ⊕*www.bestwestern.com* ➾*120 rooms, 5 suites* ⌂*In-hotel: restaurant, pool, gym, spa, laundry facilities, Wi-fi, some pets allowed, no-smoking rooms* ☰*AE, D, DC, MC, V.*

$–$$ 🖭**Buffalo Bill Village.** This downtown development com-prises three lodgings, which share many facilities. The Buf-falo Bill Village Resort consists of log cabins with modern interiors, and the Holiday Inn Convention Center and the Comfort Inn are typical chain hotels. The downtown shop-ping district begins one block to the west, and there's also a grocery store a block away. ⊠*1701 Sheridan Ave., 82414* ☎*307/587–5544 or 800/527–5544* ⊕*www.blairhotels. com* ➾*Buffalo Bill Village Resort 83 cabins; Comfort Inn 74 rooms; Holiday Inn 188 rooms* ⌂*In-hotel: restaurant, bar, pool, gym, airport shuttle, no-smoking rooms* ☰*AE, D, DC, MC, V.*

$–$$ 🖭**Irma Hotel.** This 106-year-old Victorian hotel named for
★ Buffalo Bill's daughter retains some frontier charm and rough edges, with period furniture, pull-chain commodes in many rooms, a large restaurant and an elaborate cher-rywood bar. For those looking for modern amenities and trappings, this probably isn't it. But if you want true history, be sure to stay in one of the 15 rooms of the original 1902 hotel named after local legends and not in the annex, which has standard hotel-style contemporary rooms. In summer, locals stage a gunfight on the porch Tuesday–Saturday at 6 PM. ⊠*1192 Sheridan Ave., 82414* ☎*307/587–4221 or 800/745–4762* 🖷*307/587–1775* ⊕*www.irmahotel.com*

🛏40 rooms ♿In-hotel: restaurant, bar, no-smoking rooms. ⊟AE, D, DC, MC, V.

$-$$ 🏨**Lockhart Inn.** The former home of Cody author Caroline Lockhart, this inn has rooms named after her characters and books. Western antiques decorate the rooms, many of which have claw-foot tubs. It's on the main western strip of Cody, which is convenient to area attractions. ✉109 W. Yellowstone Ave., 82414 ☎307/587–6074 or 877/377–7255 ⊕stayincody.com/lockhartinn1.htm 🛏7 rooms ♿In-hotel: no-smoking rooms, no elevator. ⊟D, MC, V ⊚BP.

$-$$ 🏨**Yellowstone Valley Inn.** Located 16 mi west of Cody and 30 mi east of Yellowstone National Park's east entrance, this sprawling and peaceful property offers basic accommodations in a mountain setting. Rooms are in the motel or duplex cabins, and campsites are available. ✉3324 Northfolk Hwy., 82414 ☎307/587–3961 or 877/587–3961 🖷307/587–4656 ⊕www.yellowstonevalleyinn.com 🛏15 motel rooms, 20 cabin rooms ♿In-room: no phone. In-hotel: restaurant, bar, hot tub, pool, laundry facilities, some pets allowed, no-smoking rooms, no elevator ⊟AE, D, MC, V.

WHERE TO CAMP

There are 31 campgrounds within **Shoshone National Forest** (☎307/527–6241 ⊕www.fs.fed.us/r2/shoshone); some have only limited services, and others have hookups and campground hosts.

$$$-$$$$ ⛺**Cody KOA.** This campground on the southeast side of town serves free pancake breakfasts. There's also a free shuttle to the Cody Nite Rodeo, and you can arrange to take a horseback ride. ♿Flush toilets, full hookups, partial hookups (electric and water), drinking water, guest laundry, showers, picnic tables, general store, swimming pool, sand volleyball pit 🛏78 tent sites, 68 full hookups, 54 partial hookups, 21 cabins, 1 cottage ✉5561 U.S. 20 (Greybull Hwy.) ☎800/562–8507 🖷307/587–2369 ⊕www.codykoa.com ⊟AE, D, DC, MC, V ⊙May–Oct.

¢ ⛺**Dead Indian Campground.** You can fish in the stream at this tent campground adjacent to the Chief Joseph Scenic Byway (Highway 296). There are hiking and horseback-riding trails, plus nearby corrals for horses. ♿Pit toilets, drinking water, bear boxes, fire grates, picnic tables, swimming (creek) 🛏12 sites ✉17 mi north of Cody on Hwy. 120, 17 mi to WY 296, then 25 mi northwest on Hwy.

7

296 ☎307/527–6241 ⊕www.fs.fed.us/r2/shoshone ⊟No credit cards ⊙May–Oct.

¢ ⛺**Deer Creek Campground.** At the head of the South Fork of the Shoshone River, this small, tree-shaded campground for tents provides hiking access to the Absaroka Range and the Washakie Wilderness. ⚐Pit toilets, drinking water, fire pits, picnic tables ☞7 sites ✉47 mi west of Cody on South Fork Hwy. (Hwy. 291) ☎307/527–6241 ⊕www.fs.fed.us/r2/shoshone ⊙May–Oct.

$$–$$$$ ⛺**Ponderosa Campground.** Within walking distance (three blocks) of the Buffalo Bill Historical Center, this is a large facility with separate areas for tents and RVs. You can even stay in a teepee or pitch your own tent or teepee in a primitive camping area (without any nearby facilities) known as the OK Corral in the canyon above the Shoshone River. ⚐Flush toilets, full hookups, dump station, drinking water, guest laundry, showers, picnic tables, public telephone, Wi-Fi, general store, play area, cable TV. ☞137 full hookups, 50 tent sites; 8 teepees ✉1815 8th St. ☎307/587–9203 ⊟No credit cards ⊙Mid-Apr.–mid-Oct.

NIGHTLIFE & THE ARTS

NIGHTLIFE

A trip to Cody isn't complete without a chance to scoot your boots to live music, usually provided by the local band West, at **Cassie's Supper Club and Dance Hall** (✉214 Yellowstone Ave. ☎307/527–5500). The tunes are a mix of classic country, the band's Western originals, and today's hits.

THE ARTS

Impromptu jam sessions, nightly concerts, and a symposium of educational and entertaining events related to cowboy music are all part of the **Cowboy Songs and Range Ballads** (☎307/587–4771 ⊕www.bbhc.org). In addition to classic range ballads there's original music by performers from across the West. Events are held over the course of a few days in early April at the Buffalo Bill Historical Center and other venues.

⊙ The two-day **Plains Indian Powwow** (✉720 Sheridan Ave. ☎307/587–4771 ⊕www.bbhc.org), in late June, brings together hoop dancers, traditional dancers, and jingle dancers from various tribes. The performances take place at the Buffalo Bill Historical Center.

Sculptures and paintings by such artists as James Bama, Chris Navarro, Frank McCarthy and Howard Post are displayed at **Big Horn Galleries** (⌧*1167 Sheridan Ave.* ☎*307/527–7587*). **Simpson Gallagher Gallery** (⌧*1161 Sheridan Ave.* ☎*307/587–4022*) showcases and sells contemporary representational art by Harry Jackson, Margery Torrey, and Julie Oriet.

SHOPPING

★ Sheridan Avenue, Cody's main drag, is a great place to browse and shop among its many Native American and Western-themed shops. Most carry high-quality goods, but for those desiring the real McCoy beware of those items claiming to be true in Native American handcraft or from local tribes. While judging an item's authenticity, be sure to determine whether it's made from natural or artificial materials. Head to the **Custom Cowboy Shop** (⌧*1286 Sheridan Ave.* ☎*800/487–2692*) to stock up on top-quality cowboy gear and clothing, ranging from hats and vests for men to women's shirts and jackets; there's even gear for your horse here. Also available are CDs by top Western recording artists such as Ian Tyson, Don Edwards, and Michael Martin Murphey.

★ **Indian Territory** (⌧*1212 Sheridan Ave.* ☎*307/527–5522*) lacking the variety of its imitators, is a small shop selling a high-percentage of handmade Arapaho, Shoshone, Aztec jewelry, wall art, shadowboxes, clothing, hair shirts, dream catchers, walking sticks, headdresses, and much more. **Flight West** (⌧*1155 Sheridan Ave.* ☎*307/527–7800*) sells designer Western women's wear, leather goods for men and women, books, gifts, and jewelry. Women shop at the **Plush Pony** (⌧*1350 Sheridan Ave.* ☎*307/587–4677*) for "uptown Western clothes" ranging from leather belts to stylish skirts, jackets, and dresses. The **Wyoming Buffalo Company** (⌧*1270 Sheridan Ave.* ☎*307/587–8708 or 800/453–0636*) sells buffalo-meat products, such as sausage and jerky, in addition to specialty foods such as huckleberry honey.

JACKSON

Most visitors to northwest Wyoming come to Jackson, which remains a small but booming Western town that's "howdy" in the daytime and hopping in the evening. For active types, it's a good place to stock up on supplies before heading for outdoor adventures in Grand Teton National Park, Yellowstone, and the surrounding Jackson Hole area. It's also a great place to kick back and rest your feet awhile while taking in the wealth of galleries, Western-wear shops, varied cuisines, a new $35-million arts center and active nightlife centering on bars and music.

Unfortunately, Jackson's charm and popularity have put it at risk. On busy summer days, traffic often slows to a crawl on the highway that doglegs through downtown. Proposals for new motels and condominiums sprout like the purple asters in the spring, as developers vie for a share of the upscale vacation market. Old-timers suggest that the town—in fact, the entire Jackson Hole—has already lost some of its dusty charm from when horses stood at hitching rails around Town Square. However, with national parks and forests and state lands occupying some of the most beautiful real estate in the country, there's 3% to 4% in unprotected ground on which to build. These limitations, along with the cautious approach of locals, may yet keep Jackson on a human scale.

EXPLORING JACKSON

The best way to explore Jackson's downtown, which is centered on vibrant Town Square, is on foot, since parking can be a challenge during the busy summer months. To go beyond downtown—the National Wildlife Art Museum or National Elk Refuge, for example—you'll need to hop into your car.

WHAT TO SEE

❷ **Jackson Hole Historical Society.** Displays at this log cabin illuminate local history. In addition to historic artifacts and photographs, the society houses manuscripts, maps, and an oral-history collection. ⊠ *105 Mercill Ave.* ☎ *307/733–9605* ⊕ *www.jacksonholehistory.org.*

❸ **Jackson Hole Museum.** For some local history, visit this museum, where you can get acquainted with the early settlers and find out how Dead Man's Bar got its name. You'll also learn how Jackson elected the first all-female town government, not to mention a lady sheriff who claimed to have killed three men before hanging up her spurs. Kids can try on vintage clothes and hats and see what they'd look like as homesteaders. Among the exhibits are Native

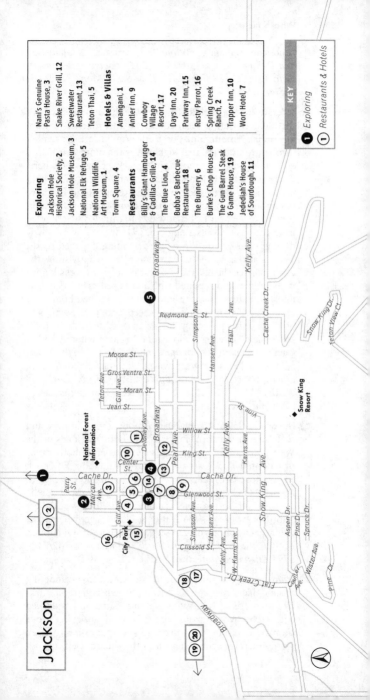

Jackson

KEY

- ◆ Exploring
- ① Restaurants & Hotels

Exploring

Jackson Hole Historical Society, **2**
Jackson Hole Museum, **3**
National Elk Refuge, **5**
National Wildlife Art Museum, **1**
Town Square, **4**

Restaurants

Billy's Giant Hamburger & Cadillac Grille, **14**
The Blue Lion, **4**
Bubba's Barbecue Restaurant, **18**
The Bunnery, **6**
Burke's Chop House, **8**
The Gun Barrel Steak & Game House, **19**
Jedediah's House of Sourdough, **11**
Nani's Genuine Pasta House, **3**
Snake River Grill, **12**
Sweetwater Restaurant, **13**
Teton Thai, **5**

Hotels & Villas

Amangani, **1**
Antler Inn, **9**
Cowboy Village Resort, **17**
Days Inn, **20**
Parkway Inn, **15**
Rusty Parrot, **16**
Spring Creek Ranch, **2**
Trapper Inn, **10**
Wort Hotel, **7**

American, ranching, and cowboy artifacts. ⊠*Glenwood and Deloney Ave.* ☎*(307) 733–2414* ⊕*www.jacksonhole-history.org* ⊠*$3* ⊙*Memorial Day–Sept., Mon.–Sat. 9:30–6, Sun. 10–5.*

★ FodorśChoice **National Elk Refuge.** Wildlife abounds on this
❺ 25,000-acre refuge year-round at the foot of "Sleep-
☺ ing Indian" mountain. But from around late November through March, the real highlight is the more than 7,500 elk, many with enormous antler racks, that winter here. There are also buffalo and limited hunts, depending on population size, to cull the herds. The Refuge Road Entrance lies about 1 mi (2 km) from the Town Square just past St. John's hospital on E. Broadway. Elk can also be observed from various pullouts along U.S. 191, or up close by slowly driving your car on the refuge's winding unpaved roads. There's also a horse-drawn sleigh ride, giving visitors the chance to see the elk stand or eat calmly as sleighs loaded with families and supplied with alfalfa pellets move in their midst. Among the other animals that make their home here are buffalo, coyote, mountain sheep, trumpeter swan, and other waterfowl. Arrange for sleigh rides through the Jackson Hole & Greater Yellowstone Visitor Center at 532 N Cache (⊕*www.fws.gov/nationalelkrefuge Sleigh Rides, below)* in Jackson; wear warm clothing including hats, gloves, boots, long johns, and coats. ⊠*532 N. Cache St.* ☎*307/733–5771* ⊠*Sleigh rides $16* ⊙*Year-round; sleigh rides mid-Dec.–Mar.*

❶ **National Wildlife Art Museum.** Among the paintings and
★ sculptures of bighorn sheep, elk, and other animals of the West you'll find fine-art representations and photographs of wildlife by such artists as John J. Audubon, Frederick Remington, George Catlin, Tucker Smith, and Charles M. Russell. The collection includes works in various media and styles, the earliest pieces dating to 2000 BC. A deck here affords views across the National Elk Refuge, where, particularly in winter, you can see wildlife in a natural habitat. ⊠*2820 Rungius Rd., 3 mi north of Jackson* ☎*307/733–5771* ⊕*www.wildlifeart.org* ⊠*$6* ⊙*Daily 9–5.*

❹ **Town Square.** You can spend an entire day wandering around Jackson's always-bustling Town Square, a park-like area crisscrossed with walking paths and bedecked with arches woven from hundreds of elk antlers. Various shops and restaurants surround the square, and there's often entertainment going on in the square itself, including a rip-roaring "shoot-out" most summer evenings at approximately 6:30. At the southwest corner of the square you can board a stagecoach for a ride around the area; it costs about $6 per adult.

GRANITE HOT SPRINGS. Soothing thermal baths in pristine outback country awaits in the heart of the Bridger Teton-National Forest, just a short drive south of Jackson. Concerted local and federal efforts have preserved the wild lands in this hunter's and fisherman's paradise where ranches dot the Teton Valley floor. The Snake River turns west and the contours sheer into steep vertical faces. By Hoback Junction there's white-water excitement. The drive south along U.S. 191 provides good views of the river's bends and turns and the life-jacketed rafters and kayakers who float through the Hoback canyon. At Hoback Junction, about 11 mi (18 km) south of Jackson, head east (toward Pinedale) on U.S. Hwy 189/191 and follow the Hoback River east through its beautiful canyon. A tributary canyon 10 mi (16 km) east of the junction is followed by a well-maintained and marked gravel road to Granite Hot Springs, in the Bridger-Teton National Forest. Drive 9 mi (14km) off U.S. 189/191 (northeast) on Granite Creek Road to reach the hot springs. People also come for the shady, creek-side campground and moderate hikes up Granite Canyon to passes with panoramic views. You'll want to drive with some caution as there are elevated turns, the possibility of a felled tree, and wandering livestock that can own the road ahead on blind curves. In winter, there's a popular snowmobile and dogsled trail from the highway. The 93°F to 112°F thermal baths at the end of the road is pure physical therapy, but it's closed from November through mid-December. There's also an admission price of $6 per person.

SPORTS & THE OUTDOORS

BICYCLING

The trip up to **Lower Slide Lake,** north of town, is a favorite of cyclists. Turn east off U.S. 26/89/191 to Kelly, and then follow Slide Lake Rd. Cyclists ride the **Spring Gulch Road,** part pavement, part dirt, off Route 22, along the base of Gros Ventre Butte, rejoining U.S. 26/89/191 near the Gros Ventre River.

Bike rentals for all skill levels and age groups are available at **Edge Sports** (✉*490 W. Broadway* ☎*307/734–3916*); the company also does on-site repairs. You can rent a mountain bike to explore on your own or take a tour at **Hoback Sports** (✉*520 W. Broadway* ☎*307/733–5335*). General tours are geared to intermediate and advanced riders, but Hoback can also custom-design a tour to suit your abilities and interests. The store also sells bike, ski, skate, and snowboard apparel and equipment. **Teton Cycle Works** (✉*175 N. Glenwood St.* ☎*307/733–4386*), the oldest shop in town, offers mountain and road bike sales, accessories, repairs, and rentals. Call for tours and family-style outings to the National Elk Refuge and intermediate or advanced tours from the top of Snow King Mountain. With **Teton Mountain Bike Tours** (✉*Box 7027, Jackson, WY 83002* ☎*307/733–0712 or 800/733–0788* ⊕*www.wybike.com*), mountain bikers of all skill levels can take guided half-, full-, or multi-day tours into both Grand Teton and Yellowstone national parks, as well as to the Bridger-Teton and Caribou-Targhee national forests and throughout Jackson Hole.

CANOEING, KAYAKING & RAFTING

South of Jackson, where the Hoback joins the Snake River and the canyon walls become steep, there are lively whitewater sections. But the Snake, whose rating is Class I and II, is a river for those who value scenery over white-water thrills. For the most part, floating rather than taking on rapids is the theme of running the Snake (with trips usually incorporating Jackson Lake, at the foot of the Tetons). As such, it's a good choice for families with children. What makes the trip special is the Teton Range, looming as high as 8,000 feet above the river. This float trip can also be combined with two or more days of kayaking on Jackson Lake. Raft trips take place between June and September. Experienced paddlers run the Hoback, too.

The Snake River's western Idaho portion has earned a strange footnote in history. It's the river that Evel Knievel tried (and failed miserably) to jump over on a rocket-powered motorcycle in the mid-1970s.

If you take a float trip with **Barker-Ewing Scenic Float Trips** (✉*Box 100-J, Moose, WY 83012* ☎*307/733–1800 or 800/365–1800* ⊕*www.barkerewingscenic.com*), you will travel the peaceful parts of the Snake River looking for wildlife as knowledgeable guides talk about area history, plants, and animals.

Rendezvous River Sports (✉*945 W. Broadway* ☎*307/733–2471 or 800/733–2471* ⊕*www.jacksonholekayak.com*) is the premiere paddle sports outfitter in the region, offering expert instruction so you can test yourself on western Wyoming's ancient rivers and lakes. The company also schedules more relaxed and scenic trips, including guided tours of Jackson, Slide, and String lakes, and rapid-shooting rides on the Hoback River down Granite Creek to the Snake River while you marvel at south Jackson's majestic canyons. Raft and canoe rentals are also available.

DOGSLEDDING

Dogsledding excursions are available through **Iditarod Sled Dog Tours** (✉*11 Granite Creek Rd.* ☎*307/733–7388 or 800/554–7388* ⊕*www.jhsleddog.com*). Veteran Iditarod racer Frank Teasley leads half-day introductory trips and full-day trips to Granite Hot Springs. It's a great way to see wintering native wildlife such as moose, elk, big horn sheep, deer, and bald eagles in the Bridger-Teton National Forest. Sled trips are offered only in season, which can begin as early as November and run as late as April.

HIKING

Bridger-Teton National Forest (✉*340 N. Cache St., Box 1888, 83001* ☎*307/739–5500* ⊕*www.fs.fed.us/btnf*) covers hundreds of thousands of acres of western Wyoming and shelters abundant wildlife. Permits for backcountry use of the forest are necessary only for groups and commercial operators such as outfitters. Contact the forest office for more information.

The guides at **The Hole Hiking Experience** (✉*Box 7779 83002* ☎*866/733–4453 or 307/690–4453* ⊕*www.holehike.com*) will take you to mountain meadows or to the tops of the peaks on half- or full-day tours. Some outings are suitable for the very experienced, others for any well-conditioned adult, and still others for families.

You can take part in wilderness camping, climbing, and exploration of alpine areas with experienced guides on day trips, overnight excursions, or as part of regular classes offered by **Jackson Hole Mountain Guides** (✉*165 N. Glenwood St.* ☎*307/733–4979* ⊕*www.jhmg.com*).

HUNTING & FISHING

Hunting is an age-old pastime in these parts. And numerous companies run hunt camps in the western Wyoming area. Some are reliable; others are not. If you head out on your own or with an experienced outfitter, make sure you bring the right equipment. Under state law, hunters must be 12 or over.

Bear Basin Outfitters (✎*Box 7207, Jackson, WY 83002* ☎*307/883–3186* ⊕*www.bearbasinoutfitters.net*) is the only company run by both veteran Wyoming lawmen and longtime locals who live to hunt elk, moose, sheep, antelope, deer, and bear. Accommodations are in either wall tents or sometimes hotels; meals are always provided in a camping environment. The real advantage to using an experienced outfitter like this is for those who love roughing it outdoors but don't love wasting their time in this pricey sport, when the most important thing is being led by professional guides who relish sharing their expertise with hunters from around the globe. Besides knowing where to bag the biggest Wyoming game from the Hoback to the Gros Ventre to Rock Springs, these safety-conscious sportsmen also know all the rules and regulations, so you won't run afoul of the law while having an unforgettable experience. **Jack Dennis Outdoor Shop** (✉*50 E. Broadway* ☎*307/733–2237 or 800/647–2561* ⊕*www.jackdennis. com*) offers guided fly-fishing trips led by nationally recognized guru Jeff Currier. The store carries high-quality fishing gear, outdoor gear, and free fishing maps.

SKIING

Jack Dennis Sports (✉*Jackson Hole Mountain Resort* ☎*307/733–6838* ⊕*www.jackdennis.com*) sells and rents skis and snowboards, plus outdoor gear for any season. Ski rental costs $25 to $44; snowboard and boot rental costs $25–$35.

☾ **Snow King Resort** (✉*400 E. Snow King Ave.* ☎*307/733– 5200 or 800/522–5464* ⊕*www.snowking.com*), at the western edge of Jackson, has 400 acres of ski runs for daytime use and 110 acres suitable for night skiing, plus an extensive snowmaking system on Snow King Mountain. You'll also find a snow-tubing park. In the summer, there's a 2,500-foot Alpine slide and miles of biking and hiking paths, all the way to the mountaintop. For $10 and under a person, you can also ride the scenic chair lift to the top and back. Or, you can stop off at the summit, which is 7,751 feet above sea-level, for a picnic and feast on the stunning 50-mi view of Jackson. From up here, on a clear day, you can see over the neighboring buttes and count the clouds passing around the Tetons. **Spring Creek Ranch**

(⊠*1800 Spirit Dance Rd.* ☎*307/733–8833 or 800/443–6139*) offers lessons and use of its groomed cross-country trails for a fee.

☾ Sleigh rides into the National Elk Refuge last about 45 minutes and depart from in front of the **Jackson Hole & Greater Yellowstone Visitor Center** (⊠*532 N. Cache St.* ☎*307/733–5771*) daily in winter, 10 to 4, about every 20 minutes. Dinner sleigh rides are available through **Spring Creek Ranch** (⊠*1800 Spirit Dance Rd.* ☎*307/733–8833 or 800/443–6139*), with dinner at its Granary restaurant.

Numerous companies in the Jackson area rent snowmobiles. **Rocky Mountain Snowmobile Tours** (⊠*1050 U.S. 89 S* ☎*307/733–2237 or 800/647–2561* ⊕*www.rockymountainsnow.com*) guides one- to five-day trips beginning at $200 per day, to such areas as Granite Hot Springs, Togwotee Pass, Gros Ventre Mountains, Grey's River near Alpine, and Yellowstone National Park.

WHERE EAT

For Dining price-category information, see ⇨Where to Eat in West Yellowstone, above.

$$$–$$$$ ✕**Burke's Chop House.** Offering fine dining in casual elegance, Burke's is considered by many to be Jackson's best steak house. The menu ranges from a variety of game dishes—venison, elk, and buffalo—to haute cuisine such as beef tournedos with truffles and foie gras. The wine list is extensive. The food and service here are first-rate, but the restaurant is usually crowded and can be noisy. A kids' menu is available, and this is a completely no-smoking restaurant. Its semiprivate dinning room seats up to 26. ⊠*72 S. Glenwood, across from the Antler Motel* ☎*307/733–8575* ⊟*AE, D, MC, V* ⊘*Closed Mar. No lunch.*

$$$–$$$$ ✕**The Gun Barrel Steak & Game House.** At Jackson's legendary game & steak lodge, all dishes are slow-cooked over an open river-rock mesquite grill. The dining atmosphere is rustic and fun, with an Old West collection of mounted game, wildlife, and memorabilia. Service is always friendly. The menu offers a wide variety of unique dishes, but some, such as velvet elk, may be too rich for those unaccustomed to game. The bar has an ample list of bourbons, scotches, and wines to sample if you just want a drink. ⊠*862 W.*

Broadway, approximately 1 mi (2 km) from Town Square in the Grand Teton Plaza ☎307/733–3287 ═MC, V ⊘*No lunch.*

$$$–$$$$ ✕**Snake River Grill.** Dine in Western, fireside elegance, with white tablecloths and an excellent wine list aimed at true oenophiles. Those looking for a brew may find the beer list lacking. Choose from fresh fish, free-range meats, and organic produce at this second-floor restaurant overlooking the Town Square and Snow King Mountain. Buffalo cowboy steaks, vegetarian pasta with mushrooms and artichokes, and grilled elk chops are among the stand-out entrees, but some may find the prices on the high side. A private party room right off the bar seats up to 16. Kids are welcome; however, there are no high chairs or children's menu. Reservations are recommended, but walk-ins will be accommodated if there is room. ⊠*84 E. Broadway* ☎307/733–0557 ═AE, MC, V ⊘*Closed Apr. and Nov. No lunch.*

$$–$$$$ ✕**The Blue Lion** For 30 years, consistently excellent, distinctive fare has been the rule at this white-and-blue clapboard house two blocks from Town Square. The sophisticated offerings range from Dijon-mustard-rubbed rack of lamb to grilled elk with port wine sauce to fresh fish dishes, including rainbow trout. There's patio dining in summer and a wine list. Early bird specials (from 6–6:30 PM) are a great value in an otherwise pricey restaurant. This is a no-smoking restaurant. ⊠*160 N. Millward St.* ☎307/733–3912 ═AE, D, MC, V ⊘*Closed Tues. from early Oct.–late Nov. and early Apr.–late May. No lunch.*

$$–$$$$ ✕**Nani's Genuine Pasta House.** The Italian menu is ever-changing (each month the menu represents a different region) at this cozy restaurant with classic checkered tablecloths. Whether Nani's is "authentic" or Americanized Italian is open to debate, but the knowledgeable staff will help you through the rotating menu. Sometimes-available favorites include braised veal shanks with saffron risotto, quail marinated with honey and balsamic vinegar, or other regional Italian cooking. Al fresco seating is possible, weather permitting, but Nani's is designed to attract gourmets, not tourists, so it's not the location that is so appealing. The wine list features a wide range of sparkling wines, regional Italian and non-Italian wines, as well as wines by the glass. Vegan choices are also offered. During April and

November, you'll find some two-for-one specials. ✉ *242 N. Glenwood St.* ☎ *307/733–3888* ▭ *AE, MC, V.*

$$–$$$ ✕**Sweetwater Restaurant.** Imaginative takes on salmon, pork tenderloin, buffalo, and pot roast are on the dinner menu in this historic log building built in 1915 with antique oak furnishings. The atmosphere is rustic, homey, and comforting. There's a great dessert menu, too. Try lemon raspberry cake with extra homemade whipped cream if they have it. For lunch, you can have a wrap, salad, or sandwich in the outdoor dining area (weather permitting), though even there the views aren't great. Reservations are essential in busy seasons. ✉ *85 S. King St.* ☎ *307/733–3553* ▭ *AE, D, MC, V.*

$–$$$ ✕**Billy's Giant Hamburgers & Cadillac Grille.** True to its name, Billy's serves big—really big—burgers and waffle fries that are really, really good, albeit greasy. Not to be outdone, there are also hot dogs and several deli-style sandwiches that you can munch around a 1950s-style lunch counter with clear views of the Town Square. The portions in general are huge. Service is quick and unpretentious. Billy's shares space with the more refined but equally fun Cadillac Grille, where you can enjoy a casual atmosphere of a few booths and tables or grab a stool—if you can find one— around its usually jam-packed circular bar. ✉ *55 N. Cache Dr.* ☎ *307/733–3279* ▭ *AE, MC, V.*

$–$$ ✕**Bubba's Barbecue Restaurant** Succulent baby back ribs and mouthwatering spareribs are the specialties at this busy barbecue joint, which evokes the Old West with its large wooden porch, wooden booths, Western paintings, and antique signs. Sandwiches and a huge salad bar with plenty of non-meat choices are also available. This is also one of the most affordable breakfast options in Jackson, but whenever you go there can be a long wait for a table. The desserts include homemade pies of the chocolate-buttermilk and fudge-pecan variety. ✉ *515 W. Broadway* ☎ *307/733–2288* ▭ *AE, D, MC, V.*

★ Fodor\'sChoice ✕**The Bunnery.** Lunch is served year-round and
$–$$ dinner is served in summer at the Bunnery, but it's the breakfasts of omelets and home-baked pastries that are irresistible; the coffee is also very good. All of the breads are made on the premises, most from OSM flour (oats, sunflower, millet). It's elbow-to-elbow inside, so you may have to wait to be seated on busy mornings, but any inconvenience is well worth it. There's also a decent vegetarian

selection here. Try a giant almond stick, sticky bun, or a piece of Very Berry Pie made from raspberries, strawberries, and blueberries. In the summer there's outdoor seating. On-street parking can be hard to find here. ✉*Hole-in-the-Wall Mall, 130 N. Cache St.,* ☎*(307)734-0075* ═*MC, V, D* ⊘*No dinner Sept.–May.*

$–$$ ✕**Jedediah's House of Sourdough.** Friendly, noisy, and elbow-knocking, this restaurant a block east of Town Square—which also has a branch at the airport—makes breakfast and lunch for those with big appetites. There are plenty of excellent "sourjacks" (sourdough flapjacks) and biscuits and gravy. Burgers are mountain-man size. The menu at the airport location tends to be more expensive than in the restaurant downtown, but it's open later. ✉*135 E. Broadway* ☎*307/733–5671* ✉*1250 Airport Rd.* ☎*307/733–6063* ═*AE, D, DC, MC, V* ⊘*No dinner.*

★ Fodor'sChoice ✕**Teton Thai.** For the best Thai this side of San
$–$$ Francisco—and maybe the entire inner-mountain west—this family-owned local favorite tops the list of everyone in Jackson. Just one block off Town Square—across from the Teton Theatre and next to Gaslight Alley—it is always packed. In winter, there's inside counter seating right in the kitchen or you can get takeout, but in summer you can sit on the patio outside, where the atmosphere can become boisterous. Service can sometime be slow, but the *tom kha gai* (coconut milk, lemongrass, and chicken soup) or tofu curry dishes are always worth the wait. ✉*135 N. Cache* ☎*307/733–0022* ═*No credit cards* ⊘*Closed mid-Oct.– mid-Nov. No lunch weekdays.*

WHERE TO STAY

There are three reservations services for Jackson Hole. You can make reservations for most lodgings in Jackson through **Central Reservations** (☎*888/838–6606*). Properties managed by **Jackson Hole Resort Lodging** (☎*800/443–8613* ⊕*www.jacksonholewy.com*) offers rooms, condominiums, and vacation homes at Teton Village, Teton Pines, and the Jackson Hole Racquet Club. **Mountain Property Management** (✉*250 Veronica La., Box 2228, Jackson 83001* ☎*800/992–9948* ⊕*www.mpmjh.com*) offers condominium, cabin, and luxury-home rentals throughout Jackson Hole.

For Lodging price-category information, see ⇨Where to Stay in West Yellowstone, above.

$$$$ ⊠**Amangani.** This exclusive resort built of sandstone and
★ redwood melds into the landscape of Gros Ventre Butte,
affording beautiful views of Spring Creek Valley from its
clifftop location. The warm hospitality is Western, but the
setting is that of Eastern (as in Asian) simplicity, with tall
ceilings, clean lines, and rooms with platform beds, large
soaking tubs, and plenty of space. The amenities here are
the best in Jackson Hole, and include horseback riding,
tennis, and nearby cross-country skiing and sleigh rides
in winter. **Pros:** extremely luxurious, impeccable service,
excellent views of the Tetons. **Cons:** very expensive, too
detached from the mundane world below (even by Jackson standards), decor seems a bit too exotic for western
Wyoming ⊠*1535 N.E. Butte Rd., 83002* ☎*307/734–7333
or 877/734–7333* ⊕*www.amangani.com* ⇆*40 suites* ⌂*In-
room: safe, refrigerator, DVD, VCR. In-hotel: restaurant,
room service, bar, tennis courts, pool, spa, laundry service,
airport shuttle* ⊟*AE, D, DC, MC, V* ⦿*EP.*

$$$$ ⊠**Rusty Parrot.** An imposing river-rock fireplace in the
cathedral lounge lends warmth to this timber inn near the
center of Jackson. You can walk the four blocks to shops,
galleries, and restaurants on Town Square. Handcrafted
wooden furnishings fill the rooms, some of which have
fireplaces and oversized whirlpool tubs. With body wraps,
massages, and facials, the spa is a nice extra. Have dinner
at the Wild Sage Restaurant ($$$$), which serves duck,
pork, halibut, Montana Legend Beef. Children under 12
are strongly discouraged. **Pros:** in town yet off the beaten
path, fine dining in the charming restaurant, good off-season deals. **Cons:** not family-friendly, limited views. ⊠*175
N. Jackson St., 83001* ☎*307/733–2000 or 800/458–2004*
⊕*www.rustyparrot.com* ⇆*31 rooms* ⌂*In-room: DVD,
VCR, Wi-Fi. In-hotel: restaurant, room service, spa, no
elevator, public Wi-Fi, no-smoking rooms* ⊟*AE, D, DC,
MC, V* ⦿*CP.*

$$$–$$$$ ⊠**Parkway Inn.** From the moment you enter its ground floor
★ "salon," a vintage ambience soothes the soul in period fur-
niture and black-and-white photographs, showing the rise
of east Jackson. Each room has a distinctive look—with
oak or wicker furniture—and each is filled with antiques
from the 19th century onward. The overall effect is homey
and delightful, especially if you plan to stay a few days or
longer. Continental breakfast is served in an antiques-filled
lounge. This quiet property is just three blocks from the
Town Square. **Pros:** walking distance to many restaurants,

7

quiet, boutique atmosphere. **Cons:** not a full-service hotel, no on-premises restaurant. ✉ *125 N. Jackson St., 83001* ☎ *307/733–3143 or 800/247–8390* ⊕ *www.parkwayinn. com* ⬭ *37 rooms, 14 suites* ⌂ *In-room: dial-up. In-hotel: pool, gym, public Internet, public Wi-Fi, no-smoking rooms.* ⊟ *AE, D, MC, V* ⌾ *CP.*

$$$–$$$$ ⬜ **Spring Creek Ranch.** Outside Jackson on Gros Ventre Butte, this luxury resort has beautiful views of the Tetons. Among the numerous amenities are horseback riding, tennis, and cross-country skiing and sleigh rides in winter. Aside from hotel rooms, there's a mix of studios and condos; many of the accommodations have wood-burning fireplaces and lodgepole-pine furniture. Wi-Fi in the lobby is free. Among the fine food served at the Granary ($$$–$$$$) are Alaskan halibut, fillet of beef, elk tenderloin, and New Zealand lamb. You can also eat in the Rising Sage Cafe. A naturalist is on the property, and astronomy lectures are offered twice-weekly in the summer. **Pros:** scenic mountaintop location, expert staff, meals included in some packages. **Cons:** not for budget-conscious; can be a tricky, winding drive in winter. ✉ *1800 Spirit Dance Rd., Box 4780, 83001* ☎ *307/733–8833 or 800/443–6139* ⊕ *www.springcreekranch.com* ⬭ *36 rooms, 76 studios and condominiums* ⌂ *In-room: kitchen, Ethernet. In-hotel: restaurant, room service, bar, tennis courts, pool, spa, no elevator, public Wi-Fi, no-smoking rooms* ⊟ *AE, DC, MC, V* ⌾ *EP.*

★ **Fodor's** Choice ✕ ⬜ **The Wort Hotel.** This brick Victorian hotel
$$$–$$$$**   near the Town Square, built in 1941, seems to have been around as long as the Tetons, but it feels fresh inside (there's even Wi-Fi in the lobby, though it's not free, yet). A fireplace warms the lobby, and a sitting area is just up the stairs. Locally made Western-style furnishings of lodgepole-pine beds, pine dressers, carpets, drapes and bed coverings in warm, muted blues and mauves. You can sip a drink in the Silver Dollar Bar & Grill ($–$$$$)—aptly named for the 2,032 silver dollars embedded on top of the bar—or amble through swinging doors into the restaurant for a fine meal. **Pros: charming old building with lots of history, convenient location in town, some good-value packages offered. **Cons:** limited views, must drive to parks and mountains. ✉ *50 N. Glenwood St., 83001* ☎ *307/733–2190 or 800/322–2727* ⊕ *www.worthotel.com* ⬭ *59 rooms, 5 suites* ⌂ *In-room: Wi-fi, dial-up. In-hotel: restaurant, room service, bar, gym, public Internet, public Wi-Fi, no-smoking rooms* ⌾ *EP* ⊟ *AE, D, MC, V.*

$$–$$$$ 🏨**Trapper Inn.** This motel is within walking distance of Town Square and has some of the best-appointed rooms in Jackson for people with disabilities. It's also undergone a major renovation geared toward turning it into an executive-stay hotel. Downstairs, you'll find an open reception desk with friendly and helpful staff, free coffee, plenty of tall windows, ample sitting space, free Wi-Fi, a stone fireplace, and vintage trapper gear big enough to snare a grizzly. **Pros:** some package deals include breakfast, walking distance to town, small pool and Jacuzzi. **Cons:** limited views, must drive to mountains. ⌂*235 N. Cache St., 83001* ☎*307/733–2648* ⊕*www.trapperinn.com* ⬎*80 rooms; 48 suites* ⬓*In-room: kitchen (some), refrigerator. In-hotel: pool, laundry facilities, no-smoking rooms* ▭*AE, DC, MC, V* ⊙|*EP.*

$$–$$$ 🏨**Days Inn.** Like other chain properties, this motel is familiar, but the lodgepole-pine swing out front, the lobby's elk-antler chandelier, and the rooms' Teton, Wind River Range, or Snake River views remind you where you are. There are ski-boot and glove dryers in the lobby, plus in-room ski racks. **Pros:** near large grocery store, rates very competitive. **Cons:** except for the grocery store there's not much close by, limited views. ⌂*350 S. U.S. 89, 83001* ☎*307/733–0033* ⬎*90 rooms* ⬓*In-room: safe, refrigerator (some). In-hotel: public Wi-fi, no-smoking rooms* ▭*AE, D, DC, MC, V* ⊙|*CP.*

$–$$$ 🏨**Antler Inn.** As real estate agents say, location, location, location, and perhaps no motel in Jackson has a better location than the Antler, one block south of Town Square. Some rooms have fireplaces, two have Jacuzzis, but otherwise they're standard motel rooms (indeed, as the neon sign says, this is the Antler Motel). In winter there's a complimentary ski shuttle. **Pros:** restaurants nearby, family-run operation with owner on premises, good prices in the off-season. **Cons:** frequently booked in summer, and can get rowdy during "Hill Climb," a snowmobile festival in March at nearby Snow King. ⌂*43 W. Pearl St., 83001* ☎*307/733–2535 or 800/483–8667* ⬎*110 rooms* ⬓*In-hotel: some pets allowed* ⊙|*EP* ▭*AE, D, DC, MC, V.*

$–$$$ 🏨**Cowboy Village Resort.** Stay in your own small log cabin with covered decks and barbecue grills. There is a ski-waxing room, and both the START Bus and Targhee Express buses that serve the ski areas stop here. **Pros:** near town, late-night dinner option next door, grills available for cooking outside. **Cons:** crowded in summer, few amenities, more like a motel with cabins than a true resort. ✉*120 S. Flat Creek, 83001* ☎*307/733–3121 or 800/962–4988* ⊕*www. townsquareinns.com* ⊷*82 cabins* ⚂*In-room: kitchen. In-hotel: laundry facilities, no-smoking rooms* ▭*AE, D, MC, V* ⋈*EP.*

WHERE TO CAMP

$ ⛰**Curtis Canyon.** Numerous trees surround this simple campground northeast of Jackson Hole. Part of Bridger-Teton National Forest, the campground is near a popular mountain-biking area and sits at an elevation of 6,600 feet. ⚂*Pit toilets, drinking water, fire pits, picnic tables* ⊷*11 sites* ✉*From Elk Refuge Headquarters in Jackson, take Flat Creek Road northeast 7 mi. No trailers longer than 30 feet. 10 day stay limit. Please keep your camp clean and free of food and other bear attractants.* ☎*307/739–5400 or 307/543–2386* ⊕*www.fs.fed.us/btnf* ⚠*Reservations not accepted* ▭*No credit cards* ⊙*June–Sept.*

$$ ⛰**Granite Creek.** Part of Bridger-Teton National Forest, this wooded, 52-site campground is a big, noisy place convenient to hiking and mountain-biking trails. An added bonus are the small pools of Granite Hot Springs ($). The elevation is 7,100 feet and there are wheelchair-accessible sites. ⚂*Flush toilets, pit toilets, drinking water, fire pits, picnic tables* ⊷*52 sites* ✉*Granite Creek Rd. off U.S. 189/191, 35 mi southeast of Jackson* ☎*307/739–5400 or 307/543–2386* ⊕*www.fs.fed.us/btnf* ⚠*Reservations not accepted* ▭*No credit cards* ⊙*Late May–Sept.*

NIGHTLIFE & THE ARTS

NIGHTLIFE

There's never a shortage of live music in Jackson, where local performers play country, rock, and folk. Some of the most popular bars are on Town Square. At the **Million Dollar Cowboy Bar** (✉*25 N. Cache St.* ☎*307/733–2207*), everyone dresses up in cowboy garb and tries to two-step into the Old West, or mosey over to the bar and slide into authentic horse saddle seats. There are plenty of pool tables, good pub grub, and live country music most nights but Sunday, not to mention free country-western dance lessons on Thursday. Downstairs is a popular restaurant serving certified Black Angus steaks. **43 North** (✉*645 S. Cache Dr. Get Dire* ☎*307/ 733–0043*), at the base of Snow King Mountain serves Continental cuisine for both lunch and dinner, with outdoor seating (weather-permitting) and a stellar view of the mountain in summer. You can also curl up inside by the stone fireplace at this locals hangout and grab a drink at a table or the antique bar. There's lots of free parking and frequent live music; call for a schedule of events. Come to the **Virginian Saloon & Lodge** (⌷ *750 W. Broadway* ☎*307/733–2792*) to shoot a game of pool, throw darts, grab a pitcher at a table, sip a drink by the fireplace, watch sports from one of four TVs, or listen to live music.

THE ARTS

Center For the Arts (⌷ *240 S. Glenwood, 83001* ☎*307/734–8956* ⊕*www.jhcenterforthearts.org*) is Jackson's new $35-million center dedicated to supporting the fine and performing arts, including theater, film, and dance. It also hosts lectures on global issues, rotating exhibits, and showcases of star talent from Hollywood to Broadway. Classes for adults are included in the center's mission.

Artists who work in a variety of media show and sell their work at the **Jackson Hole Fall Arts Festival** (☎*307/733–3316*), with special events highlighting art, poetry, and dance. Festival events take place throughout town in September, and many art galleries in Jackson have special programs and exhibits.

At the **Jackson Hole Playhouse** (⌷ *145 W. Deloney Ave.* ☎*307/733–6994*), you can attend live musical theater, including revivals of Western classics such as *Paint Your Wagon*; some of the performances are dinner shows. The theater is open from May to September.

For those seeking a more contemporary theatre experience, **Off-Square Theatre** (⌷ *Center for the Arts, 240 S. Glennwood, 83001* ☎*307/733–3021*) is a space for children and adults where theater professionals and nonprofessionals strut their stuff and sometimes go outside the box. The company is one of the leading theater companies in the region.

SHOPPING

Jackson's peaceful Town Square is surrounded by storefronts with a mixture of specialty and outlet shops—most of them small-scale—with moderate to expensive prices. North of Jackson's center, on Cache Street, is a small cluster of fine shops on Gaslight Alley.

Jackson Art Tours

Local arts impresario Tammy Christel offers visitors an enriching look at Jackson's vibrant arts scene of contemporary and traditional galleries and artists on her **Jackson Hole Art Tours**. Tours begin at Jackson's Center for the Arts, in the lobby at 240 S. Glenwood. (There are two lobbies, one on either side of the Center.) The tour meets in the Visual Arts Lobby Glenwood Street side and ends around the Town Square. Tours are roughly two hours, and cover 1 to 2 mi. Reserve if you can because these tours can sell out in the busy season. ☞ Box 3941, Jackson 83001 ☎ 307/690–1983 ⊕ www.jacksonholearttours.com ☜ $25 ⊗ Mon.–Fri. at 9:45 AM.

BOOKS

One of Gaslight Alley's best shops is **Valley Bookstore** (⊠ 125 N. Cache St. ☎ 307/733–4533). It ranks among the top bookstores in the region, with a big selection of regional history, guidebooks on flora and fauna, and fiction by Wyoming and regional authors.

CLOTHING

★ Fodor'sChoice **Hide Out Leather** (⊠ 40 N. Center St. ☎ 307/733–2422) carries many local designs and has a diverse selection of men's and women's coats, vests, and accessories such as pillows and throws. Try **Corral West** (⊠ 840 W. Broadway ☎ 307/733–0247) For authentic women's, men's and children's Western wear, this store located about a mile south of Town Square in the Grand Teton Plaza offers a wide selection of reasonably priced belts, boots, purses, leather jackets and cowboy hats with free shaping and fitting.

CRAFT & ART GALLERIES

★ Fodor'sChoice Jackson's art galleries serve a range of tastes. **Di Tommaso Galleries** (⊠ 172 Center St. ☎ 307/734–9677) has a collection of 19th- and 20th-century art as well as contemporary pieces; the gallery specializes in painting and sculpture of Western life, wildlife and Native America by artists Kate Starling, Harry Jackson, Melvin Johansen, and Conrard Schwring. Fine nature photography by Tom Mangelson from around the globe of is displayed and sold at his **Images of Nature Gallery** (⊠ 170 N. Cache St. ☎ 307/733–9752). **Trailside Galleries** (⊠ 105 N. Center St. ☎ 307/733–3186) sells traditional Western art and jewelry. The photography of Abi Garaman is highlighted at **Under the Willow Photo Gallery** (⊠*50 S. Cache St.* ☎*307/733–6633*). He has been photographing Jackson Hole for decades and has produced a wide selection of images of wildlife, mountains, barns, and both summer and winter scenes. **Wilcox Gallery** (⊠*1975 U.S. 89 N* ☎*307/733–6450*) showcases wildlife and landscape paintings, sculpture, pottery, and other works by contemporary artists. At **Wild By Nature Gallery** (⊠*95 W. Deloney Ave.* ☎*307/733–8877*) 95% of the images are of local wildlife and landscape photography by Henry W. Holdsworth; there's also a selection of books and note cards. **Wild Exposures Gallery** (⊠*60 E. Broadway* ☎*307/739–1777*) represents photographers Jeff Hogan, Scott McKinley, and Andrew Weller, all of whose work has appeared on National Geographic and BBC programs.

SPORTING GOODS

Jackson's premier sports shop, **Jack Dennis Sports** (⊠*50 E. Broadway* ☎*307/733–3270*) is well stocked with the best in outdoor equipment for winter and summer activities. It also has a store at Teton Village. **Skinny Skis** (⊠*65 W. Deloney Ave.* ☎*307/733–6094*) offers everything a cross-country skier might need. **Teton Mountaineering** (⊠*170 N. Cache St.* ☎*307/733–3595*) specializes in Nordic-skiing, climbing, and hiking equipment and clothing. **Westbank Anglers** (⊠*3670 N. Moose–Wilson Rd.* ☎*307/733–6483*) can provide all the equipment necessary for fly-fishing.

AROUND JACKSON HOLE

In this part of Wyoming you need to keep one thing straight: there is Jackson, and then there is Jackson Hole, both named for fur trapper David Jackson, who spent a great deal of time in the area in the late 1820s and early 1830s. The first is the small town; the second is the larger geographic area surrounding the town (and called a hole because it is encircled by mountains). In addition to Jackson, Jackson Hole includes Grand Teton National Park and the small towns of Kelly, Moose, Moran, and Wilson. Also here is Teton Village, the center for the Jackson Hole Mountain Resort, best known for skiing in winter but popular for summer activities as well.

Although you might headquarter in Jackson, most of the outdoor activities in the region occur out in Jackson Hole and "The Valley." The valley has a world-class ski mountain and hiking and biking trails, and the Snake River, ideal for fishing or floating, runs right through the middle of it.

TETON VILLAGE & JACKSON HOLE MOUNTAIN RESORT

11 mi northwest of Jackson via Hwy. 22 and Teton Village Rd.

Teton Village resounds with the clomping of ski boots in winter and with the sounds of violins, horns, and other instruments at the Grand Teton Music Festival in summer. The village mostly consists of the restaurants, lodging properties, and shops built to serve the skiers who flock to Jackson Hole Mountain Resort. This is possibly the best ski resort area in the United States, and the expanse and variety of terrain are incredible. In summer, folks come here to hike, ride the tram, and attend high-caliber concerts.

As it travels to the summit of Rendezvous Peak, the **Aerial Tramway** has always afforded spectacular panoramas of Jackson Hole. There are several hiking trails at the top of the mountain. The tram was closed and dismantled in September 2006, and at this writing, its replacement was not expected to be online until late in 2008 or early in 2009, though the opening date was still very much in flux. ✉*Teton Village* ☎*307/733–2292 or 800/333–7766.*

SPORTS & THE OUTDOORS

GOLF

The 18-hole **Teton Pines Golf Club** (✉*3450 N. Clubhouse St. Wilson, WY* ☎*307/733–1005 or 800/238–2223* ⊕*www. tetonpines.com*) lies south of the Jackson Hole Mountain Resort on Moose-Wilson Road. Vice President Dick Cheney owns a home here. Current greens fees run $57 to $195, depending on the season and whether or not you are a guest at the resort.

HIKING

The plus here is that much of the uphill legwork will be dispensed with the opening of the new Aerial Tramway in December 2008. From the top of Rendezvous Peak you can walk through high-mountain basins filled with wildflowers in summer or along cliff-line ridges, all against the stunning backdrop of the Tetons. The weather and wildflowers are best between July and August.

A loop of about 30 mi can be made by picking up the Teton Crest Trail, then branching off on the Death Canyon Trail. Don't necessarily expect solitude; most of the time, you're in Grand Teton National Park, an exceedingly popular tourist destination. However, this route keeps you well away from the visitor crush at the park's main gate, so you aren't likely to encounter hiker traffic jams, either.

DOWNHILL SKIING & SNOWBOARDING

★ Fodor'sChoice A place to appreciate both as a skier and as a voyeur, **Jackson Hole Mountain Resort** (⌂*Box 290, Teton Village 83025* ☎*307/733–2292 or 800/333–7766* ⊕*www. jacksonhole.com*) is truly one of the great skiing experiences in America. There are literally thousands of ways of getting from top to bottom, and not all of them are hellishly steep, despite Jackson's reputation. First-rate racers such as Olympic champion skier Tommy Moe and snowboarders Julie Zell, A. J. Cargill, and Rob Kingwill regularly train here. As Kingwill has put it, "Nothing really compares to Jackson Hole . . . This place has the most consistently steep terrain. You can spend years and years here and never cross your trail."

On the resort map, about 111 squiggly lines designate named trails, but this doesn't even begin to suggest the thousands of different skiable routes. The resort claims 2,500 skiable acres, a figure that seems unduly conservative. And although Jackson is best known for its advanced to extreme skiing, it is also a place where imaginative intermediates can go exploring and have the time of their lives. It is not, however, a good place for novices.

■TIP➔**High snowfall some winters can lead to extreme avalanche danger in spite of efforts by the Ski Patrol to make the area as safe as possible.** Before venturing from known trails and routes, check with the Ski Patrol for conditions. Ski with a friend, and always carry an emergency locator device. Ski passes range from $58 to $81 for adults depending on day of the week.

FACILITIES
4,139-foot vertical drop; 2,500 skiable acres; 10% beginner, 40% intermediate, 50% expert; 1 gondola, 6 quad chairs, 2 triple chairs, 2 double chair, 1 magic carpet.

LESSONS & PROGRAMS
☾ Half-day group lessons at the **Jackson Hole Ski & Snowboard School** (⌂*Teton Village* ☎*307/733–2292 or 800/450–*

0477) start at $90. There are extensive children's pro-
grams, including lessons for kids six to 13 years old and
day care for children from six months to two years old.
Nordic-skiing lessons start at $45. For expert skiers, the
Jackson Hole Ski Camps (⊠*Teton Village* ☎*307/739–2779
or 800/450–0477*), headed by such skiers as Tommy Moe,
the 1994 Olympic gold medalist, and top snowboarders
like Julie Zell, A. J. Cargill, and Jessica Baker, run for five
days, teaching everything from big-mountain free-skiing to
racing techniques. The cost is $890 per person.

LIFT TICKETS

Lift tickets cost $58 to $81. You can save about 10% to
30% if you buy a five- to seven-day ticket.

RENTALS

Equipment can be rented at ski shops in Jackson and Teton
Village. **Jackson Hole Sports** (⊠*Teton Village* ☎*307/739–
2649 or 800/443–6931*), at the Bridger Center at the ski
area, offers ski and snowboard rental packages starting
at $22 a day. You can buy or rent skis or snowboards at
Pepi Stegler Sports Shop (⊠*3395 W. McCollister Dr., Teton
Village* ☎*307/733–4505* ⊕*www.pepistieglersports.com*),
which is run by the famous Stiegler family. Daughter
Resi, who calls Jackson Hole home, competed in the 2006
Olympics in Torino, Italy. Pepi, her father, is a native of
Austria who won a bronze in the giant slalom at the 1964
Innsbrook games. Ski rentals cost between $25 and $44;
snowboard rentals are $25. The store is at the base of Ren-
dezvous Peak.

HELI-SKIING

In general, heli-skiing is best done when there has been
relatively little recent snowfall. For two or three days
after a storm, good powder skiing can usually be found
within the ski area. Daily trips can be arranged through
High Mountain Helicopter Skiing (⊠*Jackson Hole Mountain
Resort base area, Teton Village* ☎*307/733–3274* ⊕*www.
heliskijackson.com*).

BACKCOUNTRY SKIING

Few areas in North America can compete with Jackson
Hole when it comes to the breadth, beauty, and variety
of backcountry opportunities. For touring skiers, one of
the easier areas (because of flatter routes) is along the base
of the Tetons toward Jenny and Jackson lakes. Telemark
skiers (or even skiers on alpine gear) can find numerous

downhill routes by skiing in from Teton Pass, snow stability permitting. A guide isn't required for tours to the national park lakes but might be helpful for those unfamiliar with the lay of the land; trails and trail markers set in summer can become obscured by winter snows. When you are touring elsewhere, a guide familiar with the area and avalanche danger is a virtual necessity. The Tetons are big country, and the risks are commensurately large as well.

Alpine Guides (✉*Teton Village* ☎*307/739–2663*) leads half-day and full-day backcountry tours into the national parks and other areas near the resort, for more downhill-minded skiers. Arrangements can also be made through the Jackson Hole Ski School. **Jackson Hole Mountain Guides** (✉*165 N. Glenwood St., Jackson* ☎*307/733–4979* ⊕*www.jhmg. com*) leads strenuous backcountry tours. The **Jackson Hole Nordic Center** (✉*Teton Village* ☎*307/739–2629 or 800/450–0477*) has cross-country, telemark, and snowshoe rentals and track and telemark lessons. The center also leads naturalist tours into the backcountry. Rental packages begin at $28 and lessons start at $75, including rental equipment and a $13 trail pass. Forest Service rangers lead free snowshoe tours; the Nordic Center also runs snowshoe tours, starting from $80. Sled dog tours are available (call to inquire about prices).

TRACK SKIING

The **Jackson Hole Nordic Center** (✉*Teton Village* ☎*307/739–2629 or 800/450–0477* ⊕*www.jacksonhole.com*) is at the ski-resort base. The scenic 17 km (10.5) mi of groomed track is relatively flat. Because the Nordic Center and the downhill ski area are under the same management, downhill skiers with multiday passes can switch over to Nordic skiing in the afternoon for no extra charge. Otherwise, the cost is $13 for a day pass. Rentals and lessons are available; alpine lift tickets are also good at the Nordic Center.

WHERE TO STAY & EAT

In the winter ski season, it can be cheaper to stay in Jackson, about 20 minutes away; in summer it's generally cheaper to stay at Teton Village.

$$$$ ✕**Solitude Cabin Dinner Sleigh Rides.** Climb aboard a horse-drawn sleigh and ride through the trees to a log cabin for a dinner of prime rib, broiled salmon, or a vegetarian entrée. Live entertainment is provided; a children's menu is available. ✉*Jackson Hole Mountain Resort, Teton Village*

☎307/739–2603 ⊟AE, D, DC, MC, V ☙Reservations essential ⊘Closed Apr.–early Dec.

$$$–$$$$ ✕**Mangy Moose.** Folks pour in off the ski slopes for a lot of food and talk at this two-level restaurant with a bar and an outdoor deck. There's a high noise level but decent food consisting of Alaska King Crab legs, buffalo meat loaf, and fish and pasta dishes. The place is adorned with antiques, including a full-size stuffed caribou and sleigh suspended from the ceiling. Popular nightspot with live music and frequent concerts by top bands. ⊠3295 Village Dr., Teton Village ☎307/733–4913 ⊟AE, MC, V.

$$$–$$$$ ▦**R Lazy S Ranch.** Jackson Hole, with the spectacle of the Tetons in the background, is true dude-ranch country, and the R Lazy S is one of the largest dude ranches in the area. Horseback riding and instruction are the main attraction, with a secondary emphasis on fishing, either in private waters on the ranch or at other rivers and streams. One of the regular activities is a scenic float on the Snake River. You stay in log-cabin guest cottages and gather for meals in the large main lodge. **Pros:** authentic dude ranch experience, very popular with older kids and preteens, an absolutely beautiful setting. **Cons:** few modern trappings, not for the high-maintenance traveler. ⊠1 mi north of Teton Village on the outskirts of Grand Teton National Park, 83025 ☎307/733–2655 ⊕www.rlazys.com ⇌14 cabins ♨In-room: no a/c, no TV. In-hotel: no elevator, no kids under 7, no-smoking rooms ⊟No credit cards ⊘Closed Oct.–mid-June ⦿FAP ☞1-week minimum; rates based on double occupancy.

$$–$$$$ ▦**Alpenhof Lodge.** This small Austrian-style hotel is in the heart of Jackson Hole Mountain Resort, next to the tram. Hand-carved Bavarian furniture fills the rooms. All the deluxe rooms have balconies, and some have fireplaces and bathtub jets. Standard rooms are smaller and don't have balconies. Entrees such as wild game loaf, Wiener schnitzel, and fondue are served in the dining room, and relatively quiet nightclub that also offers casual dining. **Pros:** quaint, Old World feel, cozy surroundings. **Cons:** some rooms are more small than cozy, especially for the price. ⊠Teton Village, 83025 ☎307/733–3242 or 800/732–3244 ⊕www.alpenhoflodge.com ⇌42 rooms ♨In-room: a/c, Wi-Fi. In-hotel: bar, pool, spa, no-smoking rooms ⊟AE, D, DC, MC, V ⊘Closed mid-Oct–Dec. 1; early Apr.–May 1 ⦿BP.

$ ▥ **The Hostel X.** Although the classic hostel accommodations at this lodge-style inn are basic, you can't get any closer to Jackson Hole Mountain Resort for a better price. It's popular with young, budget-conscious people. Rooms, some of which have twins, bunks, and king beds, sleep from two to four people. Downstairs common areas include a lounge with a fireplace, game room, a movie room, library, and a ski-waxing room. There's no smoking in any of the hostel's public areas. **Pros:** superb deal for the upscale locale, truly convivial and communal atmosphere. **Cons:** not family-friendly, little privacy, no matter how you slice it this is still a hostel. ✉ *Teton Village, 83025* ☎ *307/733–3415* ⊕ *www.hostelx.com* ⇨ *55 rooms* ⚬ *In-room: no a/c, no phone, no TV. In-hotel: no elevator, laundry facilities, public Internet, public Wi-fi* ═MC, V ⑽ *coffee, hot chocolate, BBQ facilities.*

THE ARTS

In summer the symphony orchestra performances of the **Grand Teton Music Festival** (✉ *Box 490, Teton Village, 83025* ☎ *307/733–3050* ⊕ *www.gtmf.org*) are held outside at Teton Village. A winter series takes place in Walk Festival Hall. Tickets cost between $20 and $75.

SHOPPING

At the **Mountainside Mall** (✉ *Teton Village* ☎ *No phone*), not to be mistaken for a big suburban mall (to its credit), you can find goggles, snowboards, skis, and clothing ranging from parkas to swimsuits, but some items are overpriced.

WILSON

6 mi south of Teton Village on Teton Village Rd., 4 mi west of Jackson on Hwy. 22.

If you want to avoid the hustle and bustle of Jackson, Wilson makes a good alternative base for exploring Grand Teton National Park or skiing at Jackson Hole Mountain Resort. This small town takes its name from Nick Wilson, one of the first homesteaders in the area, a man who spent part of his childhood living with the Shoshone Indians.

WHERE TO EAT

★ Fodor'sChoice✕ **Bar J Chuckwagon** At the best bargain in the $$–$$$ Jackson Hole area, you'll get a true ranch-style meal in a long hall along with some of the liveliest Western entertainment you'll find in the region. The food, served on a tin plate, includes barbecued roast beef, chicken, or rib-eye steak, plus potatoes, beans, biscuits, applesauce, spice cake, and ranch coffee or lemonade. The multitalented Bar J Wranglers sing, play instruments, share cowboy stories and poetry, and even yodel. "Lap-size" children eat free. The doors open at 5:30, so you can explore the Bar J's Western village—including a saloon and several shops—before the dinner bell rings at 7:30. The dining area is covered, so no need to worry if the sun isn't shining. Reservations strongly suggested. ⊠ *4200 Bar J Chuckwagon Rd., Wilson, 83014* ☎ *307/733–3370* ▭ *D, MC, V.*

★ Fodor'sChoice✕**Nora's Fish Creek Inn.** One of those inimitable
$$–$$$ Western places that have earned its keeping as a local treasure among its many loyal customers. Look for the giant trout on the roof outside. Great spot to catch a hardy weekend breakfast of pancakes or huevos rancheros that barely fit on your plate and dinner among the talkative locals. Among the imaginative dishes served at this casual log inn are honey-hickory baby back ribs, prime rib, elk tenderloin with blackberry wine sauce, and nut-crusted trout, plus nightly specials. There are also soups such as pumpkin to warm your bones, wine by the glass, and a kids' menu. You can dine in one of two large rooms or sit at the counter for quick service. Breakfast, but not lunch, is served on weekends. ⊠ *Hwy. 22, 6 mi outside Jackson at the base of the pass.* ▭ *AE, D, MC, V* ⊗ *No lunch weekends.*

$–$$ ✕**Merry Piglets.** No pork served here, hence the name! But
★ otherwise, you'll get more-than-generous portions of Mexican fare, over a mesquite grill if you like, with a range of homemade sauces from mild to spicy for those who like the heat. Favorites include sizzling fajitas, carne asada, shrimp mango wraps, and even Tex-Mex style seafood chimichanga. It's usually noisy and jam-packed, but there's a full-service bar whipping up frozen strawberry margaritas that you can sip in this festive atmosphere while waiting for your table. ⊠ *160 N. Cache Drive, Jackson, near Teton Theatre* ☎ *307/733–2966* ⚲ *Reservations not accepted* ▭ *AE, D, MC, V.*

WHERE TO STAY

$$$$ ⊡**The Wildflower Inn.** This log country inn built in 1989 is cozy, clean, comfortable and serves gourmet breakfasts. Just down the road from Jackson Hole Mountain Resort and Teton Village, the inn is surrounded by three acres of aspen and pine trees frequented by moose, deer, and other native wildlife. Each room has a private deck and bath-

native wildlife. Each room has a private deck and bathroom, handcrafted log bed piled high with comforters, and its own alpine theme. There's also a plant-filled solarium, hot tub and a sunlit dining room. **Pros:** excellent views, perfectly situated for outdoor activities and exploration parks. **Cons:** books far in advance, 12 mi from Jackson itself. ✉ *3725 Teton Village Rd., 83001* ☎ *307/733–4710* ⊕ *www.jacksonholewildflower.com* ⌂ *5 rooms* &*In-room: refrigerator (some), Wi-Fi. In-hotel: no-smoking rooms.* ≡ *MC, V* ⌾ *BP.*

$$$–$$$$ 🏠 **Teton Tree House.** On a steep hillside and surrounded by trees, this is a real retreat. Ninety-five steps lead to this cozy lodgepole-pine B&B tucked away in the forest. Decks abound, rooms are full of wood furniture and warm Southwestern colors, and an inviting common area has a two-story old-fashioned adobe fireplace. **Pros:** scenic locale, good breakfast. **Cons:** not open in winter, must drive to town, small climb up to the B&B. ✉ *6175 Heck of a Hill Rd., 83014* ☎ *307/733–3233* ⌂ *6 rooms* &*In-room: no a/c, no TV. In-hotel: no elevator, no kids under 6, no-smoking rooms* ≡ *D, MC, V* ⌾ *BP* ⊙ *Closed Oct.–April.*

NIGHTLIFE

The **Stagecoach Bar** (✉ *WY 22* ☎ *307/733–4407*) fills to bursting when local bands play. Disco Night is on Thursday and attracts a packed house of swingers. "The Coach" is a good place to enjoy a drink and conversation at other times, and there's now a Mexican café and kitchen where one can grab a quick bite.

Yellowstone & Grand Teton Essentials

There are planners and there are those who, excuse the pun, fly by the seat of their pants. We happily place ourselves among the planners. Our writers and editors try to anticipate all the issues you may face before and during any journey, and then they do their research. This section is the product of their efforts. Use it to get excited about your trip to Yellowstone & Grand Teton, to inform your travel planning, or to guide you on the road should the seat of your pants start to feel threadbare.

GETTING STARTED

We're proud of our Web site: Fodors.com is a great place to begin any journey. Scan Travel Wire for suggested itineraries, travel deals, restaurant and hotel openings, and other up-to-the-minute info. Check out Booking to research prices and book plane tickets, hotel rooms, rental cars, and vacation packages. Head to Talk for on-the-ground pointers from travelers who frequent our message boards. You can also link to loads of other travel-related resources.

▌ RESOURCES

ONLINE TRAVEL TOOLS
Weather Accuweather.com (⊕www.accuweather.com) is an independent weather-forecasting service with good coverage of hurricanes. **Weather.com** (⊕www.weather.com) is the Web site for the Weather Channel.

VISITOR INFORMATION
The park Web site, www.nps.gov/yell, makes all its Yellowstone publications available online, in addition to *Yellowstone Resources and Issues Handbook,* a 200-page book used by park naturalists to answer many basic questions.

Contacts Grand Teton National Park. ⊘Drawer 170, Moose, WY83012 ☎307/739–3300, 307/739–3400 TTY ⊕www.nps.gov/grte. **Yellowstone National Park**

⊘Box 168, Mammoth, WY82190-0168 ☎307/344–7381, 307/344–2386 TDD ⊕www.nps.gov/yell. **West Yellowstone Visitor Information Center** ⊘30 Yellowstone Ave. West Yellowstone, MT ☎406/646–4403 ⊕www.nps.gov/yell.

▌ THINGS TO CONSIDER

ACCESSIBILITY
Yellowstone has long been a Park Service leader in providing for people with disabilities. Rest rooms with sinks and flush toilets designed for those in wheelchairs are in all developed areas except Norris and West Thumb, where more rustic facilities are available. Accessible campsites and restrooms are at Bridge Bay, Canyon Village, Madison, Mammoth Hot Springs, and Grant Village campgrounds, while accessible campsites are found at both Lewis Lake and Slough Creek campgrounds. Ice Lake has an accessible backcountry campsite. An accessible fishing platform is about 3.5 mi west of Madison at Mount Haynes Overlook. For details, contact the accessibility coordinator for

the park or pick up a free copy of *Visitor Guide to Accessible Features in Yellowstone National Park*. It's available at all park visitor centers. You can also order it by mail.

The frontcountry portions of Grand Teton are largely accessible to people in wheelchairs. There's designated parking at most sites, and some interpretive trails are easily accessible. There are accessible restrooms at visitor centers. TDD telephones are available at Colter Bay Visitor Center and Moose Visitor Center. For an "Easy Access" guide to the park, stop by any visitor center or contact the park's general information number.

Information **Colter Bay Visitor Center** (☎307/739–3544). **Grand Teton National Park** (☎307/739–3600, 307/739–3400 TTY ⊕www.nps.gov/grte). **Moose Visitor Center** (☎307/739–3400).

Park Accessibility Coordinator (✉Box 168, Yellowstone National Park, WY82190-0168 ☎307/344–2017 or 307/344–2386 TDD).

ADMISSION FEES
Entrance fees are $25 per car, $20 per motorcycle and $12 per visitor arriving on foot, ski, bicycle, or in a noncommercial bus. Entrance fees entitle visitors to seven days in both Yellowstone and Grand Teton. Guests 15 and younger are exempt from paying an entrance fee. An annual pass to the two parks costs $50. Senior Pass is $10 for U.S. citizens or permanent residents of the U.S. who are 62 or older.

Access Pass allows free admission to citizens or permanent residents of the U.S. who have been determined to be blind or permanently disabled and present such documentation.

ADMISSION HOURS
Depending on the weather, Yellowstone is generally fully open from late April through mid-October, and from mid-December through early March. From mid-October to late April only one road—from the North entrance at Gardiner to the Northeast entrance at Cooke City—is open to wheeled vehicles; other roads are used by over-snow vehicles only.

Grand Teton is open 24/7 year-round. The Craig Thomas Discovery and Visitor Center is closed only on Christmas Day. All park visitor centers are open 8 to 7 from Memorial Day through Labor Day. The park is in the Mountain time zone.

PERMITS
Fishing permits are required if you want to take advantage of Yellowstone's abundant lakes and streams. Live bait is not allowed, and for all native species of fish, a catch-and-release policy stands. Anglers 16 and older must purchase a $15 three-day permit, a $20 seven-day permit, or a $35 season permit. Those 12 to 15 need a free permit or must fish under direct supervision of an adult with a permit. Children 11 and under do not need a permit but must be supervised by an adult. Fish-

ing permits are available at ranger stations, visitor centers, and Yellowstone General Stores.

All camping outside of designated campgrounds requires a free backcountry permit. Horseback riding also requires a free permit.

In Yellowstone, all boats, motorized or nonmotorized, including float tubes, require a permit. Boat permits for motorized vessels are available for $20 (annual) or $10 (seven days). Permits for nonmotorized vessels are $10 (annual) or $5 (seven days). Permits from Grand Teton National Park are valid in Yellowstone, but owners must register their vessel in Yellowstone.

Grand Teton backcountry permits, which must be obtained in person at Craig Thomas visitor center, Colter Bay visitor centers or Jenny Lake ranger station, are $25 and required for all overnight stays outside designated campgrounds. Seven-day boat permits, available year-round at Moose Visitor Center and in summer at Colter Bay and Signal Mountain ranger stations, cost $20 for motorized craft and $10 for nonmotorized craft and are good for seven days. Annual permits are $40 for motorized craft and $20 for nonmotorized craft.

TRIP INSURANCE

What kind of coverage do you honestly need? Do you need trip insurance at all? Take a deep breath and read on.

We believe that comprehensive trip insurance is especially valuable if you're booking a very expensive or complicated trip (particularly to an isolated region) or if you're booking far in advance. Who knows what could happen six months down the road? But whether or not you get insurance has more to do with how comfortable you are assuming all that risk yourself.

Comprehensive travel policies typically cover trip-cancellation and interruption, letting you cancel or cut your trip short because of a personal emergency, illness, or, in some cases, acts of terrorism in your destination. Such policies also cover evacuation and medical care. Some also cover you for trip delays because of bad weather or mechanical problems as well as for lost or delayed baggage. Another type of coverage to look for is financial default—that is, when your trip is disrupted because a tour operator, airline, or cruise line goes out of business. Generally you must buy this when you book your trip or shortly thereafter, and it's only available to you if your operator isn't on a list of excluded companies.

Expect comprehensive travel insurance policies to cost about 4% to 7% or 8% of the total price of your trip (it's more like 8%–12% if you're over age 70). A medical-only policy may or may not be cheaper than a comprehensive policy. Always read the fine print of your policy to make sure that you are covered

Trip Insurance Resources

INSURANCE COMPARISON SITES

Insure My Trip.com	800/487–4722	www.insuremytrip.com
Square Mouth.com	800/240–0369	www.quotetravelinsurance.com

COMPREHENSIVE TRAVEL INSURERS

Access America	866/807–3982	www.accessamerica.com
CSA Travel Protection	800/873–9855	www.csatravelprotection.com
HTH Worldwide	610/254–8700 or 888/243–2358	www.hthworldwide.com
Travelex Insurance	888/457–4602	www.travelex-insurance.com
Travel Guard International	715/345–0505 or 800/826–4919	www.travelguard.com
Travel Insured International	800/243–3174	www.travelinsured.com

MEDICAL-ONLY INSURERS

International Medical Group	800/628–4664	www.imglobal.com
International SOS	215/942–8000 or 713/521–7611	www.internationalsos.com
Wallach & Company	800/237–6615 or 504/687–3166	www.wallach.com

for the risks that are of most concern to you. Compare several policies to make sure you're getting the best price and range of coverage available.

BOOKING YOUR TRIP

Unless your cousin is a travel agent, you're probably among the millions of people who make most of their travel arrangements online.

Is it truly better to book directly on an airline or hotel Web site? And when does a real live travel agent come in handy?

ONLINE

Booking engines like Expedia, Travelocity, and Orbitz are actually travel agents, albeit high-volume, online ones. And airline travel packagers like American Airlines Vacations and Virgin Vacations—well, they're travel agents, too. But they may still not work with all the world's hotels.

An aggregator site will search many sites and pull the best prices for airfares, hotels, and rental cars from them. Most aggregators compare the major travel-booking sites such as Expedia, Travelocity, and Orbitz; some also look at airline Web sites, though rarely the sites of smaller budget airlines. Some aggregators also compare other travel products, including complex packages—a good thing, as you can sometimes get the best overall deal by booking an air-and-hotel package.

ACCOMMODATIONS

If you want to stay inside either Yellowstone or Grand Teton, make your reservations as far in advance as possible (up to a year in advance for the choice properties, especially in Yellowstone). Old Faithful Snow Lodge and Mammoth Hot Springs Hotel are the only accommodations open in winter; rates are the same as in summer. Telephones have been put in some rooms, but there are no TVs. All park lodging is no-smoking. There are no roll-away beds available.

WHAT IT COSTS HOTELS	
$$$$	over $200
$$$	$151–$200
$$	$101–$150
$	$50–$100
¢	under $50

Hotel prices are per night for two people in a standard double room in high season, excluding taxes and service charges.

Be sure you understand the hotel's cancellation policy if you are reserving a room far in advance. Some places allow you to cancel without any kind of penalty—even if you prepaid to secure a discounted rate—if you cancel at least 24 hours in advance. Others require you to cancel a week in advance or penalize you the cost of one night. Small inns and B&Bs are

Online Booking Resources

AGGREGATORS		
Kayak	www.kayak.com	also looks at cruises and vacation packages.
Mobissimo	www.mobissimo.com	
Qixo	www.qixo.com	also compares cruises, vacation packages, and even travel insurance.
Sidestep	www.sidestep.com	also compares vacation packages and lists travel deals.
Travelgrove	www.travelgrove.com	also compares cruises and packages.
BOOKING ENGINES		
Expedia	www.expedia.com	a large online agency that charges a booking fee for airline tickets.
Orbitz	www.orbitz.com	charges a booking fee for airline tickets, but gives a clear breakdown of fees and taxes before you book.
Travelocity	www.travelocity.com	charges a booking fee for airline tickets, but promises good problem resolution.
ONLINE ACCOMMODATIONS		
Hotelbook.com	www.hotelbook.com	focuses on independent hotels worldwide.
Hotels.com	www.hotels.com	a big Expedia-owned wholesaler that offers rooms in hotels all over the world.
Quikbook	www.quikbook.com	offers "pay when you stay" reservations that let you settle your bill at check out, not when you book.

most likely to require you to cancel far in advance.

■TIP➔ Assume that hotels operate on the European Plan (**EP**, no meals) unless we specify that they use the Breakfast Plan (**BP**, with full breakfast), Continental Plan (**CP**, Continental breakfast), Full American Plan (**FAP**, all meals), Modified American Plan (**MAP**, breakfast and dinner) or are all-inclusive (**AI**, all meals and most activities).

▌ AIRLINE TICKETS

Most domestic airline tickets are electronic; international tickets may be either electronic or paper. With an e-ticket the only thing you receive is an e-mailed receipt citing your itinerary and reservation and ticket numbers.

The greatest advantage of an e-ticket is that if you lose your receipt, you can simply print out another copy or ask the airline to do it for you at check-in. You usually pay a surcharge (up to $50) to get a paper ticket, if you can get one at all.

The sole advantage of a paper ticket is that it may be easier to endorse over to another airline if your flight is canceled and the airline with which you booked can't accommodate you on another flight.

■TIP→ Discount air passes that let you travel economically in a country or region must often be purchased before you leave home. In some cases you can only get them through a travel agent.

▌ RENTAL CARS

When you reserve a car, ask about cancellation penalties, taxes, drop-off charges (if you're planning to pick up the car in one city and leave it in another), and surcharges (for being under or over a certain age, for additional drivers, or for driving across state or country borders or beyond a specific distance from your point of rental). All these things can add substantially to your costs. Request car seats and extras such as GPS when you book.

Rates are sometimes—but not always—better if you book in advance or reserve through a rental agency's Web site. There are other reasons to book ahead, though: for popular destinations, during busy times of the year, or to ensure that you get certain types of cars (vans, SUVs, exotic sports cars).

■TIP→ Make sure that a confirmed reservation guarantees you a car. Agencies sometimes overbook, particularly for busy weekends and holiday periods.

You will need to rent a car to explore either Grand Teton or Yellowstone. Although there are some bus tours of Yellowstone, there is also no substitute for having your own transportation. Rates in most Montana and Wyoming cities run about $50 a day and $275 to $325 a week for an economy car with air-conditioning, automatic transmission, and unlimited mileage. In resort areas such as Jackson, you'll usually find a variety of 4x4s and SUVs for rent. Unless you plan to do a lot of mountain exploring, a four-wheel drive is usually needed only in winter, but if you do plan to venture onto any back roads, an SUV (about $85 a day) is the best bet because it will have higher clearance. Rates do not include tax on car rentals, which is 6% in Wyoming. There is no tax in Montana, but if you rent from an airport location, there is an airport-concession fee.

Rental rates are similar whether at the airport or at an in-town agency. Many people fly in to Salt Lake City or Denver and drive a rental car from there to cut travel costs. Just be aware that it's a 10- or 11-hour drive from Denver to Jackson or Cody; it's about a six-hour drive to Jackson and a nine-hour trip to Cody from Salt Lake City.

In the Rockies and plains you must be 21 to rent a car with a valid driver's license. Some companies charge an additional fee for drivers ages 21 to 24, and others will not rent to anyone under age 25; most companies also require a major credit card.

Surcharges may apply if you're under 25 or if you take the car outside the area approved by the rental agency. You'll pay extra for child seats, which are compulsory for children under five (under eight in Wyoming) and cost $5 to $10 a day, and usually for additional drivers (up to $25 a day, depending on location).

CAR-RENTAL INSURANCE

Everyone who rents a car wonders whether the insurance that the rental companies offer is worth the expense. No one—including us—has a simple answer. It all depends on how much regular insurance you have, how comfortable you are with risk, and whether or not money is an issue.

If you own a car and carry comprehensive car insurance for both collision and liability,

your personal auto insurance will probably cover a rental, but read your policy's fine print to be sure. If you don't have auto insurance, then you should probably buy the collision- or loss-damage waiver (CDW or LDW) from the rental company. This eliminates your liability for damage to the car.

Some credit cards offer CDW coverage, but it's usually supplemental to your own insurance and rarely covers SUVs, minivans, luxury models, and the like. If your coverage is secondary, you may still be liable for loss-of-use costs from the car-rental company (again, read the fine print). But no credit-card insurance is valid unless you use that card for *all* transactions, from reserving to paying the final bill.

All car rental companies are required to carry a minimal level of liability coverage insuring all renters, but it's rarely enough to cover claims in a really serious accident if you're at fault. Your own auto-insurance policy will protect you if you own a car; if you don't, you have to decide whether you are willing to take the risk.

U.S. rental companies sell CDWs and LDWs for about $15 to $25 a day; supplemental liability is usually more than $10 a day.

■TIP➔ You can decline the insurance from the rental company and purchase it through a third-party provider such as Travel Guard

Car Rental Resources

LOCAL AGENCIES		
ABC Rent-A-Car	800/773-6814	www.abc-rentacar.com
Arizona Auto Rental	520/624-4548	
Fox Rent A Car	800/225-4369	www.foxrentacar.com
Major Agencies		
Alamo	800/462-5266	www.alamo.com
Avis	800/331-1084	www.avis.com
Budget	800/472-3325	www.budget.com
Hertz	800/654-3131	www.hertz.com
National Car Rental	800/227-7368	www.nationalcar.com

(⊕ *www.travelguard.com*)—$9 per day for $35,000 of coverage. That's sometimes just under half the price of the CDW offered by some car-rental companies.

GETTING STARTED / BOOKING YOUR TRIP / TRANSPORTATION / ON THE GROUND

TRANSPORTATION

▮ BY AIR

Absolutely the best connections to Montana and often the shortest flights to Wyoming are through the Rockies hub cities, Salt Lake City and Denver. Montana also receives transfer flights from Minneapolis, Seattle, and Phoenix.

If you decide to connect through either Denver or Salt Lake City, you will still have one or two hours of flying time to reach your final airport destination. Many of the airports in these states are served by commuter flights that have frequent stops, though generally with very short layovers. There are no direct flights from New York to the area, and most itineraries from New York take between seven and nine hours. Likewise, you cannot fly direct from Los Angeles to Montana or Wyoming; it will take you four or five hours to get here from the West Coast. To reach Wyoming and most Montana cities, you will have to take a connecting flight.

At smaller airports, you may only need to be on hand an hour before the flight.

If you're traveling during snow season, allow extra time for the drive to the airport, as weather conditions can slow you down. If you'll be checking skis, arrive even earlier.

Smoking policies vary from carrier to carrier. Most airlines prohibit smoking on all of their flights; others allow smoking only on certain routes or certain departures. Ask your carrier about its policy.

Airlines & Airports Airline and Airport Links.com (⊕www.airlineandairportlinks.com) has links to many of the world's airlines and airports.

AIRPORTS

The major gateways include Gallatin Field in Bozeman, MT (BZN); Jackson Hole Airport (JAC); and Yellowstone Regional Airport (COD; in Cody).

Airport Information Gallatin Field (in Bozeman) (☎406/388–8321 ⊕www.gallatinfield.com).

Denver International Airport (☎303/342–2000, 800/247–2336, 800/688–1333 TTY ⊕www.flydenver.com).

Salt Lake City International Airport (☎801/575–2400 ⊕www.slcairport.com).

Yellowstone Regional Airport (☎307/587–5096 ⊕www.flyyra.com).

FLIGHTS

United and Delta have the most flights to the region. The regional carrier Big Sky connects Montana cities; America West and Northwest (among others) provide connections to Big Sky from outside the state.

Airline Contacts **Alaska Airlines** (☎800/252–7522 ⊕www.alaskaair.com). **AmericanAirlines** (☎800/433–7300 ⊕www.aa.com). **Big Sky** (☎800/237–7788 ⊕www.bigskyair.com). **Continental Airlines** (☎800/523–3273 for U.S. and Mexico reservations, 800/231–0856 for international reservations ⊕www.continental.com). **Delta Airlines** (☎800/221–1212 for U.S. reservations, 800/241–4141 for international reservations ⊕www.delta.com). **Horizon Air** (☎800/547–9308 ⊕www.alaskaair.com). **jetBlue** (☎800/538–2583 ⊕www.jetblue.com). **Mesa Airlines** (☎800/637–2247 ⊕www.mesa-air.com). **Midwest Airlines** (☎800/452–2022 ⊕www.midwestairlines.com). **Northwest Airlines** (☎800/225–2525 ⊕www.nwa.com). **Southwest Airlines** (☎800/435–9792 ⊕www.southwest.com). **United Airlines** (☎800/864–8331 for U.S. reservations, 800/538–2929 for international reservations ⊕www.united.com). **USAirways** (☎800/428–4322 for U.S. and Canada reservations, 800/622–1015 for international reservations ⊕www.usairways.com).

▌ BY CAR

You'll seldom be bored driving through the Rockies and plains, which offer some of the most spectacular vistas and challenging driving in the world. Montana's interstate system is driver-friendly, connecting soaring summits, rivers, glacial valleys, forests, lakes, and vast stretches of prairie, all capped by that endless "Big Sky." Wyoming's interstates link classic, open-range cowboy country and mountain-range vistas with state highways headed to the geothermal wonderland of Yellowstone National Park. In Wyoming everything is separated by vast distances, so be sure to leave each major city with a full tank of gas and be prepared to see lots of wildlife and few other people.

Before setting out on any driving trip, it's important to make sure your vehicle is in top condition.. For emergencies, take along flares or reflector triangles, jumper cables, an empty gas can, a fire extinguisher, a flashlight, a plastic tarp, blankets, water, and coins or a calling card for phone calls (cell phones don't always work in high mountain areas).

In the Rockies and plains, as across the nation, gasoline costs fluctuate often.

GASOLINE

In major cities throughout Montana and Wyoming, gas prices are roughly similar to those in the rest of the continental United States; in rural and resort towns, prices are sometimes considerably higher. Although gas stations are relatively plentiful in many areas, you can drive more than 100 mi on back roads without finding gas.

In 2008, all service stations in Yellowstone will accept credit cards (AE, Conoco, D, MC, V) at the pump, 24 hours a day.

Repair services are available at Canyon, Fishing Bridge, Grant Village, and Old Faithful from late May through early September. Towing service is available from mid-May through mid-October. Repair stations can fix all common problems (including electronics, fuel pumps, alternators, brakes, bearings)—and carry a selection of replacement parts. They also receive daily, overnight parts deliveries in the summer. The nearest gasoline stations in the winter are in Gardiner and West Yellowstone.

In Grand Teton, automobile service stations are located in the park at Colter Bay Village, Dornan's, Jackson Lake Lodge, and Signal Mountain Lodge. Auto and RV repair is available at Colter Bay Village.

ROAD CONDITIONS

Roads range from multilane blacktop to barely graveled backcountry trails. Many twisting switchbacks are considerately marked with guardrails, but some primitive roads have a lane so narrow that you must back up to the edge of a steep cliff to make a turn. Scenic routes and lookout points are clearly marked, enabling you to slow down and pull over to take in the views.

One of the more unpleasant sights along the highway is roadkill—animals struck by vehicles. Deer, elk, and even bears may try to get to the other side of a road just as you come along, so watch out for wildlife on the highways.

Exercise caution, not only to save an animal's life, but also to avoid possible extensive damage to your car.

ROAD INFORMATION & EMERGENCY SERVICES

Contact the Wyoming Department of Transportation for road and travel reports October–April. For emergency situations dial 911 or contact the Wyoming Highway Patrol. Most cell phones work in the developed areas of the park, and there are emergency phones located along some park roads.

Information **Montana Highway Patrol** (☎406/388–3190 or 800/525–5555 ⊕www.mdt.mt.gov). **Wyoming Department of Transportation** (☎307/777–4484, 307/772–0824 from outside Wyoming for road conditions, 888/996–7623 from within Wyoming for road conditions ⊕www.wyoroad.info). **Wyoming Highway Patrol** (☎307/777–4301, 800/442–9090 for emergencies (#4357 [#HELP] from a cell phone for emergencies)).

SNOWY DRIVING

Modern highways make mountain and plains driving safe and generally trouble free even in cold weather. Although winter driving can occasionally present some real challenges, road maintenance is good and plowing is prompt. However, in mountain areas, tire chains, studs, or snow tires are essential. If you're planning to drive into high elevations, be sure to check the weather forecast and call for road conditions beforehand.

Even main highways can close. Winter weather isn't confined to winter months in the high country (it's been known to snow on July 4), so be prepared year-round: carry an emergency kit containing warm clothes, a flashlight, some food and water, and blankets. It's also good to carry a cell phone, but be aware that the mountains, and sheer distances from cell towers, can disrupt service. If you do get stalled by deep snow, do not leave your car. Wait for help, running the engine only if needed (making sure to keep the exhaust clear and occasionally opening a window for fresh air), and remember that assistance is never far away.

SPEED LIMITS

The speed limit on U.S. interstates is 75 mph in rural areas and 65 mph in urban zones. The speed limit on most two-lane roads is 55 or 65 mph; in Montana there are lower speed limits at night.

ON THE GROUND

▌ COMMUNICATIONS

INTERNET

If you stay at a hotel in town (West Yellowstone, Jackson, Cody, etc.), you are likely to have some kind of Internet service available. Cafés also have Internet. But if you stay in the park, your options are much more limited. A few upscale hotels in Grand Teton have Internet service, but no places in either park offer Wi-Fi.

Contacts **Cybercafes** (⊕www. cybercafes.com) lists over 4,000 Internet cafés worldwide.

PUBLIC TELEPHONES

In Yellowstone, public telephones are near visitor centers and major park attractions. Verizon cellular towers provide good service for Old Faithful, Mammoth Hot Springs, and the Canyon area, but coverage is otherwise hit-and-miss throughout the park.

In Grand Teton, public phones are located at Moose, Dornan's, south Jenny Lake, Signal Mountain Lodge, Moran Entrance Station, Jackson Lake Lodge, Colter Bay Village, Leeks Marina and Flagg Ranch. GT Medical Clinic is located at Jackson Lake Lodge. Cell phones work in most developed areas and occasionally on trails.

▌ EATING OUT

Dining in Montana and Wyoming is generally casual. Menus are becoming more varied with such regional specialties as trout, elk, or buffalo, but you can nearly always order a hamburger or a steak. Authentic ethnic food—other than Mexican—is hard to find outside of cities. Dinner hours are from 6 PM to 9 PM. Outside the large cities and resort towns in the high seasons, many restaurants close by 9 or 10 PM. The restaurants we list are the cream of the crop in each price category.

For information on food-related health issues, see Health below.

MEALS & MEALTIMES

You can find all types of cuisine in the major cities and resort towns, but don't forget to try native dishes such as trout, elk, and buffalo (the latter two have less fat than beef and are just as tasty); organic fruits and vegetables are also readily available. When in doubt, go for a steak, forever a Rocky Mountain and northern plains mainstay.

Rocky Mountain oysters, simply put, are bull testicles. They're generally served fried, although you can get them lots of different ways. You can find them all over the West, usually at down-home eateries, steak houses, and the like.

Unless otherwise noted, the restaurants listed in this guide are open daily for lunch and dinner.

WHAT IT COSTS RESTAURANTS	
$$$$	over $30
$$$	$20–$30
$$	$12–$20
$	$8–$12
¢	under $8

Restaurant prices are per person for a main course at dinner and do not include tax.

RESERVATIONS & DRESS

Regardless of where you are, it's a good idea to make a reservation if you can. In some places, it's expected. We only mention them specifically when reservations are essential (there's no other way you'll ever get a table) or when they are not accepted. For popular restaurants, book as far ahead as you can (often 30 days), and reconfirm as soon as you arrive. (Large parties should always call ahead to check the reservations policy.) We mention dress only when men are required to wear a jacket or a jacket and tie.

Reservations are a must for the more formal, sit-down restaurants in either Yellowstone or Grand Teton and for upscale places in Jackson. Otherwise, you are on your own.

WINES, BEER & SPIRITS

Microbreweries throughout the region produce a diverse selection of beers. Snake River Brewing Company in Jackson Hole, Wyoming, has won awards for

its lager, pale ale, Zonker Stout, and numerous other releases. Missoula, Montana–based Big Sky Brewing Company's bestseller is Moose Drool (a brown ale); the company also markets an award-winning pale ale and several other brews.

▌ EMERGENCIES

YELLOWSTONE

In case of emergency, dial 911 or visit one of the park's clinics or ranger stations. In addition to public phones throughout the park, there are phones outside each clinic for after hours use.

Mammoth Clinic ☎307/344–7965 is located next to the post office in Mammoth Hot Springs. It is the only medical facility in the park open year-round. A doctor is on duty all day Monday through Thursday and Friday mornings. Call for an appointment unless an emergency condition or new work injury.

Lake Clinic is located behind the Lake Hotel in Lake village.

Staffed with one physician's assistant or nurse practitioner and two nurses. No appointments.

Old Faithful Clinic ☎*307/545–7325.* is located in the parking lot behind Old Faithful Inn. Staffed with one physician's assistant or nurse practitioner and two nurses. No appointments.

There are hospitals with 24-hour emergency rooms in Jackson, Cody, and Bozeman.

Contacts **General Emergencies** (☎911 or 307/344–7381).

Bozeman Deaconess Hospital (✉915 Highland Blvd., Bozeman, MT ☎406/585–5000). **Lake Clinic** (✉Lake Village ☎307/242–7241 ☉Late-May–late-Sept., daily 8:30–8:30). **Mammoth Clinic** (✉Mammoth Hot Springs ☎307/344–7965 ☉May–Sept., daily 8:30–5; Sept.–May, Mon.–Thurs., 8:30–5 and Fri. 8:30–1). **Old Faithful Clinic** (✉Old Faithful ☎307/545–7325 ☉Mid-May–mid-Sept., daily 7–7; mid-Sept.–early Oct., Thurs.–Mon., 8:30–5). **St. John's Medical Center** (✉625 E. Broadway Ave., Jackson, WY ☎307/733–3636). **West Park Hospital** (✉707 Sheridan Ave., Cody, WY ☎307/527–7501).

Yellowstone Family Medical Clinic (✉11 S. Electric Ave., West Yellowstone, MT ☎406/646–0200 ☉May–Sept., weekdays 8–5; Oct.–Apr., weekdays 9–4.).

GRAND TETON
In case of a fire, medical, or police emergency in the park, dial 911. Park law enforcement rangers are located at ranger stations

(at Colter Bay, Jenny Lake, and Moose). Dial ☎307/739–3301 for park dispatch. The Grand Teton Medical Clinic at Jackson Lake Lodge is open daily from 10 to 6 during the summer. The closest hospital to the park is St. John's Hospital in Jackson.

Contacts **General Emergencies** (☎911). **Medical Emergencies** (☎307/739–3300).

Grand Teton Medical Clinic (✉Jackson Lake Lodge, 0.5 mi north of Jackson Lake Junction ☎307/543–2514 or 307/733–8002). **St. John's Hospital** (✉625 E. Broadway Ave., Jackson ☎307/733–3636 or 800/877–7078).

▮ MONEY

In Yellowstone, ATMs can be found in the lobbies at Canyon Lodge, Grant Village Hotel, Lake Yellowstone Hotel, Mammoth Hot Springs Hotel, Old Faithful Inn and Old Faithful Snow Lodge. They are also located at the following Yellowstone General Stores: Canyon, Fishing Bridge, Grant Village General Store and Old Faithful.

In Grand Teton, ATMs are at Colter Bay Grocery and General Store, Dornan's, Jackson Lake Lodge, and Signal Mountain Lodge. You can also find ATMs at Flagg Ranch Resort, which is north of the park before the southern entrance to Yellowstone. The nearest full-service banks are in Jackson and Dubois.

Prices throughout this guide are given for adults. Substantially reduced fees are almost always available for children, students, and senior citizens.

CREDIT CARDS

Throughout this guide, the following abbreviations are used: **AE**, American Express; **D**, Discover; **DC**, Diners Club; **MC**, MasterCard; and **V**, Visa.

It's a good idea to inform your credit-card company before you travel, especially if you're going abroad and don't travel internationally very often. Otherwise, the credit-card company might put a hold on your card owing to unusual activity—not a good thing halfway through your trip. Record all your credit-card numbers—as well as the phone numbers to call if your cards are lost or stolen—in a safe place, so you're prepared should something go wrong. Both MasterCard and Visa have general numbers you can call (collect if you're abroad) if your card is lost, but you're better off calling the number of your issuing bank, since MasterCard and Visa usually just transfer you to your bank; your bank's number is usually printed on your card.

Reporting Lost Cards **American Express** (☎800/528-4800 in the U.S. or 336/393-1111 collect from abroad ⊕www.americanexpress. com). **Diners Club** (☎800/234-6377 in the U.S. or 303/799-1504 collect from abroad ⊕www.diners club.com). **Discover** (☎800/347-2683 in the U.S. or 801/902-3100 collect from abroad ⊕www.discover card.com). **MasterCard** (☎800/627-8372 in the U.S. or 636/722-7111 collect from abroad ⊕www.master card.com). **Visa** (☎800/847-2911 in the U.S. or 410/581-9994 collect from abroad ⊕www.visa.com).

▌ LOST AND FOUND

You can turn in any found item or search for a lost object at any ranger station or visitor center. The main Lost & Found in Grand Teton can be found at the Moose Visitor Center.

▌ POST OFFICES

Post Offices in Yellowstone **Canyon Village Post Office** (✉Canyon Village 82190 ☎307/242-7323 ⊙Closed Oct.–May. **Grant Village Post Office** ✉Grant Village 82190 ☎307/242-7338 ⊙Closed early Sept.–mid-May. **Lake Post Office** ✉Lake Village 82190 ☎307/242-7383 ⊙Closed early Sept.–mid-May. **Mammoth Hot Springs Post Office** ✉Mammoth Hot Springs 82190 ☎307/344-7764. **Old Faithful Post Office** ✉Old Faithful 82190 ☎307/545-7252 ⊙Closed early Sept.–mid-May.

Post Offices in Grand Teton **Moose Post Office** (✉Visitor Center, Box 9998 Moose 83012 ☎307/733-3336). **Moran Post Office** (✉Moran Junction, 1 Central Station Moran 83013 ☎307/543-2527).

RELIGIOUS SERVICES

Religious services are held at several Yellowstone locations as well as in the communities surrounding the park during the summer and on religious holidays. For times and locations of park services, check at visitor centers or lodging front desks.

There are chapel services within Grand Teton National Park on weekends late spring through early autumn. Nearby Jackson has other services.

RESTROOMS

In Yellowstone, public restrooms may be found throughout all of the developed areas of the park, including all visitor centers, campgrounds, and entrances. West Thumb and Tower Fall also have public restrooms.

Public restrooms may be found at all Grand Teton visitor centers, campgrounds, and ranger stations. There are restrooms at the picnic area north of Moose on Teton Park Road, and at String Lake and Colter Bay picnic area.

SAFETY

Regardless which outdoor activities you pursue or your level of skill, safety must come first. Remember: know your limits.

Many trails in the Rockies and northern plains are remote and sparsely traveled. In the high altitudes of the mountains, oxygen is scarce. Hikers, bikers, and riders should carry emergency supplies in their backpacks. Proper equipment includes a flashlight, a compass, waterproof matches, a first-aid kit, a knife, a cell phone with an extra battery (although you may have to climb atop a mountain ridge to find a signal), and a light plastic tarp for shelter. Backcountry skiers should add a repair kit, a blanket, an avalanche beacon, and a lightweight shovel to their lists. Always bring extra food and a canteen of water, as dehydration is a common occurrence at high altitudes. Never drink from streams or lakes, unless you boil the water first or purify it with tablets. Giardia, an intestinal parasite, may be present.

Always check the condition of roads and trails, and get the latest weather reports before setting out. In summer, take precautions against heat stroke or exhaustion by resting frequently in shaded areas; in winter, take precautions against hypothermia by layering clothing. Ultimately, proper planning, common sense, and good physical conditioning are the strongest guards against the elements.

ALTITUDE

You may feel dizzy and weak and find yourself breathing heavily—signs that the thin mountain air isn't giving you your accustomed dose of oxygen. Take it easy and rest often for a few days until you're acclimatized. Throughout your stay drink plenty of water and watch your alcohol consumption. If you experience severe headaches and nausea, see a doctor. It is easy to go too high too fast. The remedy for altitude-related discomfort is to go down quickly, into heavier air. Other altitude-related problems include dehydration and overexposure to the sun because of the thin air.

EXPOSURE

The high elevation, severe cold temperatures, and sometimes windy weather in Montana and Wyoming can often combine to create intense and dangerous outdoor conditions. In winter, exposure to wind and cold can quickly bring on hypothermia or frostbite. Protect yourself by dressing in layers, so you don't become overheated and then chilled. Any time of year, the region's clear air and high elevation make sunburn a particular risk. Always wear sunscreen, even when skies are overcast.

FLASH FLOODS

Flash floods can strike at any time and any place with little or no warning. Mountainous terrain can become dangerous when distant rains are channeled into gullies and ravines, turning a quiet streamside campsite or wash into a rampaging torrent in seconds. Similarly, desert terrain floods quickly when the land is unable to absorb heavy rain. Check weather reports before heading into the backcountry and be prepared to head for higher ground if the weather turns severe.

WILD ANIMALS

One of the most wonderful parts of the Rockies and plains is the abundant wildlife. And although a herd of grazing elk or a big-horn sheep high on a hillside is most certainly a Kodak moment, an encounter with a bear or mountain lion is not. To avoid such a dangerous situation while hiking, make plenty of noise, keep dogs on a leash, and keep small children between adults. While camping, be sure to store all food, utensils, and clothing with food odors far away from your tent, preferably high in a tree (also far from your tent). If you do come across a bear or big cat, do not run. For bears, back away quietly; for lions, make yourself look as big as possible. In either case, be prepared to fend off the animal with loud noises, rocks, sticks, and so on. And as the saying goes, do not feed the bears—or any wild animals, whether they're dangerous or not.

When in the wilderness, give all animals their space and never attempt to feed any of them. If you want to take a photograph, use a long lens rather than a long sneak to approach closely. This is particularly important for winter visitors. Approaching an animal can cause it stress and affect its ability to survive the sometimes brutal climate. In all cases remember that the animals have the right-of-way; this is their home, and you are the visitor.

TAXES

Sales tax is 4% in Wyoming; Montana has no sales tax. Some areas have additional local sales and lodging taxes, which can be quite significant.

TIME

Montana and Wyoming are in the Mountain time zone. Mountain time is two hours earlier than Eastern time and one hour later than Pacific time. It is one hour earlier than Chicago, seven hours earlier than London, and 17 hours earlier than Sydney.

TIPPING

It is customary to tip 15% at restaurants; 20% in resort towns is increasingly the norm. For coat checks and bellhops, $1 per coat or bag is the minimum. Taxi drivers expect 10% to 15%, depending on where you are. In resort towns, ski technicians, sandwich makers, coffee baristas, and the like also appreciate tips. At hotels, it's always a nice gesture to leave a dollar or two for the maid each morning.

INDEX

ABOUT OUR WRITERS

Steve Pastorino loved every minute of his trips to Yellowstone National Park to research this book. After a 16-year career managing professional sports franchises, counting bears instead of ticket stubs was a refreshing change. A regular contributor to the *Salt Lake Tribune,* he also maintains a blog titled "Not Just a Hat Rack." He lives in Salt Lake City with his wife, Teri, and three children.

Before moving to Jackson Hole in 2005, Gil Brady, an easterner by birth, traveled America for seven years working as a movie hand, script analyst, filmmaker, columnist, reporter, and journalist. He first became enchanted by the Tetons and its national park in 1999, when he stayed at a ranch near Jackson. Since that summer, with stops in Los Angeles, North Carolina, Washington D.C., and New England, he vowed to return and learn Wyoming's storied history, unravel its still-untold legends, track down the last of its itinerant characters, and crack its many unsettled mysteries while sharing his discoveries with others. Gil's work has appeared in *The Los Angeles Times,* the *Casper Star-Tribune, New West.net* and *Planet Jackson Hole.* Along with his wife and dog, he now lives in Oregon, where he's writing about the adventures—and misadventures—of outsiders and insiders coexisting in the inscrutable west.

Acknowledgements

Steve would like to give special thanks to his cousin, NPS Ranger Sean Eagan, and Sean's wife Cynthia for helping him navigate Yellowstone figuratively and literally. Thanks also to Jan Stoddard (West Yellowstone Chamber of Commerce), Ardythe Wendt (Xanterra), Mona Mesereau (Yellowstone Association), and Bob Sadrakula (The Frugal Flyfisherman).

Gil would like to give special thanks to his my wife, former NPS ranger Rebecca Caruba Brady; the National Parks Service staff at Grand Teton National Park; the citizens of northern and western Wyoming who helped him with his research in the area; and the *Casper Star-Tribune.*